PROPHECY AND PREDICTION IN THE
20th CENTURY

Janette h Fowler.

December 1998

Jackie

£5.88

PROPHECY AND PREDICTION IN THE 20th CENTURY

Charles Neilson Gattey

Aquarian/Thorsons

An Imprint of HarperCollins*Publishers*

The Aquarian Press
An Imprint of HarperCollins*Publishers*
77–85 Fulham Palace Road,
Hammersmith, London W6 8JB

Published by The Aquarian Press 1989
3   5   7   9   10   8   6   4   2

A catalogue record for this book
is available from the British Library

ISBN 0 85030 830 5

Typeset by MJL Limited, Hitchin, Hertfordshire
Printed in Great Britain by Mackays of Chatham, Kent

To Rosemary Shelly

Man's perceptions are not bounded by organs of perception. He perceives more than sense (though ever so acute) can discover.

William Blake

Contents

Introduction

Much has been written about the paranormal. My purpose in this book has been to assemble the evidence, both anecdotal and experimental, concerning prophecy and prediction in our century that I consider of significance and to do this objectively and covering as varied a field as possible.

Is it extra-sensory perception or, to use Paul Daniels' phrase, extra-sensory deception? In 1987, due to the tragic death of David Penhaligon MP, a by-election was held at Truro and wide publicity was given in the press to the claim that the votes cast for all three candidates had been correctly foretold by a Liberal councillor, Stephen Wells, on a sheet of paper placed in a locked box some weeks prior to polling day and kept under lock and key in the office of Radio Cornwall's manager, Michael Hoskin. I wrote to Michael Hoskin and he confirmed this, adding that Mr Wells had the only key to the box and did not see the box again until he unlocked it in Mr Hoskin's presence just after the election result had been announced on 12 March. The sheet of paper had been sealed in an envelope, across the flap of which Michael Hoskin had signed his name. He went on: 'The votes cast for the three main candidates were correct — they had been written in ballpoint pen.'

When the General Election was announced, I wrote to Mr Wells suggesting that he might send me his forecast of how the political parties would stand after the event, which I would entrust to my bank. He did not reply. In early January 1988, answering an enquiry from me regarding Stephen Wells's further activities, Michael Hoskin said: 'He did not make any forecasts about the General Election as far as I am aware. I do know that, fired by his publicity over the Truro by-election forecast, he abandoned his position as a county councillor in Cornwall. When last heard of, he was engaged as a conjuror at a Butlin's Holiday Camp.'

This revelation led to my probing deeper into the case. I learned that Mr Wells, using the stage name 'Stephen Magus', had a reputation for performing similar feats, usually at clubs and concerts in Cornwall, that he had not given any-one at Radio Cornwall any explanation for his ability to predict the by-election result, and that the studio staff believed that they were dealing with legerdemain rather than the use of paranormal powers. Then Michael Hoskin rev-ealed: 'One of my colleagues noted that after the declara-tion of the result (but before the opening of the envelope) Mr Wells excused himself for a couple of minutes and went to the cloakroom with a newspaper. When the newspaper was examined after his departure, we found that the actual details of the result had been scribbled in the margin. Of course, we have no idea as to how these details found their way into the envelope!'

So it would appear that this might well have been a case of extra-sensory deception. But the discovery of one black sheep does not mean that all white sheep are really black, and in the pages ahead most of the cases discussed cannot be so easily faulted.

C.N.G.

CHAPTER 1

The Hitler Predictions

Frau Elsbeth Ebertin, born at Görlitz in 1880, was the most accomplished German astrologer of this century and is best known for casting Hitler's horoscope with what proved to be remarkable accuracy. In her twenties, she earned her living as a graphologist, supplying character assessments for a few pfennigs a time to readers of popular newspapers and magazines who sent in specimens of their handwriting. In 1910, a woman Frau Ebertin met, who claimed to be a professional graphologist too, offered to give her a reading, but asked for the date of her birth as well as a sample of her handwriting. What the woman then told Frau Ebertin was so accurate in its details that the latter questioned her closely and discovered that she was really an astrologer, and had pretended to be a graphologist to avoid being harassed by the police. She obtained her information solely through casting horoscopes.

This impressed Frau Ebertin so much that she herself now studied astrology assiduously and soon found that she had a definite flair for it, and in 1917 she brought out the first of her almanacs, *Ein Blick in die Zukunft* ('A Glance into the Future'), which, written in a lucid, arresting manner, became an annual best-seller. By 1920, she was also being consulted privately by a large clientèle from all classes, including ex-King Ferdinand of Bulgaria.

In 1923, Frau Ebertin was busy preparing her almanac for the following year when she received a letter from a woman in Munich, a member of the National Socialist German Workers' Party, which was busy stirring up trouble in Bavaria and holding meetings to which Hitler's oratory drew the crowds. She wanted to know what the future held in store for him and gave the date of his birth but not the hour.

Without mentioning Hitler by name, Frau Ebertin included her reply in the 1924 edition of her almanac, which was published in late July 1923. She wrote:

A man of action born on April 20, 1889, with Sun in 29° Aries at the time of his birth, can expose himself to personal danger by excessively uncautious action and could very likely trigger off an uncomfortable crisis. His constellations show that this man is to be taken very seriously indeed; he is destined to play a 'Führer-role' in future battles. It seems that the man I have in mind, with his strong Aries influence, is destined to sacrifice himself for the German nation, also to face up to all circumstances with audacity and courage, even when it is a matter of life and death, and to give an impulse, which will burst forth quite suddenly, to a German Freedom Movement. But I will not anticipate destiny—time will show, but the present state of affairs at the time I write this cannot last.

As Frau Ebertin's annual predictions were mainly applicable to the year ahead, the one made in the opening sentence was regarded by her readers as having been fulfilled when that November Hitler's Putsch led to his breaking his shoulder in the rioting, being brought to trial in February 1924, found guilty, and imprisoned for nearly six months in the Landsberg prison.

In her next year's almanac, commenting on her success, Frau Ebertin wrote that, when preparing her predictions, she never read the daily newspapers, because she did not want to be influenced by their contents. Therefore she had limited her research to studying Hitler's constellations so as to be able to write 'a few quite impartial remarks' about him. There had not been time to write for his birth hour, so she had cast a provisional horoscope for the day of his birth, based on the sun's position at noon on 20 April 1889. From this she had deduced that he had an unusual character, and that, no matter whether born in the morning or the evening, he would not be favoured by good fortune—because of the coming Saturn—sun opposition—if he were confronted with a major action or allowed himself to become involved in one.

Before the trial, Frau Ebertin, in collaboration with L. Hoffmann, a Bavarian journalist, wrote *Sternenwandel und Weltgeschehen* ('The Stars in their Courses and World Events') and such was the interest roused by her Hitler prediction that some 20,000 copies of this astrological pamphlet were soon sold. The final part was written by Hoffmann and was an account of what Frau Ebertin had told him about the Hitler prediction. She revealed that she had sent a copy of her 1924 yearbook to the *Völkischer Beobachter*, the newspaper owned by the National Socialist German Workers' Party, and her friends had shown Hitler the passage in question. His response to her warning had been to exclaim impatiently: 'What on earth have women and the stars got to do with me?' Frau Ebertin revealed that she had tried to explain to some of his followers that their Führer would have very critical aspects in November, and one had retorted: 'At this moment, when he's got something so important ahead of him, the aspects can't be good enough!'

Hoffmann wrote that Frau Ebertin had now discovered from the baptismal register at Braunau am Inn that the time of Hitler's birth was 6.30 p.m. She had also attended one of his meetings and had spoken briefly to him. It had seemed to her that he was rather shy off the platform, but on it became 'like a man possessed, like a medium, the unconscious tool of higher powers'. She added prophetically: 'It will turn out that recent events will not only give this movement inner strength, but external strength as well, so that it will give a mighty impetus to the pendulum of world history.'

Once Hitler became Chancellor, astrologers with conflicting opinions about him published horoscopes based on different times for his birth. One, maintaining that he had been born 12 hours earlier than recorded in the register, angered the Führer's followers by interpreting the new time as indicating that he had 'destructive and rapacious tendencies'. Another, Frank Glahn, swung a pendulum over Hitler's chart which selected 5.45 a.m. as the time of his birth. And Frau Ebertin in her 1934 *Ein Blick in die Zukunft* wrote that she now believed that he had been born between 6.22 and 6.26 p.m. and not 6.30 p.m.

The Propaganda Ministry regarded all this astrological divination with increasing distaste, and publication of any references to Hitler and prominent Nazis was suppressed from 1934 onwards.

Ellic Howe in his fascinating book about the strange world

of the German astrologers, *Urania's Children*, quotes a passage from the autobiography of Hans Blüher, a founder of the Wandervögel youth movement. Shortly after the Rohm *Putsch* of 30 June 1934, he asked Count Finckenstein, an astrologer friend of his, to tell him what he had gathered from studying Hitler's horoscope. The Count looked cautiously round the Berlin restaurant to make sure that no one was listening to their conversation, then he leaned towards Blüher and whispered into his ear through a cupped hand: 'He's a homicidal maniac!'

The 1937 edition of Elsbeth Ebertin's almanac was the last to be published, and even before the outbreak of war in 1939, Ellic Howe says, astrology in Germany had been driven underground. Frau Ebertin lost her life in an air raid on Freiburg im Breisgau in November 1944. Her son, Reinhold, also an astrologer, wrote in *Kosmobiologie*: 'My mother saw the crisis coming for she knew the horoscopes of many people living in the neighbouring houses. However, if she had left, it would have caused a terrible turmoil and she would have been picked up by the Gestapo because people were saying: "As long as Frau Ebertin is here nothing serious can happen to us!"'

I have already told in detail the story of Karl Ernst Krafft, the remarkable Swiss astrologer, in my book about visionaries and seers, *They Saw Tomorrow*, so I will limit my references to him now to a summary of his predictions. Through offering his services to Dr Heinrich Fesel of Himmler's secret intelligence service, he was employed in a free-lance capacity in 1939, and on 2 November Fesel was startled to receive a sheet of paper on which Krafft stated that the Führer's astrological aspects showed that his life would be in danger between the 7th and 10th of that month and added: 'There is a possibility of an assassination attempt through the use of explosive material.'

Fesel kept the memorandum, but did not pass on its contents as there was a ban on all predictions concerning Hitler. Then, on the evening of the 8th, when the annual celebration of the 1923 Putsch took place in Munich, a bomb hidden behind a pillar on the rostrum exploded, only a few minutes after the Führer had left earlier than originally planned.

When the news broke next day, Krafft decided that he

must not miss this opportunity of furthering himself, so he immediately sent a telegram to Rudolf Hess stating that he had predicted the assassination attempt in a letter to Dr Fesel six days previously. He warned that Hitler would still be in danger for the next few days. The wire was seen by Hitler and Goebbels soon after it arrived, and the same day the Gestapo arrested Krafft. After close interrogation he satisfied them that he was not involved in the attempt on the Führer's life.

When, two years later, Rudolf Hess landed in Scotland on Saturday 10 May 1941, the Nazis were quick to blame his defection on the astrologers he had constantly consulted and to claim that in consequence he had lost his reason. *The Times*, on 14 May, included a report from its Swiss correspondent stating: 'Certain of Hess's closest friends have thrown an interesting light on the affair. They say that Hess has always been Hitler's astrologer in secret. Up to last March, he had consistently predicted good fortune and had always been right. Since then, notwithstanding the victories Germany has won, he has declared that the stars showed that Hitler's meteoric career was approaching its climax.'

Incidentally, on 10 May, the *Sunday Chronicle's* Gypsy Petulengro had a remarkably correct prediction spoilt by the interference of a sub-editor who altered the astrologer's copy to read: 'Hitler's right hand man will die this week'—whereas not 'die' but 'be lost' had been typed by Petulengro. Jimmy Drawbell, the paper's editor, commented only a few days later that the regrettable change had been made because the original was regarded as ambiguous.

In Germany, all Hess's associates were taken into custody, on 7 June Martin Bormann ordered the arrest of all 'astrologers, fortune-tellers and other swindlers', and two days later the Gestapo put this ruthlessly into operation all over the country. This upset Himmler, who was always seeking advice from astrologers and clairvoyants. A jest circulated that Goering cared only about the stars on his epaulettes and Himmler about the stars in his horoscope.

The Gestapo were particularly suspicious of Ernst Schulte-Stathaus, who had been in an administrative position on Hess's staff for many years and who was an earnest amateur astrologer. When arrested, he denied their charge that he had told Hess 10 May would be a propitious date for his flight. What he had said was that a unique major conjunction would take place on 10 May 1941, with six planets coinciding with a full moon, and he might have said that such a date would prove an unfortunate time for Hess. He swore that he knew nothing of his chief's intention to leave the country on that day. Schulte-Stathaus was nevertheless kept in prison until the spring of 1943.

Ellic Howe spent a good deal of time when in Germany in trying to find the astrologers who might have advised Hess to take the course he did. He received some interesting information from Dr Rainer Hildebrandt, author of a biography of his close friend Professor Albrecht Haushofer of Berlin, a prominent participant in the underground movement against Hitler. Haushofer was a convinced believer in astrology and fascinated by the subject of Hitler's horoscope and what it portended for him and for Germany.

Dr Hildebrandt wrote to Ellic Howe that Hess had flown to Scotland on his peace mission because he was convinced that despite the risks everything possible must be done to end hostilities without delay, because at the end of April and at the beginning of May 1941 Hitler's astrological aspects were unusually malefic. Hess interpreted these aspects to mean that he, personally, must take these dangers that threatened the Führer upon his own shoulders in order to save Hitler and restore peace to Germany. On several occasions, Hess's astrological adviser had told him that Anglo-German relations were threatened by a deep-seated crisis of confidence. Indeed, at this time there were very dangerous planetary oppositions in Hitler's horoscope. Haushofer, who dabbled a great deal in astrology, seldom left his friend Hess without a hint that something unexpected could happen in the near future.

Among those arrested, according to Dr Hildebrandt, was Hess's astrologer, Dr Ludwig Schmitt, who was also a well-known Munich physician.

Dr Goebbels's propaganda machine made considerable use of the fascination the occult had for the populace. German agents wrote articles for large-circulation magazines in neutral countries. All planetary aspects showed certain victory for Hitler's forces, they asserted.

The British Secret Service countered this by sending over Louis de Wohl in the guise of a private astrologer. Beginning his campaign in New York, he asserted that Hitler's horoscope showed the planet Neptune in the house of death, and that this implied his days were numbered. At the national convention of the American Federation of Scientific Astrologers at Cleveland, Ohio, in August 1941, he compared the astrological charts of Napoleon and Hitler and pointed out that both had the same Saturn position, which meant that the Führer would fall from power within a few years. Although he could not have known of Eva Braun's existence, de Wohl said that Hitler had a mistress who would die violently, which was in itself an extraordinary prediction, as was his next one. The Russian campaign had just begun and, according to de Wohl, all the astrological aspects indicated eventual disaster.

Back in England, de Wohl worked for Sefton Delmer's secret 'black' section in the Political Warfare Executive, writing the text for faked issues of *Der Zenit*, the German astrological magazine, which were smuggled into Germany, mainly into ports. The issue dated April 1943, for example, which predicted when U-boats would be sunk, was actually printed three months later, by which time Delmer had received details from the Admiralty of the dates on which U-boats had been destroyed in the interim. This would make the remaining crews in German ports believe that the astrological correspondent of *Der Zenit* possessed genuine powers, and they would become demoralized when in the same issue they read predictions that Germany would suffer serious reverses on the Eastern front.

Both Britain and Germany used faked texts of the celebrated sixteenth-century seer Nostradamus to their own advantage. As the German armies were sweeping over the Belgian border, the Luftwaffe dropped leaflets over northern France containing quatrains predicting certain victory for the Germans which helped to spread a mood of defeatism among the credulous.

Professor Trevor-Roper, in his book *The Last Days of Hitler*, quotes from what Hitler's Minister of Finance, Count Schwerin von Krosigk, wrote in his unpublished diary, which came into British hands when he was captured at Flensburg in May 1945. Two horoscopes were in Himmler's custody, the horoscope of the Führer prepared on 30 January 1933, and that of the Weimar Republic dated 9 November 1918. The documents were examined and, according to Krosigk, both horoscopes had astonishingly predicted the outbreak of war in 1939, the victories till 1941, and then the series of defeats culminating in the worst disasters in the early months of 1945, especially in the first half of April. There was to be an overwhelming victory in the second half of April, stalemate till August, and in August peace. After the peace, there would be a difficult time for Germany for three years, but from 1948 onwards she would rise to greatness again.

'Next day, Goebbels sent me the horoscopes,' Krosigk continued. 'I could not fathom everything in them; but in the subjoined interpretation newly drawn up, I found it all; and now I am eagerly awaiting the second half of April.'

What Krosigk does not mention is that in Hitler's horoscope Neptune was at the cusp, the beginning degree of the twelfth field of his chart in April, and Neptune was his 'death significance'. This might mean his own death, although that event was not likely to occur before Saturn was at an angle of 180° to Hitler's moon position, which would be the case on 1 May. It could be interpreted as the death of an enemy. Himmler's astrologer, Wilhelm Wulff of Hamburg, was consulted, and to avoid Hitler's wrath tactfully suggested that the aspect might augur the death of the Führer's worst enemy.

On Friday 13 April, Goebbels learned of the death of President Roosevelt, ordered champagne to celebrate with his entourage, and phoned Hitler to congratulate him. 'It is written in the stars,' he crowed. 'The second half of April will be the turning point for us. It is the turning point!'

But, as Wulff told Himmler privately, it was Hitler's own death that was foretold, and this took place a day earlier than predicted on 30 April.

Wilhelm Wulff himself was an extraordinary character. After the First World War, he became a professional sculptor and took up astrology as a hobby, and he found that through casting the horoscopes of missing persons he was able to help in tracing them. In 1923, like Frau Ebertin, he cast Hitler's horoscope for the first time and found that for about 24 hours on or about 8–9 November, Mars and Saturn were particularly threatening. There were indications of violence with disastrous consequences. This was fulfilled when Hitler's Putsch failed and he was imprisoned.

Eventually, Wulff became so successful as an astrologer that he was able to earn his own living entirely from such work. In June 1941, when all known astrologers were rounded up by the Gestapo, Wulff too was arrested. After spending four months in a concentration camp, he was released on promising not to practise astrology any longer, and was given employment by a former client named Zimmermann in his factory. Then, six months later, Wulff was ordered by the authorities to take up new duties as a research assistant in an institute in Berlin attached to naval headquarters. Following the outbreak of war in 1939, such institutes had been set up for the army and the Luftwaffe to test any new inventions sent in by members of the public. To his amazement, he discovered on arrival that the Nazi leaders proposed not to limit experiments to conventional science but to include the supernatural.

In his autobiography, *Zodiac and Swastika*, Wulff describes how he found himself in a top-secret milieu run by a naval captain and among a strange assortment of sprirtualists, astrologers, astronomers, ballistics experts, and mathematicians. The institute had been instructed by Naval Command HQ to pinpoint the position of British convoys at sea by means of pendulums and other occult paraphernalia, so that U-boats could be certain of sinking them. 'Day in, day out, the pendulum practitioners squatted with their arms stretched out over nautical charts,' wrote Wulff. 'The results were pitiful.' In the hope that bracing sea air might produce better results, this motley crew were moved to the island of Sylt but with no improvement in their performance.

Wulff soon found himself back working for Zimmermann, through whom he met Felix Kersten, Himmler's personal physician and masseur, who then exploited Wulff's astrological knowledge to make himself more interesting in the eyes of his patient and the SS top brass. Now Wulff was having to work under great pressure on 'the most ridiculous commissions and having to produce infallible results was both trying and dangerous'.

On 28 July 1943, two Gestapo officials called at Wulff's home unexpectedly and drove him to the Berlin HQ of the Kriminalpolizei, where he was taken before General Arthur Nebe, its chief and one of the finest criminologists of this century. Nebe asked Wulff whether he could use his astrological powers to discover the whereabouts of Mussolini, who had been abducted two days previously. Wulff says that Indian astrology provided a method for achieving this which he had successfully tried out in another case and now repeated, with the result that on the afternoon of the same day he was able to tell Nebe that Mussolini was then hidden not further than 75 miles south-east of Rome. Later it was confirmed that at that time the Duce was imprisoned on the island of Ponza, the position of which was where Wulff had indicated.

Nebe also handed Wulff the birth particulars of a certain Franz Schwarz, who, he said, was a factory manager, and asked him to prepare a detailed horoscope. In a letter dated 8 May 1963, a lawyer, Dr Ernst Teichmann, was later to tell Wulff how a few weeks after he had first been consulted by Nebe, the latter called Teichmann, then his personal assistant, into his office and handed him the Schwarz horoscope to read and asked what he thought of it. He realized at once from the birth data that 'Schwarz' was really Nebe himself and said so, adding: 'And I am astonished to see how accurately the astrologer has characterized you.' To his horror, Nebe turned pale and shouted at him to read the rest.

Teichmann wrote that he was almost struck dumb by the grim prediction which followed:

a professional and personal debacle, persecution, and a dreadful death were prophesied for 'Herr Franz Schwarz' in the near future. Nebe did not take his eyes off me as I tried to pooh-pooh the prophecy and pass it off with a joke. From that day on, Nebe was frightened. Subsequently, he became more and more nervous and was subject to severe depressions. I do not think I am mistaken in assuming that his psychological condition prompted his precipitate flight after the assassination attempt (on Hitler's life) of July 20, 1944.

As predicted, Nebe was hanged on 4 March 1945, in a cruel and terrible way after being found guilty of involvement in the plot.

In January 1944, Wulff cast the horoscope of Walter Schwellenburg, then in charge of counter-espionage and head of Department VI in the Reich Central Security Office, who admitted that it was 'absolutely true', but nevertheless maintained that he could not take astrology seriously. He referred to Dr Goebbels's use of astrology for propaganda purposes by printing faked quatrains of Nostradamus predicting victory for Germany and circulating these in neutral countries—which had backfired when Spanish and Swedish newspapers had carried the headline 'WHO IS NOS-TRADAMUS?' and had followed this a few days later with the answer: 'NOSTRADAMUS IS ADOLF HITLER'.

When Schwellenburg and Wulff became more friendly, the young SS general confided that he thought the Third Reich could be saved only by Hitler's removal. Wulff replied that this could not change the course of events: far too much had happened for that. He had been studying Hitler's horoscope for some 20 years. Hitler would probably lose his life in 'enigmatic' circumstances in which a woman would play a leading part. Neptune was extremely strong in his horoscope, and it was always to be expected that his great military projects would have a dubious outcome. As far as Stalin was concerned, he could expect highly favourable planetary directions in 1945–6, and so too could Great Britain and the United States, whose constellations would reach their peak in mid-May 1945.

Wulff's meeting with Schwellenburg led to a well-cloaked visit to Himmler's castle retreat of Aigen. The SS leader told his guest that he was sorry he had had him sent to a concentration camp together with the other astrologers, but none could be allowed to follow their calling except those who worked for the National Socialists. He revealed that he had received details of what Wulff had said about Hitler's horoscope and asked what the astrologer thought ought to be done to prevent Germany's losing the war. Wulff dared to suggest that Himmler might have Hitler arrested and was told that this would be difficult. Wulff urged him to do so as his police force was still intact and he could easily take over the government. For the immediate future, his constellations were favourable whilst Hitler's were bad. Himmler said that he would think about it, and after discussing the international situation and astrology Wulff left.

Back in Berlin, Wulff was taken to see Schwellenburg, who had delivered the horoscope details to Himmler in person and arranged the meeting at Aigen in the hope that it might make the vacillating SS leader act accordingly. Wulff told the counter-espionage chief that he had spent five hours with

Himmler which Schwellenburg regarded as a good sign, commenting that he rarely spent so much time with anyone.

The visit had taken place in May 1944. On 6 June the Allies landed in Normandy, then on 20 July came the attempt on Hitler's life, which failed, with the result that Himmler had second thoughts about leading a rebellion and dealt ruthlessly with the conspirators. Wulff's own standing with Himmler was unaffected by the course of events because, when regularly consulted by him, he had insisted that, according to Hitler's horoscope, he would not die at the hands of an assassin. And now, as the tide of war turned against Germany, Wulff was continually being pressed for astrological reports by Himmler, who continued to vacillate but whose faith in Wulff had been strengthened by the fact that he had foretold an escape from a serious accident on 9 December 1944. This happened, for on the night of 9 December, driving above the Black Forest railway, Himmler ran off the road and down the hill just as a train was approaching, and only just managed to get out of the way in time.

Whenever Wulff told Himmler that Hitler's constellations indicated a mysterious death and that the SS leader could succeed if he arrested him, Himmler would argue that he had sworn a soldier's oath to Hitler and could not break it. Wulff had to prepare the horoscopes of Churchill, Montgomery, and Eisenhower so as to provide guidance in the proposed peace negotiations, and also those of five prominent Germans to see if the stars approved of their forming a new government. And so it went on, with Wulff having to supply a daily list of planetary aspects. Himmler would shriek hysterically over and over again 'Tell me what to do!' but did not take Wulff's advice when he told him to flee the country. Captured by the British, Himmler committed suicide in the summer of 1945.

CHAPTER 2

Wolf Messing—Seer to Stalin

Wolf Grigorievich Messing, who died in 1972, was probably the most remarkable hypnotist and telepathist of this century. For his accomplishments in this field he was appointed a Meritorious Artist of the Soviet Union. He was a Jew born in the village of Gora Kalwaria near Warsaw on 10 September 1899. His parents were poor and very religious, and he was gifted with such a fine memory that by the age of six he was so conversant with the Talmud that the rabbi told his pleased parents that he must go to a special school and be trained for the rabbinate. Very unwillingly he obeyed, but life at the religious school did not suit his temperament, and at the age of 11 he ran away.

Jumping on to a passing train, Wolf hid under a seat and fell asleep. On being awakened by the conductor demanding to see his ticket, he pulled a scrap of newspaper out of his pocket and held it out as he stared into the other's eyes, desperately willing him to accept it as a ticket. Recalling this initial success as a hypnotist, Messing wrote later: 'The man took it and in an odd way turned it over in his hands. . . then he punched it in his machine and handing it back to me said: "Why ever do you want to lie under the seat when you have a ticket? Get up! In a couple of hours we'll be in Berlin."'

In the German capital, young Wolf earned a miserable living as a messenger boy. One freezing day, he collapsed unconscious from near-starvation, was carried to a hospital, pronounced dead, and removed to a morgue; and that would have been the final chapter in his life had not a medical student detected that Messing's heart was beating feebly. He was brought back to the hospital, where his case attracted the attention of a neuropathologist and psychiatrist, Dr Abel, who after three days brought him back to full life.

Abel told Wolf that he had been suffering from abnormal drowsiness and took him under his personal care. Soon he concluded that the boy could self-induce catalepsy and had paranormal powers. He, together with another colleague and his wife, Mr and Mrs Schmidt, conducted telepathic tests with Wolf. The results were impressive.

The penniless youth managed to earn a living through exploiting his strange gifts. A Herr Tselmeister exhibited him every weekend lying in a crystal coffin in the Berlin Panopticon, for which he paid him five marks a day. During the rest of the week, he would tell fortunes in the market place. According to Wolf, he was able to pick up the thoughts of the people there and would then find answers to their problems and have visions of what was going to happen to them. He spent the pittance thus earned on private lessons to further his education.

Having developed the ability to make any part of his body immune to pain, Wolf increased his income by acting as a fakir in the Berlin Wintergarten and allowing outsize needles to be stuck deep into his chest.

In 1915, the 16-year-old 'wonder boy', as he was billed, obtained an engagement to appear in Vienna, where he made a considerable impression and was invited by Albert Einstein to meet Sigmund Freud. The latter asked Wolf if he would submit to a telepathic test with Freud himself sending out an order mentally to him. Wolf agreed and succeeded with ease. He went to the bathroom cupboard, removed some tweezers and, approaching Einstein, he said, hesitantly: 'Herr Freud wants me to pull three hairs from your magnificent moustache.' The great mathematician smiled and nodded, and the youth removed the required hairs with a care, Einstein said, that would have done credit to a surgeon.

After the end of the First World War, Messing travelled widely giving public demonstrations. In India, Gandhi carried out a test similar to Freud's. He willed Messing to take a flute from off a table and give it to a certain person in the room. The message was successfully transmitted and obeyed. Then there was an unexpected sequel: the man started playing the flute, whereupon a basket shook and a snake reared up out of it and swayed rhythmically to the music.

Messing's base was still Poland, and the police started asking for his assistance in solving cases that had baffled them. A leading member of Warsaw society, Count Czastoryski, had been robbed of the family jewels and offered Messing a reward of a quarter of a million zlotys if he could help in recovering them. Flown to the Count's castle, he employed psychometry like the Dutch psychic Hurkos to pick up impressions. This trail brought him into the bedroom of a little boy, a servant's son. He touched all the toys in turn, then he pointed at a large stuffed bear. 'They are all inside that,' he announced and when it was cut open the missing jewels cascaded on to the carpet, together with an assortment of knick-knacks and trinkets. When questioned, the child confessed that he could not resist making off with glittering objects and hiding them in this way.

In 1937, during a demonstration of his gifts in a Warsaw theatre, Messing was asked if he had any predictions concerning Hitler. 'He will die if he turns towards the East,' came the reply. As a result, Messing was placed on the list of people to be arrested when the German army swept across the Polish frontier on 1 September 1939. He immediately went into hiding, but when taking the air in a back street one morning he was unfortunate enough to encounter a Nazi officer who, recognizing him, struck him in the mouth, knocking out six teeth as punishment for what he had said about the Führer.

Messing was then taken to a police station and thrown on to the floor of a room. He wrote in his reminiscences that, realizing drastic action was imperative in order to save his life, he willed all the police to come into the room where he was confined. Such was the pull of his extraordinary mental power that they found themselves doing so, including the sentry. Messing pretended to be unconscious, but he had wriggled as near as possible to the door. When his captors were gathered together, he willed them to look away from him, then, jumping up, he dashed into the corridor and shot the iron bolt across the door. Somehow he managed to cross into Russia before dawn and thus avoided the terrible fate of his father and all his other relations, who were massacred by the Nazis with the other Jews in the Warsaw Ghetto.

On reaching Brest Litovsk, Messing visited the Ministry of Culture and told his interviewer what he did for a living.

The man snapped that fortune-telling was banned in the Soviet Union, and as for telepathy, that too was completely bogus. Messing asked to be allowed to demonstrate his gift. This was reluctantly allowed, and despite their materialistic outlook those judging him were so impressed that he was given permission to tour with his stage programme.

Wolf Messing's fame as both a hypnotist and a telepathist spread, and audiences packed the theatres where he appeared, presenting what were billed as 'Psychological Experiments'. Then, one evening in 1940, in the city of Gomel, two of the secret police strode on to the stage half-way through the show and addressed the audience. The entertainment was at an end. They must go home.

The police led Messing outside, pushed him into a car, and drove off into the night. After a long drive, they reached what in the darkness looked like a hotel in large grounds well guarded by soldiers. Messing was marched into a room and left, and then he was taken into another room. After a while a man entered whom he recognized as Stalin and who proceeded to question him closely about the opinions of people in Poland and those of its leaders. Once the interrogation had ceased, Stalin left, saying that he would be seeing him again shortly.

When Messing next visited Stalin it was in Moscow. The dictator revealed that he had been reading reports of Messing's hypnotic powers and wanted him to demonstrate them by obtaining 100,000 roubles from the Moscow Gosbank, where he had no account and was unknown. Messing accepted the challenge, went to the bank, walked up to the cashier, presented him with a blank sheet of paper taken from a school exercise book, and, without saying a word, he concentrated on willing the cashier to pay him the huge amount. The trusted and experienced employee looked at the paper, then like an obedient puppet he walked over to the safe, took out the required packet of notes, and handed them to Messing, who packed them into the attaché case which he had ready open on the counter and went out to show the money to two of the Russian ruler's aides waiting in a car. They were astounded. Then Messing walked back into the bank and started returning the bank notes to the bewildered cashier, who, no longer hypnotized, examined the paper he had previously been handed and collapsed on to the floor with a heart attack. Fortunately, he recovered.

Not completely convinced, Stalin then set Messing a second and more difficult test. He was led to a room in the heart of the Kremlin and given the task of leaving the building and hypnotizing three security guards in turn into accepting the blank cards he showed them as official passes. This he achieved without difficulty, and when he emerged outside he could not resist turning and waving at his chief 'minder' watching incredulously from the top-floor room Messing had left only a few minutes before.

But Stalin was still not satisfied. He next submitted Messing to the most difficult task of all—to penetrate, without producing any pass and looking like a complete stranger, the ruler's country retreat at Kuntsevo, which bristled with secret police and guards. Not very long after this, Stalin was working at the desk of his inner sanctum, the whereabouts of which inside the dacha no outsider could possibly know, when those guarding the doorway moved aside and Messing walked in.

The man of steel was for once in his life bewildered and inwardly unnerved. 'However did you manage it?' he demanded. According to Messing's own account, he explained that he had mentally suggested to all those who would normally have barred his way that he was Laurenti Beria, the dreaded chief of the secret police, whom he in no way resembled, not even having attempted the most superficial of disguises by wearing a pair of pince-nez.

After this remarkable feat, Messing enjoyed Stalin's complete support in all he did and was employed by the Ministry of Culture to travel anywhere he liked in the Soviet Union. The account of his experiences quoted is taken from his reminiscences published in two issues of the Russian journal *Science and Religion* in 1965. These were stated to be extracts from his autobiography, which would be published by Sovietskaya Rossiya. The autobiography never appeared and the suspicion lingers that the authorities stopped publication because too much would have been revealed. It is highly probable that Stalin consulted Messing on later occasions—and even possible that Stalin learned from Messing how to hypnotize in order to maintain his own supremacy.

* * *

In May 1942, the titanic struggle between the attacking Germans and the heroic Russians defending Kharkov was raging. A weary defender, soldier Kolya Zvantsov, while on night watch had fallen asleep from exhaustion. He dreamed that, across the quiet fields ahead of him, squadron after squadron of German tanks bore relentlessly forward in a surprise attack on the weak places in the Soviet defences, supported by wave upon wave of decimating dive-bombers. Next morning, he described his dream to his commanding officer, who had become interested in the paranormal through attending Messing's demonstrations. He regrouped his troops accordingly, barely in time to wipe out, with an unexpected barrage from heavy guns, the vanguard of the enemy's tanks, and thanks to the warning dream the Nazis were hurled back.

Although any form of prediction was forbidden in the Soviet Union, Messing flouted this ban on various occasions. Whilst the Russian–German accord was still in operation, he foretold at a private meeting in Moscow: 'Soviet tanks will within a few years enter Berlin.' This caused concern in diplomatic circles, and the Germans made an official protest to the Kremlin. After some deliberation, they were told that the Soviet government could not accept responsibility for an entertainer's predictions.

Messing's words were remembered during the dark days of 1943 when so much of the Soviet Union had been ravaged and conquered by the Germans. Addressing an audience in Novosibirsk's opera house in Siberia, he promised: 'The war will end victoriously for Russia in May 1945, and most likely in its first week.' The actual date proved to be 9 May.

After the war, in 1945, Messing went to present his 'Psychological Experiments' in Ashkhabad, and on the very first day he felt increasingly alarmed. This sensation became so strong that he cancelled all his performances and returned to Moscow. Three days later, Ashkhabad was destroyed by an earthquake and some 50,000 people died.

Attempts have been made by Russian scientists to explain how Messing proved so consistently correct in his telepathic performances. Yuri Filatov observed that he always made a point of either taking the man or woman volunteering by the hand or causing the other to seize hold of his own. Filatov believed that the subconscious muscle movements accompanying human thought played a vital role in enabling Messing to read a person's mind. Messing himself has disclosed that physical contact was an aid because it enabled him to concentrate to the exclusion of his surroundings, but he refuted the allegation that he read minds by close observation of people's reactions.

Messing in fact preferred to perform blindfolded so that he could not see his subjects. Their thoughts became images with colour and depth in his own mind. He once said that he found it easiest of all to read the thoughts of the deaf and dumb. These he perceived 'more vividly and distinctly'.

Robert Kyucharyants, editor of the Novosti Press Agency, who interviewed Messing just before he died, asked him to explain how he could predict future events so accurately. He answered:

By straining my will-power, I suddenly see the culminating result of many events. I call it 'direct knowledge'. I don't see anything supernatural about it. The future shapes itself from the past and the present, and there are certain bonds between them. Understanding the mechanism of this direct knowledge is at present inaccessible to us, because our ideas of the essence of time, of its links with space, with the past, present and future, are as yet indefinite.

CHAPTER 3

'The Sleeping Prophet'

Edgar Cayce, born on a Kentucky farm in 1877 and who died in 1945, became known as 'the sleeping prophet'. He was poorly educated and yet later, in semi-trance, he was for some 40 years to make pronouncements worthy of experts specializing in a variety of subjects and, as well, to make controversial predictions. According to Cayce himself, it all began when as a seven-year-old he was walking in a wood and he stopped to sit in an open space, which was suddenly filled with a bright light from which came a voice asking him what he would most like to do in his life. He replied that he wanted to help others and, in particular, children who were ill.

After this experience he could think of nothing else, so that next day at school he neglected his lessons and later could not concentrate on his homework. Forced by his father to stay up until he had completed the task, he was bent drowsily over his books, unable to take in what he read, when the voice spoke again, saying repeatedly: 'Sleep, we will help you.' This he did and next morning was delighted to find at school that he was able to answer correctly all his teacher's questions.

Cayce claimed he had had visions as a child. In the garden one day he saw chariots of fire rushing through the sky, and a sixth sense told him that a great war would break out. This proved to be the First World War.

According to Cayce, that was how he began to act as a channel for the 'Universal Mind'. Shortly afterwards, rendered unconscious by a baseball hitting his spine, he was yet able to prescribe for himself, telling his mother what plants to use in the poultice she applied to his neck.

Thus began the 'health readings' for which Cayce was to gain a worldwide reputation. He earned his living from running a small photographer's shop at Virginia Beach, where he also twice a day diagnosed illnesses and prescribed remedies for people consulting him. During his lifetime he was consulted by some 15,000 people.

Cayce would stretch himself out on a couch, loosen his clothes, place his folded hands over his stomach, shut his eyes, and await the flashing of a white light as he sank into a state of trance. The term 'reading' was used to describe what he then said, as he seemed to be reading from a book. He would employ medical terms that made the treatment all the more remarkable coming from someone of such limited education.

Once, Cayce prescribed a certain remedy prepared from the plant clary, but no pharmacist could trace it. Cayce's patient, a railway magnate, James Andrews, even went to the trouble of advertising in the medical press for information. During a later 'reading', Cayce was able to dictate in detail the formula for the preparation. Eventually, Andrews learned that a doctor in Paris had marketed a patent medicine the composition of which corresponded exactly with what Cayce required—but this had ceased being marketed 50 years previously.

Edgar Cayce married and had a son who, when fooling about with matches at the age of eight, exploded some magnesium and lost his sight. A specialist wanted to remove one eye. Horrified, Cayce sought guidance whilst in a trance and, forbidding the operation, insisted that bandages steeped in tannic acid should be placed over the eye instead. Within a fortnight the boy's sight was restored.

Cayce was able to treat patients successfully no matter how far they were from him, providing he knew where they would be at the time when he went to 'sleep' at Virginia Beach. He could also on occasion demonstrate his telepathic powers. To convince a sceptical Kentucky businessman, he agreed to describe to him over the telephone when he reached his office the route he had taken from his home. Cayce achieved this, adding correctly that the man had stopped at a shop on the way to buy one more cigar than usual.

One day, in his 'sleep', Cayce dictated four complicated

prescriptions which proved to be needed to treat the complaints of four people who consulted him two days later. On another occasion, he recommended the use of a drug called Codiron, giving the name and address of the manufacturing chemists that could supply it. A phone call to the firm in Chicago was received with amazement, for the preparation's formula had only just been fixed and its very name chosen an hour earlier.

Cayce asserted that, on awakening, he had no knowledge of what he had been saying. He believed that he obtained his medical knowledge in most instances through telepathic communication with the brains of those possessing it. He admitted, however, that he could be wrong at times, and would refund the fee he had charged to any dissatisfied person consulting him. Once he warned a man to take the greatest care over his diet as he had something seriously the matter with his blood. The enquirer then consulted a specialist and, told that he was in perfect health, denounced Cayce as a misguided charlatan who had caused him unnecessary worry— but three years later he died of leukaemia.

The police sought Cayce's assistance on occasion when unable to detect criminals. One of the most remarkable instances of his proving correct was when he solved a murder that had been perpetrated in an isolated part of Canada. He told the police that the victim had been shot by her sister in a fit of jealousy because both these spinsters had been infatuated with the same lover. Not only did he say that the woman had pushed the weapon down the drain, but he also gave the serial number stamped on the pistol. When it was found, the sister admitted her guilt.

On the morning of 5 March 1929, Cayce warned a man consulting him not to invest in stocks and shares. Then, in the afternoon, a stockbroker described a dream that had worried him and the 'sleeping' prophet said that it signified a downward movement of long duration, including even blue chips, and advised him to sell his entire portfolio.

On 6 April of that year Cayce told another financier: 'There must surely come a break when there will be a panic in the money centres not only on Wall Street, but a closing of the banks in many centres and a readjustment of the actual specie.'

In the thirties, when 20 young men acting as leaders in

the Scouts met in his house, Cayce suddenly walked out of the room. Asked afterwards the reason for this, he said that he had seen three of those present dying in another war, and in fact the ones he named lost their lives in the Second World War. On later occasions, he predicted the defeat of Hitler and India's coming independence.

From 1923 onwards, Cayce took on the role of an Old Testament type of prophet and, lying on a bed in trance, dictated lectures on many subjects obtained, so he said, by becoming a channel for what he termed the 'Universal Mind'—possibly the equivalent of Jung's 'collective unconscious'. In 1934, he made one of his most fantastic predictions: that there would be born in America two years later a baby to be named John Penniel, 'who would be beloved of all men in all places when the universality of God in the earth has been proclaimed'. He would come 'as a messenger, not a forerunner' and give to the earth 'a new order of things'. As a sign that this was shortly to pass, 'the sun will be darkened and the earth shall be broken in several places' No part of this prediction has as yet been fulfilled.

In the same 'reading', Cayce continued: 'The greater portion of Japan must go into the sea. The upper portion of Europe will be changed as in the twinkling of an eye. Land will appear off the east coast of America. There will be upheaval in the Arctic and in the Antarctic that will make for the eruptions of volcanoes in the torrid areas, and there will be the shifting then of the poles'—so that countries where the climate is 'frigid or semi-tropical' will become tropical. This would occur before 1998 'when His Light will be seen again in the clouds'.

So far the most in the way of natural disasters that Cayce's followers have been able to find to support the prophecy were the Alaskan earthquake of 1964, the Mount Etna eruptions in 1960 and 1971, the appearance of a volcanic island, Surtsy, off the east coast of Canada in 1963, and a major earthquake in Hokkaido Island in June 1973.

In 1941, Cayce predicted: 'Portions of the now east coast of New York, or New York City itself, will in the main disappear.' The same fate, but much sooner, would befall southern Carolina and Georgia. Little has happened since then to indicate eventual fulfilment of such a forecast, though the sea level between Maine and Virginia is now rising at a small but accelerating rate, while Rhode Island with its low coastline is shrinking.

During the same 'reading' in 1941, Cayce said: 'In the next few years, lands will appear in the Atlantic as well as in the Pacific.' Not even an island came into view before Surtsy in 1963 and a volcanic islet south of Tokyo in 1973.

Cayce's record regarding climatic and geographical changes is therefore hardly impressive. He has had more success in the political field. Following the fulfilment of his predictions that there would be a financial crash on Wall Street in 1929, two years later he forecast definite improvements for the spring of 1933 which were realized with Franklin D. Roosevelt's election and the New Deal. In 1939, he foretold social riots preceding and following the death of the 'Second President' and that he would die while still in office.

Those who long for the legendary to be proved true were heartened when Cayce claimed that Atlantis did exist. In several hundreds of his 'readings' between 1923 and 1944 he maintained that a great civilization had flourished there about 10,700 BC and that divine punishment for the inhabitants' loose living had led to its being ravaged by three earthquakes, causing it to sink beneath the Atlantic in about 9700 BC.

In 1940 Cayce predicted that in 1968 and 1969 'Poiseda' would be the first part of Atlantis to rise again to the surface, and that it would be in the vicinity of the Bimini Islands near Florida's east coast. In these very years, Dr J. Manson Valentine of the Miami Museum of Science, Count Pino Turolla, an archaeologist, and others exploring this area came across important remains that ocean currents altering their course had revealed where the sea had receded. These consisted of the walls and massive steps of a stone building and a man-made roadway. There were flat circular stone slabs arranged in a pattern, and 44 marble pillars set in a circle, some still erect and others that had fallen down. Scientific tests established these artefacts as dating from 10,000 BC.

In 1969, too, a ship with experts from Duke University came across light-coloured granite rocks in the area which, according to Dr Bruce Heezen, might have once been part of the core of a subsided continent. He explained that a granite base would have to be there to support such a land mass. Four years later, Dr Valentine received cool reactions from his conservative colleagues to his theory that Cuba and the West Indies were what remained of a continent that had once filled the Atlantic between America and Europe and had vanished from view about 9500 BC. This supports Cayce's case.

Despite all the derision from sceptics, belief in Atlantis remains as strong as ever among the romantically inclined. Cayce also said that before 9700 BC what is now the Mississippi basin was beneath the ocean and that at that time today's United States consisted of the regions that are now part of Nevada, Utah, and Arizona. The lowlands along the Atlantic coast, Cayce declared, were then part of Atlantis.

In recent years, the explorations of geologists such as James Burkland and Lorin Raymond of Appalachian State University and Dr David E. Pettry have produced evidence indicating that the Virginian mystic's utterings may not be as fanciful as some consider them. In 1977, deep-sea diver Charles Berlitz discovered a pyramid 500 feet tall in the Bermuda triangle; and a human skull considered to be 10,000 years old was retrieved by archaeologist William Cockrell working under water off south-west Florida. This is many thousand years older than any discovered on land.

Prophets are inclined to copy each other, and this was particularly true in the case of Edgar Cayce. The grimly disastrous earthquakes that he foretold would wreck the West Coast of the United States and sink California have led to other psychics making similar prognostications. For instance, in April 1969 a number of them joined together in describing a frightful fate that was about to befall Hollywood. To prove that they believed in their nightmarish predictions they packed and moved miles away, but no disaster occurred.

Nevertheless, certain of Cayce's international predictions are not only of a more cheerful sort but show signs of coming to pass, such as that China would become more democratic, and that Communism would end in Russia, which, allied to the United States, would become the hope of a new society based on international co-operation.

With the approach of the year 1982 a 'reading' of Cayce's recorded some 45 years earlier was remembered. He wrote that Neptune and Uranus would then be in Sagittarius and Jupiter in Scorpio, where it would be joined by Mars in September, and Saturn would be in Libra.

In the autumn when the sun passes through the signs of Virgo and Libra, it is logical to assume that Venus and Mercury will be nearby, although I have not calculated their exact position as yet, and the Moon will also join them. The planets will therefore be all in a bunch as it were and will disturb the equilibrium of the Sun. Traditionally, this is said to signify the commencement of the Aquarian Age.

As I see it, the planetary forces will be manifested through the last four signs of the Zodiac only, which is bound to accentuate certain tracks both in nature and in people which will make for imbalances for we are all part of the cosmic whole.

I will plump for increased instability, social upheavals, a few earthquakes, and the discarding of outworn ideas about society generally.

At the start of 1982, there was great excitement among astrologers because all the planets in our solar system would be in the same segment of sky for a time, each one of them moving through a series of conjunctions with one or more of the others. This occurred only once every 179 years. It was believed, as Cayce mentions, that the combined pull of their gravities would affect the sun, which in turn would tug at the earth. Something would have to give way, and that was likely to be where the earth's crust was weakest. Such a region of geological instability is the San Andreas fault running down the coastline of California, and a devastating earthquake was predicted. Fortunately, the prophets of doom proved wrong.

Edgar Cayce died in 1945 leaving some 14,249 transcripts of his 'readings' from 1923 onwards now stored and available for inspection at ARE—the Association for Research and Enlightenment, run by his two sons and Gladys Turner, the stenographer who took down his words for 22 years. He predicted correctly if ambiguously the date of his own death from cancer saying, 'in the evening of the fifth day I shall definitely be healed'. But he will be back, according to a dream he had in 1921, when he saw himself reincarnated in Nebraska in AD 2100. Wishing to know how things were, he found himself flying through the air in a cigar-shaped cabin at a fantastic speed and landing amid the ruins of a vast city which hordes of workmen were busy rebuilding. 'Where am I?' he enquired. 'Why, New York City!' one replied.

CHAPTER 4

'The Wizard of Utrecht'

In December 1945, after Professor Willem Tenhaeff, the distinguished director of the Parapsychology Institute at the University of Utrecht and one of the leading pioneers in this field, had given a lecture, he was approached by a man with penetrating eyes, 36-year-old Gerard Croiset, who was practically penniless as a result of the failure of his business as a grocer. Croiset claimed that he had developed paranormal powers and offered to take part in stringent tests to prove the authenticity of his claims. Professor Tenhaeff agreed with some misgivings, for Croiset was almost illiterate, but as the experiments progressed the Professor was astonished to find that the man had an extraordinary facility for tracing missing people as well as animals and objects, and for solving crimes. He could see what had happened miles away, in the past, what was happening in the present, and what would happen in the future with equal facility.

In the years ahead, Croiset would bewilder and impress sceptics and become internationally celebrated as 'the wizard of Utrecht with the X-ray mind' whom Professor Tenhaeff termed a 'paragnost'. He did not appear to go into a trance, but needed to establish contact with missing persons by either handling something belonging to them or speaking often over the telephone to someone closely connected with them. He would then describe whatever images or sensations came into his mind. Croiset himself has described how his gift functions:

When a warning feeling disturbs me, I get a vibration which is like a full-up feeling and I expand like a balloon. I grow attentive. The paragnost in me is now at work... When somebody with a real problem comes to me, I see a lot of colours. These colours spin around in me very fast until they form a picture. These pictures shoot out as if they were flashing forward like a three-dimensional film.

To Gerard Croiset's credit, he made no attempt to enrich himself through milking his gift's commercial possibilities. He was self-centred, however, and when prominent scientists came from abroad to the Parapsychology Institute to talk to Professor Tenhaeff, Croiset would brag that they had really come to watch him at work. His vanity extended to keeping books of his press cuttings in every language, with the latest in his pocket to show everyone he met.

The two men were once returning from Italy and Croiset had with him a figurine he had bought believing it to be an antique, but Professor Tenhaeff, after examining it, was sceptical. As they neared the Dutch frontier, Croiset began worrying that the Customs would make him pay duty on it. Tenhaeff assured him that he would not have to do so, but did not explain why. When the Customs officer inspected the figurine, he noticed what Croiset had failed to spot. It was stamped 'Made in Holland'. On this occasion, Croiset's insight failed him, but the reverse was usually the case.

It was the Dutch police who first approached Professor Tenhaeff with the suggestion that Croiset and any others similarly gifted might be able to help them—for example, in murder cases through psychometry by handling the weapon. Suppose a detective were convinced that a certain person was guilty. His conviction might be so strong that he might influence the paragnost telepathically into naming as the criminal someone he unjustly suspected. Croiset therefore had to take the utmost care to guard against this happening.

Thus began Gerard Croiset's career as a crime detective. On many occasions he displayed remarkable precognitive powers. Thanks to Professor Tenhaeff's scrupulous supervision, Croiset's cases concerning missing persons and crimes are fully documented, and together with tape recordings are kept under the heading of 'Psychoscopic Experiments on Behalf of the Police' in the archives of the Parapsychology Institute in Utrecht. Some typical cases in which this occurred follow.

In October 1959, Carol, a Kansas professor's daughter suffering from a nervous breakdown, vanished from the hospital where she was being treated. Six weeks later her father, despairing that the police would ever trace her, rang Tenhaeff in Utrecht and enquired if Croiset were ever able to solve such cases at such a distance. Tenhaeff replied that he could sometimes do so, and an appointment was made for Croiset to talk to the father over the transatlantic telephone at 3 p.m. Kansas time next day.

Croiset reacted at once and described as if he were watching a film what his sixth sense told him. On escaping from the hospital, Carol had obtained a lift first in a lorry and then in a very large red car. She was still alive and her father would have good news of her after six days. As predicted, Carol was reunited with her parents. She had indeed been given a lift in a lorry and then in a red car.

The following year, one Saturday evening, 21 May, when Croiset was at home with Professor Tenhaeff and his chief assistant Ms 'Nicky' Louwerens, a Mr Schuenmaker phoned from Eindhoven, 50 miles away. A neighbour's four-year-old son, Toonje Thooner, had been missing for a whole day and the police had no clues as to the boy's whereabouts. Could Croiset help? His response is interesting as it illustrates how he could focus his mind on the circumstances of the case in question and arrive at the correct solution. He asked the neighbour over the phone: 'Was the playground where the child was last seen in a new suburb?...When you leave it on the left, is there some open ground?...When one follows the edge of this open ground, does one come to a canal?...Is it some two to five hundred metres from the playground? ...' The neighbour replied 'Yes' in every case. Croiset then told him that the child was already dead and that in about three days' time the body would be found in the canal close to a bridge and near a zinc bucket. His prediction proved correct.

Croiset also wished he had not been right in a case reported in full in the *Haagsche Courant* of 23 April 1963. On the 11th of that month another boy, Wimpje Slee, was reported missing from Voorburg on the outskirts of The Hague. Crowds of people from the town searched for him. The police dredged the Vliet canal. Clairvoyants seeking to outdo Croiset put them to fruitless trouble bulldozing the sands and rubbish dumps and hunting under factory barrels.

The boy's uncle, meanwhile, tried to contact Croiset, who

was away in Paris. When he returned Croiset said that
Wimpje, having slipped into the canal, had been drowned.
They would in due course come across the body by a bridge.
When more dredging failed, the uncle, at Croiset's invita-
tion, visited him in the hope that contact with the man would
help the paragnost to get further impressions. It did.

On the morning of Friday 19 April, Croiset drew on a sheet
of paper a sketch of the locality where he predicted that on
the following Tuesday the boy's body would be found floating in the Vliet canal between two bridges and near a small
building with a weathercock on its roof. Any more dredging by the police would be unsuccessful before then. Nevertheless, they did continue with their futile search.

At a quarter to eight on the morning of the day mentioned,
the drowned Wimpje Slee was retrieved from the place indicated by Croiset.

Not all Croiset's cases had unhappy endings. In many
instances, he was able to trace missing persons of all ages
as well as animals and to predict the place and time of their
reappearance. On 5 June 1958, a patient vanished from a psy-
chiatric hospital in Apeldoorn. When after three days he
could not be found, Dr W.J. de Haan, the hospital's medical director, appealed to Croiset for his help which he had
successfully provided on earlier occasions. Croiset gave a
detailed description of the place and the shed where he said
the fugitive would be lying when caught. Three days later,
he was discovered there. In his account of this case Professor Tenhaeff wrote that it provided another example of
precognition, for the patient had not reached this location
when Croiset was consulted.

If uncertain as to whether his powers would work, Croiset
refused to help the police in their investigations lest he accuse
someone who was innocent. He preferred to take part in
cases where he felt the outcome would be a fortunate one.
For example, at 2 a.m. on Sunday 23 June 1963, a policeman from Utrecht roused him to say that a worried father
had reported that his two sons aged eight and eleven had
not returned home. Standing half-awake at the front door,
Croiset found himself informing the policeman that he saw
the boys asleep in a barn near a cornfield with their bicycles
beside them. They would be home by ten next morning—
and they were.

A year earlier another case involving a missing child and a bridge provided an example of a different kind for Gerard Croiset's gift. A boy had disappeared from the village of Slik-kerveer and Croiset told the parents that he had a vision of the boy sitting by a large bridge as he spoke to them. He was assured that there was no bridge of any kind for miles around. Nevertheless, Croiset insisted that he was right. Then a police officer discovered that plans had been prepared for such a bridge to be built, and the missing boy was found alive but lost in the very spot shown on the blueprint. A few years later, the bridge was erected.

On 10 August 1949, Croiset was taken by Professor Ten-haeff to the courthouse at Assen, the capital of Drenthe, where the public prosecutor had asked for assistance in a complicated sex crime. Taken into a room where several wrapped objects lay on a table, Croiset picked one up and said correctly that it contained a tobacco box. He described two middle-aged brothers, one of whom had carried the box in his pocket and had a broken tooth in the left side of his face.

At his request, Croiset was allowed to open a second package and took out a sack. Holding it, he seemed to relive the crime. The brothers had kidnapped a mentally retarded child, a girl, wearing wooden shoes, one of which was broken at the top. They had put her in the sack and had then raped her in a hay shed near where a fair was in progress.

Croiset pointed at a cigarette holder which was one of the exhibits. It had belonged to the other brother. He touched the remaining objects and indicated which brother had owned each one. They had committed further crimes. He heard the name Hendrik, which was in fact the name of one of the brothers, and went on to describe the characters of the two men. This, together with everything else he had said, proved accurate. The suspects had already been arrested. That afternoon, when the man with the tobacco box appeared in court, Croiset was present, and afterwards he correctly predicted that the man would hang himself within a few weeks.

French parapsychologists maintain that it was in Paris in the 1920s that the first organized experiment was staged to discover whether precognition could be proved to function in a closely supervised environment. The author, Pascal Forthuny, claimed to have a gift of precognition, and he agreed to submit to certain tests conducted by Eugene Osty. After leading Forthuny into a lecture theatre and selecting a chair at random, Osty would challenge him to describe in detail the person who, when the audience arrived later, would sit in it. Every care was taken to guard against any collusion, and a high proportion of Forthuny's descriptions were correct.

Professor Tenhaeff suggested to Croiset that he might take part in 'chair' tests on the same lines. He agreed, and a successful première led to its becoming a classic form of demonstrating precognition in an entertaining yet convincingly credible form to the public. It was to be repeated by scientists all over Europe. Full detailed accounts of the 'chair' tests with Croiset and supporting recordings on tape have been preserved at the Parapsychology Institute at Utrecht.

A seating plan would be prepared with numbered seats for a meeting to be held in a location the whereabouts of which were often not disclosed to Croiset himself. Seats were never allotted in advance to individuals attending. A chair was then chosen at random by whoever was in charge—always someone entirely independent and neutral. This done, Croiset predicted at times varying from one hour to a month prior to the event the sex, general appearance, and background of the person who would sit in the chosen chair. This information, recorded on tape, was sealed in an envelope or kept in a safe until the day and was then opened in full view of the audience. The detailed predictions regarding the individual occupying the chair were read out, and he or she was asked to comment on their accuracy. Croiset proved so accurate that it was impossible to explain away his success by attributing it to coincidence or deception.

Croiset thus described beforehand, a police inspector who, he said, would on the night have a fountain pen leaking in his pocket and ruining the lining. But there were times when Croiset failed to record anything in advance, and it was then found that nobody sat in the chosen chair at the meeting. On other occasions, his statements were confused, and this proved to be when someone had sat in the chair and had then moved elsewhere and a second person had sat there.

This novel form of experiment was tried out in Amsterdam for the first time in October 1947 before Holland's Society for Psychical Research. So astonishingly successful was it that a stream of similar tests followed. Four years later, the German parapsychologist Dr Hans Bender, with Professor Tenhaeff's co-operation, tested Croiset independently and with favourable results at the University of Freiburg. Croiset underwent tests as well in Austria, England, Italy, and Switzerland, and in 1961 the professor published a book, *De Voorschoun*, giving comprehensive accounts of these demonstrations of Croiset's precognitive versatility.

Croiset submitted to several hundreds of tests, and as time went on Professor Tenhaeff, anxious to dispel doubts, tightened his safeguards against possible deceptions.

Here are some examples of Croiset's predictions. In March 1948, he foretold that the second seat from the right in the fifth row would be taken by a man whom he described. He had a vision of him walking—some years previously—near a large villa up on a hill, then coming across a woman in a light dress lying unconscious on the ground. At the meeting, a man in that seat corresponding with the paragnost's advance description of him agreed that Croiset was correct. Twelve years previously, whilst living in such a place, he had found his wife knocked out by a car near this villa.

On 6 January 1957, Croiset, Professor Tenhaeff, his assistant Nicky Louwerens, Professor L.H. Bretschneider, a biologist, and Professor J.H. Smit, a physicist, met at the Parapsychology Institute of Utrecht. Croiset was shown a seating plan for a meeting that would take place on 1 February in the house of a resident of The Hague who had never met Croiset.

Tenhaeff asked Croiset who would be seated in chair number 9 on Friday 1 February 1957. Croiset held the chart in his hands for a minute and then started dictating his impressions on to a tape recorder. Next day, 7 January, Tenhaeff telephoned Mrs C.V.T. to say that she could now send out her 30 invitations to the meeting.

Croiset's impressions were then typed out and 40 copies made. To ensure that the chairs were chosen at random two packs, each containing 30 cards, all numbered, were made ready at the Institute the day before the experiment. One was cut, shuffled several times, and securely sealed. The other was left alone.

Next evening at 7 p.m. Professor Tenhaeff and four others reached Mrs C.V.T.'s house, where the unsealed cards were laid in numerical order on the chairs arranged in six rows of five each in a first-floor room. At the same time, in the basement, the 30 people taking part, all strangers, had the purpose of the experiment explained to them by the Professor and were handed a copy of what Croiset had foretold about the occupant of the chosen chair. They were asked to read it and if anything applied to them to write a note to that effect in the margin.

The sealed pack containing the other 30 numbered cards was then opened and every participant was handed one by Nicky Louwerens on going upstairs. They were warned not to touch any chairs as they made their way to the ones corresponding to the numbers on their cards.

At 8.15 p.m. Gerard Croiset arrived after driving from Utrecht to The Hague with instructions not to appear any earlier lest his being there might in any way influence the proceedings. Everybody having had time to study his predictions, they were now read aloud and a Mrs M.J.D., sitting in chair 9, was asked whether any of Croiset's 12 statements applied to her. She replied that most of them did. Croiset's success became even more startling when the remaining 29 participants attested that nothing on the list fitted them.

The telling facts predicted and recorded by Croiset 26 days earlier included the following: that a few days before the meeting, when working on her housekeeping accounts, Mrs M.J.D. would alter the figure 5 to a 6 and that this would lead to a dispute with her husband; that the first opera she had even seen performed was *Falstaff* and she had fallen in love with the tenor; that she had received a recent visit from a short, stout woman friend approaching her middle forties, wearing a dress with large pleats, who confided sex problems to her and whom she had advised to see a psychiatrist; and that she had recently soiled her hands handling an old-fashioned box. As regards the last statement, Croiset had added: 'Did she hurt herself slightly with that? The middle finger of her right hand.' Mrs D. said that about the same time she had cut her finger opening a tin. Croiset was partly wrong here.

After Croiset had finished helping the police in a case at their headquarters in Hengelo at 9.30 p.m. on 15 November

1949, an inspector took down at Croiset's dictation his forecast as to who would sit in the fourth place from the right in the third row at a chair test arranged for the next evening at Enschede. It would be a slim young man in a dark suit with hair combed high talking all the time to a young woman beside him, who would wear a red jumper and have a damaged nail to the middle finger of her right hand. She would have next to her an elderly woman with sharp blue eyes wearing a black dress, whose habit of playing with what she had in her hands irritated her stout and balding husband, sitting beside her, who had a scar under his left knee. She had a son, wearing a naval uniform, who had been killed in a torpedo explosion.

These particulars were typed out, sealed in an envelope, and read out by the chairman at the meeting next day. Croiset then made one correction. He said that it was the young man who had the scar under his left knee. This was correct, as were the other facts, except that the elderly woman had no sailor son.

A Miss W. van B., sitting elsewhere, then got up and disclosed that her brother had been a sailor who had lost his life when his ship was torpedoed off Plymouth. Just before the meeting, she had passed up a ring with a request for Croiset to give her a psychometric reading, and he had put it between the pages of his pad, saying that he would do so during the second half of the proceedings.

Before the meeting, Croiset told Professor Tenhaeff that he had in his precognitive vision of the elderly woman noticed correctly that she had dirty finger-nails, but he had thought it tactful not to get the police inspector to write this down.

In October 1952, when Professor Tenhaeff asked who would occupy chair 18 at a meeting to be held in Rotterdam, Croiset could get no impressions at all. The question was switched to chair three, and Croiset replied that a woman with facial scars from a motor accident in Italy would sit there.

On the night there was a snowstorm and one person failed to arrive, with the result that no one sat in chair 18, whilst the woman in chair three revealed that her disfigurement had been caused in the way Croiset had described.

Dr Hans Bender, the German parapsychologist, was in

charge of a chair test held at Neustadt on the evening of 2 June that same year. The seat number was chosen in the morning at Kaiserslautern and Croiset predicted that the chair was to be occupied by a slender, blonde-haired woman with a green shawl worn over a blouse. He thought he saw her looking at a crucifix from which the figure of Jesus was missing. Next to her would sit a stout man, whose face was inclined to redden when he lacked confidence and who indulged in day-dreams regarding travel. He had recently been in a shop selling clothes and owned a picture painted about 1850 depicting a lady with a lace cap. He had almost bought a long-playing record. Croiset also saw a white house, something to do with tombstones. Did the man's friend, Carl, live in the United States or close to them?

The predictions proved to be correct, but mixed up between the two persons involved, probably because they were sitting touching each other and at an angle. The woman had just been to her husband's grave, which had a plain stone cross above it. Nearby was a white house occupied by a stonemason. In her living-room was a painting of a 'Lady with a Lace Cap', painted in the mid-nineteenth century. She had been brought up in Mexico, where Carlos, an old family friend, lived, and her relatives owned a clothing store which she frequently visited and where she had just purchased some material.

As regards the man, he did blush when he was outwitted or made to feel inferior, and he was very much of an armchair traveller. Three weeks previously he had almost bought a long-playing record. Indeed, he had once been the manager of a store's record department. But he was not stout—that was Croiset's only mistake in his forecast.

Three and a half years later, on 3 March, 1956, the chair tests were made more difficult for Croiset. He was in Munich staying with the German parapsychologist Professor Anton Neuhäusler, who invited him to choose a chair for a meeting to be held next day in the boardroom of Verona's Museum of Natural History. There were to be 36 participants seated in six rows and they were to be invited *after* Croiset had made his predictions and not before as previously. The Professor asked him who would be seated in the fourth chair to the left in the third row. The paragnost dictated his impressions, which were written down in German by Neuhäusler and sealed in an envelope. Later they were translated into Italian and again sealed in an envelope, which was not opened again until the distinguished scientists Dr de Boni and Professor Zorzi, who had no knowledge of what was written inside, did so at the start of the experiment.

As Croiset had foretold, the seat was taken by a girl with dark hair, wearing a light-coloured blouse and shoes with cracked uppers, who lived near a ladies' hairdressing salon, had beautiful handwriting, loved animals, and owned a picture of a squirrel. When walking home, she could see at the end of her street a small square that had a unique round building with arches. There were several other accurate predictions—perhaps most unexpected of all that a few days earlier a dead chicken, hanging above the entrance to a shop, had fallen before Rita as she went past.

A chicken figured in a case where a young man, depressed because he was out of work, consulted Croiset privately and was told that he would get a remunerative post that had something to do with a black chicken. A year later this came about when he was employed as a salesman for a liqueur— Black Chicken.

In January 1969, a film was shot in Holland in which Croiset described a man and a woman he did not know who, he said, would be at a meeting in Denver, Colorado, some weeks later. The man he described as wearing 'a coat with green spots, spattered on it by a chemical from his work in a scientific laboratory'. The woman he said had had 'an emotional experience dealing with page 64 of a book she was reading'.

The rest of the film was shot at Denver, where people were handed forms on which they answered questions about themselves. A man corresponding with the one described was present, and also a woman who had read a book on cats and had been upset by the description of the death of a cat on page 64.

In 1953, the First International Congress of Parapsychological Studies, sponsored by the Dutch Ministry of Education and Eileen Garrett's Parapsychology Foundation of New York, was held in Utrecht, and Professor Tenhaeff acted as host. Professor J.B. Rhine of Duke University, who had pioneered experiments in extra-sensory perception using

Zener cards, did not attend. His absence was believed to be due to Tenhaeff's having refused to use Zener cards in experiments because he believed that this one-sided quantitative method of investigating the paranormal created unnatural conditions and stifled inspiration. To quote his words later: 'I find that the overwhelming majority of paragnosts like Croiset are not only disinterested in Zener card experiments but often manifest an aversion to them. I believe that testing should always be adapted to a paragnost's nature and interests.'

Nevertheless, Professor Tenhaeff did not completely ignore quantitative research. His assistant, Nicky Louwerens, tested the telepathic talents of 1,188 children in 15 Utrecht kindergartens, in groups of a dozen. Teachers, concealed behind screens, would turn over 25 pictures of toys consisting of five in each case of an orange, a deer, a red doll, a green ball, and a blue motor lorry. These were arranged in a loose-leaf book in the order selected at random by a stranger in a room some distance away. A member of the staff signalled to the teacher when to start concentrating on the pictures and when to turn over. The children, each sitting at well-separated individual tables, then tried to guess which picture the teacher was staring at.

The results were remarkable; some children regularly scored 15 correct guesses out of 25. The experiment was supervised by a mathematician from the Dutch university of Delft, who reported that there were an impressive number of accurate guesses and that the chance of coincidence was about one in 10 million. Girls did better than boys, and children whose parents and teachers were affectionate did better than those who felt they were neglected.

Professor Tenhaeff did not limit his studies with adults to Croiset. In the *Proceedings of the Utrecht Institute* of December 1962, he reported on his long-term investigations of the powers of 40 paragnosts including Croiset. His conclusions make interesting reading. Many showed signs of paranormal ability before they reached the age of 10. The eldest child in a family was the least likely to be so gifted, the last the most likely. Indications were that the faculty was inherited. Women were more psychic than men, and among animals dogs and horses were the most likely to have 'second sight'. The typical paragnost was unsociable and was unwilling 'to accept disturbing influences which becomes apparent in his choice of brown in the colour pigment test'.

CHAPTER 5

'The Man with the Radar Brain'

The man who became celebrated as Peter Hurkos was born in Holland on 21 May 1911, and his real name was Pieter van der Hurk. He had hardly any education. At the age of 14 he went to work in the summer painting houses with his father, and in the winter he was employed on ships sailing overseas. When the Second World War broke out and the Germans occupied Holland, he earned his living camouflaging plane hangars and barracks. In June 1943, he fell 30 feet off a ladder and fractured his skull. As he recovered slowly in hospital, after being in a coma for two days, it was not long before there were signs that the concussions had triggered off his sixth sense. Later, medical opinion concluded that he had been injured in the mid-brain and that this had upset the pineal or pituitary gland.

In his book *Psychic*, Hurkos relates that there was a man in the next bed who was a complete stranger. He had never spoken to him and yet he found facts about him coming into his conscious mind. To test whether they were correct, he said: 'You're a bad man. When your father died a short while ago, he left you a large gold watch and you've already sold it.' The other man was astonished because he thought no one knew this. When a nurse Hurkos had not seen before took his pulse, a picture flashed into his mind and he told her that he could see her in a train with a suitcase belonging to a friend. She might lose it. The girl gaped at him. She had just returned from visiting Amsterdam and had left a borrowed suitcase in the dining-car. How had he found out? Hurkos comments that this was a question he was to ask himself innumerable times in the future.

Four or five days after Hurkos's accident, another patient came up to his bed to bid him goodbye before leaving the hospital. As they shook hands, Hurkos claims that his sixth sense briefed him that the man was a British agent and he saw him being shot in The Hague a few days later. Shocked by this sensation, Hurkos tightened his grip. As the man struggled to free himself, a nurse approached and asked why Hurkos was behaving so strangely, whilst with difficulty she forced him to release his hold. The man then ran out of the ward and Hurkos shouted: 'Stop him! He's going to be killed! He is a British agent! He will be killed on Kalver Street!'

Two days afterwards, this British agent was shot dead by the Gestapo on that street. Later Hurkos discovered that the Gestapo had known all along who he was, but had not arrested him hoping he would unwittingly lead them to his contacts in the Dutch Resistance.

A week or so following these events, the resident doctor and the nurse who had witnessed Hurkos's prophetic outburst came up to him with a stranger who demanded to be told how he had known so much about the agent and accused him of being connected with the Resistance movement. Whilst the doctor and the nurse pinned Hurkos down, the stranger seized a pillow and started smothering him with it. As Hurkos fought for his life, he found himself crying out repeatedly, without knowing what the words meant: '*Como aborrezo la matanza. Como aborrego dar la muerte.*'

Suddenly the stranger raised the pillow and stared down in amazement at Hurkos. The doctor enquired what was wrong, and the man replied: 'He said what I was thinking—how I hate killing! Sometimes when I am under strain I think in Spanish—but how could he know?'

Hurkos insists that he knew no Spanish, yet he had read the other man's thoughts. The incident entirely changed his attacker's attitude. Saying that he now believed Hurkos to be innocent and that he was sorry, he left. But that did not end Hurkos's ordeal. For weeks, he had to submit to intensive interrogation from the hospital psychiatrist, Dr Pieters. Hurkos, the psychiatrist realized, had developed a sort of second sight, enabling him to reveal at times personal secrets that both members of the staff and patients had thought it impossible for anybody to learn about—and he would foretell which patients were going to die.

Eventually Hurkos was discharged. His mother arranged to collect him in a taxi, and he correctly predicted that she would be an hour late because the taxi driver had forgotten about the booking. He now found himself unable to settle down or to look for work. He would roam the streets and suddenly start babbling to strangers, displaying an uncanny insight into their private affairs and prophesying what would happen to them.

Worried about this, Hurkos returned to the hospital to consult Dr Pieters, who he knew believed in ESP. Dr Pieters was sympathetic and helped him to come to terms with his abnormality. He sent him to a mental hospital at The Hague for tests, as the authorities thought Hurkos might be putting on an act so as to retain the weekly allowance he had been paid since his accident. The doctors there were divided in their diagnosis. Some considered he should be certified insane. Others maintained that he was malingering and ought to be discharged and made to earn his own living again.

In view of these conflicting opinions, a psychiatrist was asked to arbitrate. He treated Hurkos's accounts of his paranormal experiences with derision, but completely changed his attitude when Hurkos said he saw him wearing a pair of new pyjamas with initials embroidered in green and gold on the pocket, which had been bought by a woman who was not his wife.

As a result, the psychiatrist arranged for Hurkos to continue receiving sick pay for a further four months. This saved him from being sent off to do forced labour in Germany and provided him with a cloak for his activities in the Dutch Resistance. When Goozens, one of its leaders, told him about a plan to rob a bank that was in Nazi hands, Hurkos had a premonition that they would be walking into a trap set by the Gestapo. Heed was taken of his warning and a disaster was avoided.

Hurkos continued assisting the underground, using his second sight to their advantage on several occasions. Later he himself fell under suspicion and was imprisoned in Buchenwald for a year. On arrival he weighed just over 12 stone and by the time he was released he had lost nearly five stone. Whilst there, he warned his fellow prisoners that an air-raid would take place at nine o'clock the next night and that two planes would be shot down. He foretold an Allied invasion of France on 4 June, which was only two days out, and also the date of the German surrender.

On returning to Holland, Hurkos had difficulty in finding employment. He still could not concentrate on anything for long, and his lack of education handicapped him. He did not fancy becoming a common labourer, so he started earning a living through employing his sixth sense, charging people who visited him at home for advice and using psychometry as his medium.

Hurkos's success led to his being invited by a popular comedian, Bernard Barens, to give nightly demonstrations during his show at the Kaas Lange theatre in The Hague. He did this for five weeks and was paid 100 guilders a performance. It went so well that Barens wanted him to take part in a European tour, but he refused, for by now he had built up a considerable clientèle that flocked to his consulting-room at the Hôtel Le Roi Albert in Antwerp. The police, too, were now calling on his services to trace missing persons.

On a visit to Paris, Hurkos made a favourable impression when he demonstrated his powers as part of the programme given in aid of an old soldiers' organization. As a result of the press publicity, the police asked him if he would be willing to submit to a test. He agreed and this took place in the court-room of the Palais de Justice before 20 judges, the chief of the police, and some 40 of his officers. The assistant director of police, who had approached Hurkos in the first instance, conducted the experiment through an interpreter. The test involved a new case that Hurkos could not possibly know anything about, neither would anyone present answer any questions. The assistant director pointed at a comb, a pair of scissors, a watch, a cigarette lighter, and a wallet laid out on a table. Some of these were connected with the case.

Hurkos commenced in his usual fashion by holding each object in turn. He said that only three of them had anything to do with the crime. He could see a bald man in a white coat (probably a doctor), a railway, and a hill. Below the latter he saw a small house. He paused and drew a sketch of the scene and held it up. Now he could see a barn and a body lying between it and the house. There was someone or something named Nicole. He saw a bottle of milk. There was a body, that of a woman, and the bald-headed man had murdered her. He saw him dead in his cell. That was all he could see, Hurkos said in conclusion.

There was a momentary silence, then excited voices told Hurkos that he had triumphed. He was correct about most of the details in the case. The scene of the crime resembled what he had sketched. The bald-headed man was a doctor who had killed his wife with poison concealed in a bottle of milk. The woman's body had been found between the house and the barn, and she had owned a pet poodle called Nicole. The doctor, however, was still alive and was in prison awaiting trial.

But Hurkos had seen into the future. Five days later, the police informed him that the doctor had hanged himself in his cell. This so impressed them that they asked for Hurkos's help in solving a puzzling robbery, and through his strange gift he gave them information that led to an arrest. He remained in Paris for a time, assisting the police on cases.

Regarding Hurkos's use of psychometry, the researches of the Soviet mathematician and neurophysiologist Dr Genady Sergeyev are of interest. He postulates that everybody makes an impression on their surroundings because we are continually radiating energy, which is indestructible and preserved by the objects near to us. Thought is energy, he says, and every human being leaves 'an energetical imprint, as well as an informational imprint on objects that he touches or is close to'. Those under great emotional strain vastly augment the number of electrical impulses they emit, so objects kept on one's person for many years, like jewellery, watches, and photographs, or furnishings and the walls of rooms where much emotion has been generated, become imprinted with thoughts and feelings. This would explain how psychometry works. Incidentally, Dr Sergeyev also believes that people may in this way unconsciously assimilate information from the past, giving rise to the delusion that they have lived previous existences.

Back in Holland, Hurkos was on holiday in the country with two friends when at about 8.30 one evening he had a vision of a farm ablaze near a small canal, which he recognized as belonging to a man named Janson. It would happen at 9 p.m. They drove there and, as they approached, flames leaped up into the sky ahead. When at last the fire had been put out, Hurkos inspected the shed where it had started and took away with him the padlock that had been wrenched off the door and thrown on the ground by the arsonist. It was the latest in a series of arson cases which had baffled the police. Offering to find the culprit, Hurkos persuaded them to collect photographs of everyone in the locality.

Next day, at the police station, Hurkos settled down to his task. He placed the padlock on each photograph in turn, concentrating hard all the while. After some hours had passed, he pointed at one and told the police chief: 'This is the one.' The man was astounded and told Hurkos that the boy he was accusing was the cleverest and best-behaved in the district, the son of one of the wealthiest and most highly regarded men in Holland. But Hurkos insisted that he was right, and under interrogation the suspect was eventually caught out in his lying and admitted his guilt.

Early in 1952, Hurkos dreamed in advance of the worst floods for years that swept over Holland in the autumn. Later that year, when in Madrid, he claimed to have had the strongest feeling that Adolf Hitler had been there following the war and long after he was supposed to have died in the Berlin bunker. He had seen him in a 'vision' travelling in Spain disguised as a monk, but he was not then in the country. Hurkos felt certain that Hitler had remained there for a long time before he went somewhere else.

'Hitler is alive,' Hurkos told some Spanish newspapermen. 'I will stake my life and reputation on it.'

According to Hurkos, the following night two men, once close to Hitler, visited him. They were Robert Steiner, a Nazi, and Léon Degrelle, a former Belgian Fascist leader, both of whom had fled to Spain to avoid trial. They warned him not to go on making such statements or he would end up with a bullet in his head. Hurkos wrote in his autobiography, published in 1961: 'I do not know whether Hitler is alive today, but I know that he was living at that time.'

By 1954, Hurkos's continued success led to his being consulted by the police of several European countries when they were faced with an impasse. In Antwerp, he co-operated with Dr René Dellaerts, a professor of psychology at the University of Louvain, in tests with photographs of people unknown to him. Hurkos would hold each one in his hand

and dictate his impressions in turn. Almost half were photographs of people who had died, and in practically every case he was able to differentiate between them and the living. As a further experiment, Dr Dellaerts would fix an electro-encephalograph to Hurkos's head to measure the responses in his brain. When he fingered the photographs of the dead, the graph moved about wildly, for these would cause a disturbing mental reaction in Hurkos.

In 1956, Hurkos was invited to America by the wealthy owner of a department store, Henry Belk, who thought that the 'Man with the Radar Brain', as Hurkos was termed by the publicist he employed, might help in making the store more efficient.

Hurkos agreed to be tested first by Dr Andrija Puharich, with both the encephalograph and the Faraday cage, at the Round Table Foundation in Glen Cove, Maine. There was a dramatic opening to his association with Dr and Mrs Puharich. At dinner with the couple and their guests, he startled them by spilling the contents of his soup plate over the table as he suddenly grasped his head. He apologized, explaining that his behaviour had been caused by a vision of a military plane leaving Hawaii and then crashing, killing all the occupants. Forty-eight hours later, such a plane dived into the Pacific and none of the soldiers on board survived.

As regards predictions, Hurkos operated best when stirred by a human predicament, and he made a number of remarkably accurate ones for Puharich and those he met through him. He told one man that he had 'seen' his brother with blood dropping from the slashed veins in his wrists. The man was extremely upset, for he had a brother confined in a home following a nervous breakdown. He went to see him and, finding his condition had deteriorated, moved him to a place where he could be more closely watched and where anything that might be used in a suicide attempt was removed from him. Despite this, a few weeks later, he broke the lenses in his spectacles and slashed his veins with the splintered pieces. Fortunately, he was caught doing this and his life was saved.

Henry Belk was very impressed with Hurkos and put him to work on the records of personnel in the store at Charlotte, North Carolina. Holding each photograph in turn, he astonished John Mark, the manager, with the accuracy of the facts he reeled off about the staff, disclosing how some were defrauding Belk.

At social functions, Hurkos lacked tact in the way he relentlessly poured out his disclosures. He hurt people not only through predicting deaths but also through revealing to a wife or husband the other partner's love affairs. His own wife, embraced by him on his arrival at the airport, once joked: 'Are you kissing me because you love me or are you checking on what I've been doing away from you?'

This lack of tact was due to the way Hurkos's sixth sense operated. His impressions flowed so fast that he had no time to consider the consequences likely to follow his revelations. When he did start to pause to guard against giving offence, he became less accurate.

In June 1957, Belk's 10-year-old daughter was missing from home and they searched for her in vain. Frantic with worry, Belk telephoned Hurkos, who was then living in Miami. Hurkos could get no impressions as to what had happened but promised to ring back when he did. Some minutes later, Belk received a phone call from him. Hesitantly, he said: 'Henry, I don't know how to tell you but her body is in the river near your home. She's drowned.'

Shocked, Belk asked where and was told: 'By a clump of bushes at the river's edge.' And that was where the distraught father found the girl. In his anguish, he complained that if Hurkos could see into the future, why couldn't he have warned him beforehand that she was in danger so that precautions could have been taken?

Belk had hoped that Hurkos might help him to become a millionaire, but although he predicted that the store-owner would find uranium in Utah, he found none, and the two shops Hurkos advised him to open failed to make headway, though they did succeed later under new owners.

Hurkos's primary interest by now was to make money for himself, so he charged huge fees to those who consulted him and he employed agents to exploit his gift to the utmost financially. An agent in Milwaukee, Wisconsin, approached an oil magnate to see if he might be interested in engaging Hurkos to locate oil deposits for him, but the terms demanded—expenses, a search fee, and a large royalty on all oil pumped up—were unacceptable to Maguire, who decided that the terms of geological engineers were much more moderate and their record of past successes a good one, whereas Hurkos was entering a field in which he had no experience.

In 1959, *This Week* magazine invited Hurkos to see if he could predict the result of the major-league baseball contest. Completely ignorant of anything to do with the game, he paid several visits to the camps in Florida where the teams were training that spring. There he fingered all the equipment to try and pick up sensations that would aid him in his task.

The Milwaukee Braves had been the National League champions in previous years, so Hurkos attended an exhibition match in St Petersburg's Al Lang Field and focussed his attention on catcher Del Crandall. At last, looking exhausted from mental strain, Hurkos came out and told the reporter accompanying him that the Braves were a superb team that he felt would be in the lead for the greater part of the year, but that at the very end of the season they would come second to the Los Angeles Dodgers, outsiders who no one thought had the slightest chance of winning. The experts, in fact, reckoned they would come seventh. Hurkos's forecast was published in the 26 April 1959 issue of *This Week*. He was correct.

When it came to predicting which team would become the American League champions, Hurkos failed. His choice was the New York Yankees, champions for several years running. It seems that he could not make up his mind, and those seeking an excuse for his failure suggested that he spent too much time with the team and was overwhelmed by the colossal self-confidence they exuded, which made it impossible for him to let his psychic sense function freely.

As regards boxing, Hurkos claimed that he could name the victor in nine out of ten fights he watched on television, and when the result proved to be a knock-out he could foretell the round in which this would take place. Two months before the second heavyweight contest between Ingemar Johannson and Floyd Patterson, Hurkos correctly assured a journalist from Associated Press that Johannson would be knocked out.

Later, five months before the two boxers fought each other for the last time, Hurkos predicted that Johannson would not last seven rounds and described in detail how he would be floored twice. On the evening of the match, sitting with his lawyer, John Burggraf, Hurkos watched the bout being televised live. Hardly had it begun than Patterson was knocked down by his opponent. Hurkos had not predicted to Burggraf that this would happen and could tell from his expression that he thought his client was going to be proved wrong. But Patterson was back on his feet before the bell rang and went on to floor Johansson twice before finally knocking him out in the sixth round.

Hurkos missed no opportunity of appearing on television in America, astonishing viewers with his success on the Jack Paar show in January 1962, when the producer took careful precautions against the possibility that those chosen from the studio audience might be in collusion with Hurkos. Holding personal objects belonging to those invited on to the platform, he impressed with the correctness of his statements, and made predictions that were fulfilled.

On the rare occasions when he failed with a member of the audience during a television programme, Hurkos was quick at retrieving his reputation for accuracy by quick-fire revelations about his interviewer's ailments, prescribing how they should be treated. As Joe Hyams, the Hollywood film columnist, was peering over his notes, Hurkos touched the man's arms and said, correctly, that there were times when they felt so heavy that Hyams could barely move them. He ran his hand down Hyam's back and, pausing, told him to go to a chiropractor and get him to work on his spine at that particular spot, which would cure the trouble with his arms.

Before Hyams could speak, Hurkos was telling him that he had a watch on him that needed a new mainspring and that his son had ear trouble. Hyams took his advice. A session with a chiropractor cured his arm trouble and his watch did need a new mainspring—and the son had ear trouble. Later, he too consulted Hurkos, who was able to dispel the inflammation through psychic healing.

Hurkos proved as successful as Gerard Croiset in solving puzzling crime for the police. When working on a case, Hurkos wanted to be on his own at the scene of a crime, picking up clues through psychometry. It surprised the police that he did not ask questions and that when they volunteered information he did not listen. If anyone interrupted him when he was speaking, he would tell them to be quiet.

In his autobiography, Hurkos described how by touching the corpse he received a vision of the murderer, the last person seen by the victim before he or she died. This, he believed, was because the mind was like a photographic plate storing image after image, never discarding any. 'The eyes transmit what they see to the "negative" of the brain. When a person dies, there is no longer any transmission, but the images fixed there prior to death remain as long as there is anything left of the body.' He also obtained his impressions by handling the weapon or whatever the murderer might have touched or owned. Describing the 'visions' that provided him with the solutions, he wrote: 'It's like a film being played only for me. I can see things in great detail and I can describe what I see.'

Hurkos knew that in order to be sure of the maximum co-operation from the American police he must impress them from the start. For example, when he first met Inspector Jack Hall of the Virginian State Police, he startled him by saying that Hall was unnecessarily worried about his wife. Hurkos said he could see her on the way to keep a medical appointment at mid-day, and he predicted that she would be annoyed on getting there to have to wait as the doctor would have to attend to three emergency cases. Hurkos added that the Halls hadn't had any children for 18 years and weren't expecting any more, but they would have another child, a girl, and she would be born about a year from then. In fact, he could give the date—24 June 1961. According to the inspector, Hurkos proved 100 per cent correct.

Dr Regis Riesenman first met Hurkos on the latter's arrival at Washington Airport on 10 June 1960. The distinguished psychiatrist and criminologist, when searching in his wallet, accidentally let a photograph of his father fall out which the Dutchman picked up. Holding it for a minute, he told his host-to-be that his father was aged 82 and had suffered accidents in the previous two years. His health was going to get worse, the blood vessels in his head being adversely affected. Death would occur between six months and a year from then.

Riesenman was taken aback because, although all the other details were accurate, his father's physician and the specialists believed he would last at least another five years. However, eight months later he died.

Hurkos had not finished seeking to impress (and depress) Riesenman. Becoming a weather prophet, he foretold fine weather during his stay with him and that his departure would be marked by a storm. This too happened, and a cloudburst flooded the Riesenmans' cellar. Hurkos, was, however, remembered with gratitude by the family. The youngest of the Riesenmans' seven children, then two and a half years old, could not walk and had been examined by five doctors and specialists in turn. All had diagnosed the cause as cerebral palsy and had said that she would never be able to walk.

Hurkos placed a hand on Mary Alice's back and said, though ignorant of the date, that she would take a few steps for the first time on her birthday, 21 December, and at Christmas she would walk to the tree to collect her presents, and she would continue to walk. His prediction came true, and the girl then grew up strong and sturdy.

There is a postscript to this story involving the psychic Jeane Dixon. As a result of the fulfilment of Peter Hurkos's prediction, Mary Alice was given corrective exercises to develop her leg muscles, and then, four years later, Dr Riesenman happened to show Jeane a family photograph. She pointed at a little girl in the photograph and asked if she were Mary Alice. He nodded.

Jeane crossed the room with an exaggerated duck walk and, throwing her right leg up and out, started to climb the stairs. Dr Riesenman was astonished, for that was exactly the way Mary Alice moved about. 'But you have never seen her walk,' he said. 'How did you know this?'

'Do you know why she does this?' Jeane asked, avoiding replying to his question.

Dr Riesenman answered that all the specialists had diagnosed cerebral palsy.

Jeane said that this was not the cause and continued: 'Mary Alice was born with a congenital dislocation of her hips. At this time nature is forming new sockets and she will continue to improve and will begin to walk better. She will not need surgery.'

Mrs Dixon proved right. Dr Riesenman took his daughter to see an orthopaedic specialist—and X-rays confirmed what Jeane Dixon had said.

*   *   *

The 'Yorkshire Ripper' murders of 1979 and 1980 in England and the failure of the police to catch the killer led to many would-be emulators of Peter Hurkos offering their services and solutions. None proved of any real help, so when Shirley Davenport, a reporter on the *Yorkshire Post*, went that October to interview a Mrs Nella Jones in her South London home she felt it would prove a waste of time. All the same, she wrote down in shorthand everything Mrs Jones told her. The murderer's first name was Peter. Mrs Jones had seen him in a vision sitting at the wheel of a lorry which had 'C something' painted on its side, the name of the firm for which he worked. The story sent in by Shirley to her editor in York was filed but never published.

In January 1980, Mrs Jones asked to see Shirley Davenport again and said during a second interview that another vision had revealed to her that Peter lived in a large house with the number six on its front door, which had a flight of stone steps leading up to it from a wrought-iron gate. Shirley made notes, but did not send in any further report to her editor.

Then, in early November 1980, Shirley heard from Nella Jones that she had 'seen' the thirteenth victim being murdered by Peter. It would occur on either the 17th or the 27th of that month. The first date proved correct.

When at last, in 1981, Peter Sutcliffe was arrested, Shirley Davenport was sitting watching the news on television. The moment she saw a picture of where he lived, 6 Garden Lane, Bradford, she was astounded to discover how accurate Mrs Jones had been in her description. And not only was the Ripper's first name Peter but he was also a lorry driver employed by a firm whose name began with a C—Clark Transport.

CHAPTER 6
Eileen Garrett

When Eileen Garrett died, aged 77, in 1970, the world of parapsychology lost one of its most colourful and controversial protagonists. From her childhood in County Meath she displayed psychic gifts, and in the 1920s became one of the most highly regarded of trance mediums. She also had precognitive experiences both in dreams and in other ways. She claimed that when her first baby was five months old and went on crying until she shook him in exasperation, a disembodied voice chided her, saying that he would not be with her much longer. The little boy died soon after. She had similar warnings regarding her next two sons, who also did not live.

During the First World War Eileen Garrett's husband was fighting in France. One day when she was dining at the Savoy, she said, the room around her faded and she heard a shattering explosion and had a momentary vision of him dying. Two days later, her husband was reported missing and she learned that he had never returned from a wire-cutting expedition.

Mrs Garrett wrote later that it was extremely disturbing to discover that she could foresee coming events. This sudden experiencing of some future catastrophe affected her health. She concluded that she had two separate selves:

In this difficult time I stumbled on the technique of autosuggestion though I did not know it by that name. If I relaxed, the extraneous impressions would rush in, but if I made a conscious appeal to my 'other self', the invasions would diminish, and this method of self-protection became a regular exercise... I gradually controlled my visions by permitting their manifestation only during a time set aside for practice and contemplation.

As Eileen Garrett's assurance grew, the events she foresaw were in the lives of others and rarely to do with herself. She would hear fragments of conversations including names which meant nothing to her, then a few days later she might find herself in a room with people and to her astonishment would hear repeated the same conversations. When this occurred, she was conscious of 'an increasing pressure behind the forehead' and at the same time she had 'a feeling of a channel being gently opened up from a point between the eyes the cerebellum'. Images registered behind her forehead and appeared to move out, and beyond, into space. She used to compare the process to 'a kind of mental magic lantern with the lens for the projection of the pictures located behind the forehead'.

At the British College of Psychic Science, Eileen Garrett spent five years developing mediumship under Hewart McKenzie, whom she described as 'one of the toughest-minded and least doctrinaire of spiritualist researchers'. When she was in trance, a control personality, Uvani, took over. She herself had doubts as to whether he was an Oriental spirit and thought he might be only 'a split off' of her own subconscious mind. Later, she was to suggest that her powers might perhaps derive in part from the hypothalamus gland, or from the vestigial animal brain at the base of the skull. In ages past, animals used this for survival, sensing friend and foe from miles away.

In 1926, Mrs Garrett had a vision of an airship in difficulties over Hyde Park, then two years later she 'saw' it again, in worse trouble. Lashed by the wind, it seemed about to plunge down to earth. Then, the following year, the dirigible 'appeared' right above her, discharging smoke before exploding. On 5 October 1930, these visions became reality when the R-101 crashed near Beauvais in France killing 46 people, including its commander, Flight Lieutenant H.C. Irwin.

Two days later, a seance was held at the National Laboratory of Psychical Research with the purpose of attempting to contact the spirit of Sir Arthur Conan Doyle. Present also was Australian journalist Ian Coster, who had asked for the seance to be arranged, and his secretary, Ethel Beenham. Describing what then happened, Coster wrote that Mrs Garrett was seated in an armchair 'yawning her head off'. The others were grouped round a table with Miss Beenham ready at her notebook. The medium closed her eyes and went on yawning. She breathed heavily and relaxed into 'a sort of mournful slumber, tears flowing down her cheeks'.

Then Mrs Garrett's control, Uvani, announced that someone called Irving or Irwin wanted to speak. A man's distraught voice cried: 'The whole bulk of the dirigible was too much for her engine capacity...Useful lift too small. Gross lift computed badly...Elevator jammed. Oil pipe plugged ...' On and on went the voice of the dead Irwin, describing in technical detail exactly what had caused the catastrophe, referring to confidential matters that only a few could know about and to fatal mistakes, quarrels, and obstinacy. None of this, and in particular the technical terms, could possibly be known by anyone except those who had lost their lives, and the scientists and planners on the ground. All was taken down in shorthand by Ethel Beenham and read later by experts at the Royal Airship Works in Bedford, who called it 'an astounding document'.

On a later occasion during a seance for Major Oliver Villiers, Irwin apparently spoke again through Mrs Garrett's mediumship, clarifying other obscurities about the crash.

In 1929, Hewart McKenzie died and Eileen Garrett was invited to the United States by the American Society for Psychical Research. She visited Professor J.B. Rhine's Parapsychology Laboratory at Duke University and took part in tests using Zener cards. Her scoring was unexceptional, for which her explanation was that she could never rouse enough interest to get herself into the right frame of mind for something so mechanical and tedious. But when Rhine's assistant, Dr J. Gaither Pratt, put her actual mediumship to the test by recording her impressions of people she did not know and who were separated from her by a screen, she was astonishingly successful.

By now, Mrs Garrett had become convinced that Uvani and other 'spirit' controls were manifestations arising out of her own unconscious. This led her to make an important decision: from now on, she would devote her life to the investigation of psychic phenomena. In 1951, with the financial backing of a millionairess, the former Cleveland Congress woman Mrs Frances Bolton, she started the Parapsychology Foundation in New York City. The Foundation gives grants for research, maintains the finest reference library in the world on parapsychology, and publishes several journals with reports of the most recent research.

Eileen Garrett continued to impress even the most critical with her paranormal gifts. The *Journal of the American Society for Psychical Research* for 1968 contains an authenticated account of a case in which she demonstrated both her clairvoyance and her precognitive gifts. Lawrence Le Shan, a parapsychologist of repute working at Mills College in New York, wrote that he called on her by appointment and produced a small piece of a shirt worn by a doctor the day before he vanished from home. Le Shan had never seen the doctor, but the doctor's wife had been at school with his wife. The two women had met again when Mrs Le Shan had visited the Midwest.

In two sessions 10 days apart, with Le Shan present, Eileen Garrett in trance recorded on tape the following: 'A man disappeared...He is upset, and seeking his whereabouts...I see him at La Solla...I am sure he thought of going to California and then on to Mexico.' She correctly described the doctor as being 5 feet 10 inches in height and in his middle forties. He had latterly lost weight, had been exceptionally intelligent as a child, and when he was a boy in his teens his father had died. The second time Le Shan visited Mrs Garrett, she predicted that the doctor would get in touch with his wife almost immediately. Two hours later, a letter from the doctor in La Solla reached her, in which he wrote that he had made up his mind to come back home and face his problems.

Eileen Garrett preferred to use her gift positively if possible. An example of this occurred in the case of a man who had consulted her on the recommendation of a well-known American architect, Ferdinand Bligh Bond. After he had sat with her for some time, she could get no impressions of any kind. She told him so, but as he was leaving she heard a desperately anxious 'voice' ordering her to remove a gun from the man's pocket. She ran after him and found herself saying: 'Your mother tells me you have a gun in your pocket. She is terribly distressed because you plan to use it.'

The visitor gaped at the medium, then fainted. It was only some time later that she learned through Bond that his friend was a business man from Detroit who, faced with a huge financial loss, had written a farewell letter to his wife and had reserved a room at the Piccadilly Hotel in New York City with the intention of committing suicide there. He had then kept his appointment with Eileen Garrett and she had heard what appeared to be his mother's interceding voice.

There was a happy outcome to the affair. Moved by the message, the man went back home, worked extremely hard, managed to pay off his debts, and prospered once more in business.

In her autobiography, *Many Voices*, Eileen Garrett wrote that when she had premonitions she was aware of some external sensory stimulation that made her receptive to the thoughts of and conditions affecting people she knew. The brain accepted material that was forever flowing towards and around it. It processed the material for our comprehension much in the way a computer deals with the data that is fed into it, the difference being that while the computer material is the material that has been prepared, 'the brain is dealing with some as yet unsuspected modifications of the energy that surrounds it'. Mrs Garrett believed mind was non-material and had its being in space. 'Eternity is here and now and all aspects of the self are contained within the absolute.'

CHAPTER 7

Visions in Washington

Thanks to her considerable success as a predictor of events concerning the internationally famous and to constant media publicity, Jeane Dixon has become this century's best-known specialist in the field of prophecy. The cynical might describe her as a soap opera prophetess, for she lives in an elegant old house in north-west Washington DC, with her wealthy business man husband, James, sleeps in a lace-canopied bed which she boasts once belonged to the Empress Eugénie, and on one of the room's pale-blue walls hangs a gold crucifix, the gift of the late German Chancellor Adenauer. Her days are divided between her duties as Secretary-Treasurer of her husband's business; supervising the activities of Children to Children, Inc., to which good cause all the proceeds from her prophesying are donated; working with the staff she employs to deal with the piles of mail she receives daily from people anxious to know what the future holds in store for them; being interviewed at home, on the radio, and on television; lecturing; and preparing her syndicated daily horoscope column. To those who regard the latter form of mass prediction as an easy and deplorable way of making money by pandering to the credulous, she replies that she sincerely believes she is providing a guideline 'for some people which, if followed reasonably, can beneficially affect their daily lives' and says that the 'science' of astrology was taught to her as a girl by Father Henry, a Jesuit priest of 'exemplary goodness', at Loyola University in California.

The only daughter of Catholic immigrants from Germany, Jeane Dixon claims that as a child she predicted that one of her four brothers would become a famous footballer, and that when she was eight she startled her mother by asking if she could see a letter bordered in black. This mystified the family until, a fortnight later, the postman delivered a black-edged envelope containing the news that her maternal grandfather had died.

In *My Life and Prophecies*, Jeane Dixon tells a colourful, novelettish story of how her mother took her to see a gypsy fortune-teller who, pointing at the child's right palm, cried: 'She has the Star of David in her hand, and here's the Half Moon. Your child, madam, in both her hands has all the markings of a great mystic.' Then the gypsy disappeared into her wagon and returned with a crystal ball which she placed in the girl's hands, saying: 'Take it—tell me what you see.'

Jeane says that when she did so she saw a wild rocky coast in a far country. The gypsy exclaimed that Jeane was describing her homeland and added: 'Keep the ball. It is yours. It can do more in your hands than in mine.'

Through that experience, Jeane Dixon says, she began to realize that she had been chosen for a specific purpose in life. She asserts there are many different ways in which the future is revealed to her. Sometimes she receives 'divine revelations' of events certain to occur that concern international situations—and are never intended for any one individual. Another way, she says, is through shaking people's hands and feeling their vibrations. She claims she can see even more if she is able to *touch* their hands with the tip of the ring finger of her right hand. This enables her to pick up signals so clear and so real that they often reveal to her what happened to people at an early age as well as what will happen to them until the end of their lives.

A third manner in which Jeane Dixon maintains that she receives signals is when she prays and meditates and asks for divine guidance. It was at these moments that many 'events in the making' seemed to close in on her. Often, when she needed an answer to a specific question, she would concentrate, meditate, and pray knowing that God would reveal the answer to her. It was almost like hearing the wind blowing on a stormy night: the stronger the wind, the more clearly you can hear its sound. Frequently, the answer to her question was already being worked out in other people's minds, but she was not aware of it until God allowed her to 'tune in' on their frequencies. This enabled her to pick up their thoughts and conversations without being present.

Telepathy was another means of reading people's minds. When she asked those consulting her to look into her crystal and concentrate, it enabled her to tap their subconscious minds. She would see things that had been there for years without their knowing it.

Franklin D. Roosevelt invited Jeane Dixon to the White House on 4 November 1944 for a private meeting. She predicted: 'China will go Communist and become our greatest trouble. Africa will be our biggest worry in the foreign field.' He asked her how much longer he had 'to finish the work I have to do'. Her answer was: 'Six months or less.' Should she have said that? Did she unconsciously scare him to death, for on 12 April 1945 a cerebral haemorrhage proved fatal for him.

Sitting in a Hollywood beauty parlour with her hair under a dryer, Jeane Dixon overheard the blonde in the chair beside her mention that she was shortly going on a war-bond-promoting campaign. Jeane found herself exclaiming 'Don't make that trip!' Carole Lombard tossed a coin into the air. 'Heads, I don't go—tails, I do!' she cried. 'Tails' it was—and she lost her life when the plane she was in nosedived into a mountain.

James Dixon fortunately heeded his wife's warnings against flying from Detroit to Chicago and went by train instead. The plane crashed and there were no survivors. Her close friend Eleanor Baumgartner, too, was grateful that she had taken Jeane's advice against travelling in the same plane as Dag Hammarskjöld, the United Nations Secretary-General, when he perished with all the other passengers in Northern Rhodesia on 18 September 1961. Then that autumn, Jeane Dixon claims to have made another tragically accurate prediction, that Marilyn Monroe would commit suicide within the next year.

When he was in Washington in 1945, Sir Winston Churchill asked Jeane if she could foretell the result of the forthcoming General Election and was told that the Conservatives would be defeated. He was taken aback and objected that he could not believe that the British would be so ungrateful as to throw him out of office after all he had done for them. She was able to give him some comfort by saying that he would make a comeback later.

It was only natural that Jeane should upset some people. In 1948, when she predicted that Truman was certain to be elected President, a leading Republican hostess declared that unless Mrs Dixon publicly changed her mind, she would be excluded from all the party's social functions. Jeane retorted: 'My mind has nothing to do with it.'

When the Republican national convention was held in 1952, those campaigning for Taft tried to persuade Mrs Dixon to be photographed seated next to a large picture of him as she gazed into a crystal ball and predicted that he would become the Republican candidate for the Presidency. Although she was favourably disposed towards him, she declined, saying that there was no possibility at all of that happening.

Jeane Dixon foretold Eisenhower's election to the White House. Then, in 1956, she claimed to have had a vision of the President menaced by a dark cloud and phoned a friend of his suggesting that he should not play so much golf. Shortly after this, Eisenhower went down with ileitis.

A prediction that took some years to be realized was made by Mrs Dixon in 1949 to a former US Treasurer, Ivy Baker Priest: that Richard Nixon would eventually become President. She repeated this in 1953, and in the *Washington Daily News* of 21 October 1968 she wrote: 'Nixon will become our next President...A wire-tapping scandal which I have predicted previously is yet to come.' Then, after his downfall, she said that he would be regarded as 'a great President' by posterity.

Jeane Dixon's prophecies have also concerned Indian affairs. In 1946, she attended a Washington reception given by Sir Girja Shankar Bajpai, Agent General for India, and told a diplomat that his country would be partitioned on 2 June 1947. When this occurred, she received considerable publicity in the press. In June 1947, she foresaw that Gandhi would be assassinated on 3 January 1948 'by someone they least suspect'. Next, in 1956, she was asked what lay ahead for Nehru and she predicted that he would be followed as Prime Minister of India within eight years by a man whose name began with 'S'. Nehru died in May 1964, and his successor was Lal Bahadar Shastri.

From the early fifties onwards, Jeane Dixon has been regularly interviewed on television. On 14 May 1953, on NBC,

Joseph Davies, a former American Ambassador in Moscow, asked her what the future held in store for Malenkov, who had succeeded Stalin. After gazing into her crystal ball, she replied that he would be replaced within two years.

Davies looked sceptical and told Jeane Dixon that he had never known any Russian head of state to be replaced. They either died a natural death like Stalin or they were shot. But Jeane insisted the she would be proved right and went on to describe the appearance of his successor—'a portly military man with wavy hair, green eyes and a goatee'.

Davies stared more sceptically than ever at the seer of Washington and commented that in all the many years he had spent in the USSR he had never come across any Russian who looked remotely like that.

Jeane Dixon responded that she was in no position to contradict him, but that was what she had seen in the crystal. Gazing into it again, she said that she now saw a silver ball spinning into space. It came from the East, which led her to believe that Russia would be the first to send a satellite into orbit. Now the ball was turning into a dove which stuck its claws into the scalp of an entirely bald man, but without making it bleed. And then the dove looked eastwards, which she interpreted as signifying that some day Russia would bring about peace by its own decision.

One month short of two years later, Malenkov was replaced by Marshal Bulganin, who had been described with such astonishing accuracy by Jeane, and in 1957 *Sputnik* soared into space.

Jeane Dixon's most famous prediction is that concerning President Kennedy. According to her, when she was praying in St Matthew's Cathedral, Washington, in 1952, she had a vision in which the White House appeared before her in dazzling brightness coming out of a haze. The numerals 1-9-6-0 appeared above the roof. Then a black cloud covered the numbers. She looked down and saw a tall young man with a shock of brown hair and vivid blue eyes standing in front of the main door. She says she was still looking at him when a voice came out of nowhere, telling her that he would be assassinated when in office.

In *A Gift of Prophecy*, which has done much to promote Jeane Dixon's reputation, Ruth Montgomery wrote that while two reporters from *Parade* magazine were interviewing Jeane in 1956 about her predictions she suddenly exclaimed: 'A blue eyed Democrat elected in 1960 will be assassinated.' Startled by the bluntness of her statement, they suggested this might be more tactfully put as 'die in office'. She retorted: 'Say it as you like but he will be assassinated.'

The interview appeared in the 13 May 1956 issue of *Parade,* and the reference to Kennedy is limited to: 'As for the 1960 election, Mrs. Dixon thinks it will be dominated by Labor and won by a Democrat. But he will be assassinated or die in office though not necessarily in his first term.'

Following John Kennedy's election, Jeane Dixon claimed to have another vision, this time of his coffin being carried out of the White House. Then in October 1963, she told her journalist friend Ruth Montgomery and the psychiatrist Dr Regis Riesenman of another vision, in which the Vice-President's plaque was removed from Lyndon Johnson's door. The man responsible for doing this had a two-syllabled name with five or six letters. She added: 'The second letter was definitely an S and the first looked like an O.' The name of John Kennedy's assassin was, of course, Lee Harvey Oswald.

On 1 November 1963, while having lunch with a Washington society woman, Mrs Harley Cope, Jeane suddenly looked very disturbed and exclaimed: 'He's going to be shot!' Mrs Cope was puzzled and asked who. 'The President, of course,' was the reply.

Between then and the fatal event, Mrs Dixon confided her fears to others, such as the daughter of Samuel Hall, a prominent philanthropist, who knew the Kennedys well. Kay Hall discussed the warning with Mrs Alice Roosevelt-Longworth, but nothing further was done about it.

On Tuesday 19 November, Mrs Dixon, it appears, again had one of her visions and said: 'The President has been shot.' Then, on the Friday, reacting to a vision of the White House shrouded in black when at the breakfast table, she declared: 'This is the day—this is the day—it has to happen.'

Could Oswald have heard of Mrs Dixon's prediction and been influenced by it? Appearing on an all-night radio panel show with Long Nebel a few weeks before the assassination, she suddenly announced, much to the dismay of her fellow panellists, that the President would be shot dead. We know that Oswald listened to this programme, for he phoned its producer just before the crime to ask a question about Cuba.

There were others apart from Jeane Dixon who predicted that John F. Kennedy would be assassinated. Some heard voices, like Adrienne Coulter of Flushing, New York, who during the 1960 campaign heard one saying: 'Nix on Nixon. Kennedy will become President and will be assassinated.' Others had visions, like Mary Tallmadge of New Jersey, who saw Kennedy standing by a coffin with the Stars and Stripes at half-mast. Even a calendar seemed to have fore-knowledge—one for 1963 through a misprint showed the fatal day, 22 November, as a national holiday.

Beverley Nichols relates in his book *Powers That Be* that in 1963 he was commissioned by the Canadian Broadcast-ing Company to give a talk about British royalty which would be recorded in London. He planned to conclude with a colourful description of Queen Elizabeth II proceeding down the Mall in her golden coach accompanied by the Horse Guards. He was in the studio and about to embark on this description when suddenly his head ached so violently that it made him feel sick. His mental picture of the Queen and her cavalcade was obliterated as if the electric power had sud-denly failed for a moment in a play. Then it was succeeded by another mental picture, which was extremely vivid, of President Kennedy riding in an open car, escorted by motor-cyclists. Nichols heard the snarl of their exhausts. 'And, as though it were being dictated to me, I began to describe this scene. Speaking very quickly, I followed the procession down the street until it vanished round the corner.'

This, in fact, appealed to the radio producer, as it enabled Nichols to compare the close security employed to protect the President with the far more modest measures regarded as sufficient for the Queen of England.

The recording completed, the two men had just left the studio when they met a white-faced man who blurted out: 'President Kennedy has been assassinated. Six minutes ago.'

Commenting on this episode, Nichols reveals that he did not have a vision of Kennedy in Dallas but at the Park Avenue end of East 72nd Street in New York City, where the previous winter Nichols had been staying in a ninth-floor apartment and had often watched Kennedy from the window driving down the Avenue to lunch at the Carlyle Hotel. Was it merely a coincidence, he wondered, or could it be explained by the 'group mind' theory?

As far as coincidences are concerned, there are some extraordinary similarities between the lives of Abraham Lincoln and John F. Kennedy. Their surnames had the same number of letters, and each had a child who died in the White House. The former was elected in 1860, had a secretary named Kennedy, and was murdered in Ford's Theatre; the latter was elected in 1960, had a secretary named Lincoln, and was murdered in a Lincoln automobile. Both were tall, and were shot from behind in the head on a Friday with their wives present. John Wilkes Booth, a Southerner, born in 1839, with 15 letters in his name, shot Lincoln in a theatre then fled into a warehouse, and was killed before he could be tried. Lee Harvey Oswald, also from the South and with 15 letters in his name, born in 1939, shot Kennedy from a warehouse then ran into a theatre, and was killed before he could be tried.

Andrew Johnson, born in 1808, Lincoln's Vice-President, had been a Democratic Senator from the South. Kennedy's Vice-President, Lyndon Johnson, born in 1908, had the same surname, the same number of letters in his given name, and a similar political past.

There is also the possibility that Oswald was telepathically influenced by the mass power of thought into committing the crime. It has been estimated that at least 50,000 people claimed to have had premonitions that President Kennedy would be assissinated. In most instances, knowledge of the Presidential 'jinx' may have caused these. Ever since William Henry Harrison, cursed by a Shawnee Indian, passed away two months after becoming President in December 1840, at 20 year intervals the holder of that office had died before the end of his term. Abraham Lincoln, first elected in 1860, was shot dead five years later. James A. Garfield, the voters' choice in 1880, dreamed correctly that he would be murdered in the same way. William McKinley, elected for the second time in 1900, was obsessed by feelings that such a fate would befall him, and it did. Warren G. Harding, who took over in the White House 20 years later, at least expired naturally there in August 1923. The year after the Second World War broke out, Franklin D. Roosevelt was elected for the third time and died in 1945. So it was obvious that the superstitious should have expected John F. Kennedy, elected in 1960, to fall victim to this jinx. That he himself brooded over it is mentioned by Dr Janet Travell, his physician at the White House, in her book, *Office Hours, Day and Night*. Soon after his election he asked her what she thought about it, and she did her best to dismiss it as rubbish, but he did not seem reassured.

Abraham Lincoln himself had several premonitions of death. Once, following the 1860 election, something suddenly roused him from the nap he was taking on the sofa in his Springfield home, and in a mirror opposite he was astonished to see two images of himself. He rose to make a closer inspection, but one of them faded away. He stretched himself down again and once more the second image appeared. He stared keenly at it, noticing how cadaverously pale it was. When he related this to Mary, his wife, she thought it might have been a phantasm signifying that he would die while President if elected for a second term. This experience had a profound effect upon him. He told friends that he felt his days were numbered and said some months later to Mary: 'I am sure I shall meet with some terrible end.' Then, only a fortnight before his assassination, he replied to her suggestion that they might visit Europe: 'You can but I never shall.' When she enquired why, he replied: 'Something tells me so.'

Lincoln was a fatalist, and he saw no reason why the prophetic dreams and visions enumerated in the Bible should not also occur in his time. Ward Hill Lamon, a trusted friend, has described how he was told by Lincoln that 'the star under which he was born was at once brilliant and malignant: the horoscope was cast, fixed, irreversible and he had no more power to alter or defeat it in the minutest particular than he had to reverse the law of gravitation'. Lincoln also confided to Lamon that he had gathered from his dreams that he would rise to the peak of worldly success, then plunge down without warning.

In early April 1805, Lincoln had the same dream on three successive nights, and he wrote down the following account. He seemed to be standing in a corridor of the White House. Everything was quiet except for subdued sobs, as if a number of people were weeping. He went from room to room.

No living person was in sight, but the same mournful sound of distress met me as I passed along. It was light in all the rooms, every object was familiar to me, but where were all the people who were grieving as if their hearts would break?...Determined to find the cause of a state of things so mysterious and so shocking, I kept on until I arrived at the East Room, which I entered. There I met with a sickening surprise. Before me was a catafalque, on which rested a corpse wrapped in funeral vestments. Around it were stationed soldiers, who were acting as guards, and there was a throng of people, some gazing mournfully upon the corpse, whose face was covered, others weeping pitifully.

'Who is dead in the White House?' I demanded of the soldier. 'The President,' was his answer. 'He was killed by an assassin.' Then came a loud burst of grief from the crowd which awoke me from my dream.

On Friday 14 April, Lincoln held a cabinet meeting, at the close of which he said: 'Gentlemen, something extraordinary is going to happen, and that soon.' He went on to describe the persistent dream.

That afternoon, Lincoln told his bodyguard, William Crook, that he felt there were men about who wanted to take his life, and that he had no doubt they would, for 'it would be impossible to prevent it'. When they parted, Crook recalled later, the President said 'Goodbye' instead of his customary 'Good night'—and it was to be the last time Crook met him alive.

Jeane Dixon foresaw the murder of Senator Robert Kennedy, but she describes her visions in this case as telepathic. 'Men planned his death,' she wrote. 'I simply tuned in on their channels and their plans were exposed to me.' Asked after her speech at a convention held in January 1968, in Miami Beach, Florida, whether he would ever become President, she replied that he would not. Then questioned further that evening in her hotel suite by Frank Callahan, a public relations executive, she replied that she was certain Kennedy would never attain the Presidency because she had the feeling that he would be assassinated in California that June.

Some weeks later, on 29 March, while speaking in Fort Worth, Texas, she remarked impulsively to members of a greeting committee that Robert Kennedy would be shot while in California. On 4 April, she told Frank and Occlo Boykin that Martin Luther King, Jr, would be shot, followed by Kennedy.

According to Jeane Dixon, despite these premonitions regarding the Senator, she was convinced that he did not have to die as she predicted, but the feeling became stronger and stronger. On 28 May, after addressing a convention in the Grand Ballroom of the Ambassador Hotel in Los Angeles, she was once more asked if he would become President. The answer, she says, came to her with 'a fierce, unrelenting finality'. She had an immediate vision of a black curtain falling in a flash from ceiling to floor, blotting out the audience, and she responded: 'No, he will not. He will never be President of the United States because of a tragedy right here in this hotel.'

After the meeting, Jeane Dixon told Captain George Maines of the American Legion and Mrs June Wright, mother-in-law of the lieutenant governor of Florida, about her experience. Did they think the hotel management should be told about it? Maines begged her not to do so, as Robert Kennedy was due to speak there the following week and it would only worry them. Mrs Wright thought otherwise and tried three times without success to phone her friend Mrs Rose Kennedy, Robert's mother, who happened to be staying at the hotel that night.

As the trio left the ballroom and walked along the kitchen corridor, Jeane Dixon claims that she suddenly sensed death. The entire surroundings were filled with 'everything that was dark and evil' and 'threatening currents closed in on her from all sides'. She recoiled, and when Maines asked why she looked so stricken she explained: 'Robert Kennedy...This is the place where he will be shot, George! I see him falling to the floor covered with blood.'

Jeane Dixon feels certain that she was reading the mind of Sirhan Bishara Sirhan, whose diary entries supported her belief that he had selected the spot for assassinating Robert Kennedy before 5 June.

Several others also predicted that Martin Luther King as well as Robert Kennedy would be murdered. The most remarkable case is that of Jeanne Gardner of Elkins, West Virginia, who claimed that voices told her what was going to happen. A year before Robert was killed, one of these voices, she says, began predicting a violent death for him.

On 2 June 1968, Mrs Gardner travelled to Washington hoping to see Mrs Bea Moore, an editorial director of Simon & Schuster, who would be there for the annual booksellers' convention, to submit a manuscript for possible publication. Next day, Mrs Gardner was about to leave her bedroom in the hotel where she was staying when the voice spoke and instructed her to write down in her journal that Robert Kennedy would be shot dead early on 5 June by a short, swarthy man. She heard the voice utter the words 'Tirhan Tirhan' and wondered if this might imply that the killer came from some part of Iran. The voice then said that there would be requiem masses at St Patrick's Cathedral in New York and at Hyannisport.

Mrs Gardner then made for the convention at the Shoreham Hotel and persuaded a sceptical Mrs Moore to read what she had written down. Next morning, not knowing what to make of it all, Mrs Moore had to return to New York on business. As the day passed, Jeanne Gardner felt increasingly disturbed. That evening, unable to keep her feelings to herself any longer, she made for the Simon & Schuster hospitality suite at the Shoreham Hotel where, bursting into tears, she told the startled gathering that Robert Kennedy would be assassinated early next morning. Returning exhausted to her hotel, she went to bed. At 3 a.m. something caused her to wake, and no sooner had she switched on the radio than the announcer read out the grim news she was expecting.

In September 1969, Simon & Schuster published Jeanne Gardner's book, *A Grain of Mustard Seed*, in which the full story of her Robert Kennedy and other predictions were given.

Jeane Dixon claims to have had telepathic visions of Soviet testings of missiles, and that on occasion she becomes so ultrasensitive that 'many channels of communication seem to open up all at the same time, exposing hitherto recent man-made plans'.

In September 1965, Mrs Dixon first met Jean Stout, wife of the Chief, Mission Operations, of the Office of Manned Space Flight, then directly involved in the Apollo space programme. Shortly afterwards, she had a vision in which she received a puzzling series of technical terms that seemed to have to do with space flight and which did not make sense to her. So she telephoned Jean Stout and asked her to write down what she dictated and pass the particulars over to her husband as she was certain they were of great importance to him. Fred would be involved in selecting the 'window' for the first manned lunar firings, but this would not occur for at least another three years. He might, however, be interested to know that she saw him over an 83-hour span watching what appeared to be a unit made up of two television sets. There was also some sort of a slide arrangement, looking like a red-hot triangle that moved up and down. Jeane Dixon ended: 'Tell Fred. He'll want to know this!'

Commander Stout was astounded when his wife repeated these details to him. How could Mrs Dixon have found out? he wondered. He explained that 'window' was the term used to describe the period of time during which they could launch a spacecraft, whilst the 'slide' and the two television sets accurately described a space capsule's re-entry pattern.

Over a year later, on 20 December, 1966, when the two women were lunching together at the Mayflower Hotel in Washington, Jean Stout asked Jeane Dixon for her impressions of how the Apollo programme was going to turn out. Jeane said that she needed something to help her to concentrate on the project, and would Mrs Stout hand her the cube she had in her purse?

'How did you know I had it? Fred got it only yesterday and dropped it into my purse as we drove in this morning,' the commander's wife asked, producing a gold plastic cube containing an Apollo tie clip. Jeane Dixon did not reply as she removed the top of the tiny module and gazed down at the three miniature astronauts reclining on their couches. A terrible feeling came over her, and she told her friend that three men would die in the capsule through negligence, but not necessarily in flight. It could be avoided if the wiring were carefully checked and examined. Otherwise the disaster would occur before the end of January.

There was something strange about the capsule's floor, Jeane Dixon added. It seemed so thin that a dropped tool would go right through it, and under the floor she saw a clump of tangled wires. She had a vision of the astronauts dying in an uncontrollable fire.

Fred Stout, understandably, tried to throw doubt upon

Jeane's prediction, pointing out that the Apollo would not be flying until a long while after January. His wife replied that Jeane had not said that the disaster would occur in flight.

On 27 January 1967, as foretold, the catastrophe occurred, and three young astronauts were burned to death while the Apollo capsule was being tested at Cape Kennedy. When eventually the final official report on the course of the disaster was issued, it was supported by a photograph of a tool trapped in a tangle of wires.

According to Jeane Dixon, she does not use her crystal ball often, but when she does she seems to see something of enormous significance. This was so in May 1965 when, concentrating on Europe, she saw two objects of Russian origin, one of which bore the initials MIRV, orbiting the earth in a path which appeared as a blue belt. She says that it was not until the Christmas of the following year that, on catching a closer vision in the crystal, she realized the other object was 'a multi-test vehicle, testing a propulsion system using cosmic rays and magnetic forces.' She saw these forces attracting and repelling themselves in a way which would harness them to drive a spaceship into outer space.

Continuing to gaze into the crystal, Jeane Dixon told herself that the MIRV resembled 'an atomic missile-firing submarine'. Then she realized it was 'an earth-orbiting missile carrier, capable of firing atomic missiles through its torpedo-like tubes'. Peering once more into the crystal, she noticed 'separate electronic guidance systems' in each missile, enabling it to seek out its own target.

In 1965, describing the MIRV as a 'submarine of the sky', Jeane Dixon warned the US Secretary of Defense, Robert McNamara, of the threat to the country's eastern cities posed by the warheads placed in these Soviet satellites. She says that it was not until 1 June 1967 that she knew what the initials MIRV stood for, and that it was not until later that year that McNamara admitted the Russians were producing a MIRV—two and a half years after her warning.

On 5 February 1962, Jeane Dixon announced that she had experienced an extraordinary vision. Awakening at dawn in her Washington bedroom and looking out of the window towards the east, she had been amazed to see not the familiar city street with bare trees but the equivalent of a Hollywood set depicting a desert coated with gold by the rising sun and revealing Queen Nefertiti holding the hand of her husband, the Pharaoh Akhnaton, and cradling in her arms a new-born babe wrapped in rags. Nefertiti then handed the baby over to a multitude of people before walking away. Thirsty and tired, she rested beside a water jug, and just as she cupped her hands to drink, a sudden thrust of a dagger in her back ended her life. Jeane said that her eyes now focused on the child, who had suddenly grown into a man encircled by a crowd of worshippers from the whole human race.

Mrs Dixon interpreted her vision as meaning that a descendant of Queen Nefertiti, and of humble parents, born shortly after 7 a.m. that day, would become a great leader, transforming the world and uniting its people in one all-embracing faith, the basis for a new Christianity, with Catholics and Protestants, Hindus and Mohammedans, and all other warring sects brought together in harmony through this good man. He would reveal himself to the careworn people of our wretched world in the early 1980s, and during the ensuing decade, thanks to him, conflict and cruelty would be banished from every part of the globe. His influence would increase until 1999, when people everywhere would probably become wholly aware of the entire significance of the vision.

Asked what her reactions had been on having such a vision, Mrs Dixon said: 'I felt suspended and enfolded, as if I were surrounded by whipped cream. For the first time, I felt that I would never again need food or sleep, because I had experienced perfect peace.'

Jeane Dixon was not alone in believing that a new world teacher would be born on 5 February 1962. Others deduced that this would occur on account of the extraordinary conjunction of planets on that date. Some thought the new Aquarian Age then dawned, others that this would happen in 1982. In her 'vision', she was possibly influenced by those occultists who maintain that this pharoah and his queen were incarnations of the Apostle Simon Peter and his wife.

A few years later, however, Mrs Dixon completely changed her mind about the child's character. Far from becoming a power for good, he would turn out to be the Antichrist. Another vision, she explained, had revealed this to her. He had already been taken by his parents to Egypt from where he was born. In 1974 he would become aware of his purpose in life, and by 1992 he will have become a world leader propagating a new religion that is a mixture of Christian dogma and Eastern philosophy. Posing as a prince of peace, he will dupe the world with his spurious spirituality, hiding his atheist convictions under this veneer. Christian education in the schools will almost end.

Mrs Dixon paints a chilling picture of this Antichrist's military power and his political domination based on Jerusalem. Using an intercontinental network of television stations he will corrupt the world, but gradually the masses will repudiate him and a slow return will be made to true Christianity.

This is all very fanciful stuff, and it is when Mrs Dixon assumes the mantle of a modern biblical prophet and allows her religion and her politics to colour her pronouncements that she becomes least credible and has been proved wrong—as when she predicted a short stay in power for Fidel Castro and that the Chinese Communists would embark on a world war of conquest in 1958.

As a Catholic, Jeane Dixon is particularly interested in her church's future, and she believes that between now and the end of the century it will undergo more drastic changes in doctrine and tradition than ever before. An increasing number of priests will leave to marry, and doctrinal differences will split the church into factions. In 1969, she predicted that before the year 2000 one pope would suffer grievous bodily injuries and another, the last ever to reign as absolute head of the Church, would be assassinated and replaced by the cardinals with one more to their liking.

Jeane Dixon claims that the exercising of her precognitive gift does not conflict with the tenets of her religion, for she maintains that according to the Bible 'all events are foreshadowed'. She has refused to take part in the Rhine type of experiment with Zener cards on the grounds that her powers cannot be made to operate to order. The fact that she has been wrong in the timing of some predictions she has explained by pointing out how relative time is, arguing that a day to us on earth is 24 hours but to an astronaut up in the sky it is an hour and a half. Still, she insists when she sees an actual date in the crystal or in a vision, she is invariably correct. Her alibi in other instances is an ingenious one: 'I see symbols. They are always right, but I can misinterpret them.'

In February 1976, on a visit to London, Jeane Dixon was invited by the *Sun* newspaper to predict what would happen in Britain during the rest of the century, and they published her response. Harold Wilson, she believed, would be knighted on leaving office and would remain in the House of Commons. Should he resign before the end of 1978, then there was a strong possibility that, following a General Election, Mrs Thatcher would become Prime Minister. Jeane Dixon was wrong in adding 'but only for a short time', as she was in predicting that Eric Varley would 'leap into the spotlight' and have 'a tremendous triumph', probably in 1978. Far from this occurring, he has now quit politics.

On the other hand, Jeane Dixon's prediction that Sir Geoffrey Howe will eventually attain the Premiership might well come true. More startling is her forecast that by the late 1990s there will be so many parties in the House of Commons that no Government will ever have a majority, with the result that the military will be forced to intervene to restore order.

Jeane Dixon was right in foreseeing that Prince Charles would marry an English girl, and in auguring a gloomy future for the Shah of Iran, whom a revolution would drive abroad, but she was mistaken in predicting that after living in seclusion for a time he would once again 'stride into the world spotlight'.

Another seer who has come into the limelight as a result of the publication of Donald Regan's sensational book, *For the Record*, in May 1988, is Joan Quigley the San Francisco astrologer, whose advice, he claimed, may have helped shape some of the most momentous decisions to emerge from the White House during President Reagan's administration. Mrs Reagan was worried following his election in 1980 that the '20 year cycle' of Presidential deaths that had occurred since 1840 would be repeated in his case. Consequently, the First Lady consulted Miss Quigley, who after studying Reagan's horoscope warned that 'something bad' was going to happen in March 1981, and that he risked a violent death. Nancy therefore persuaded her husband never to leave off wearing his bullet-proof waistcoat, with the result that, although seriously wounded, he survived the assassination attempt that month.

Later, according to Donald Regan, Joan Quigley correctly foresaw the bombing of a TWA plane over Greece in 1986, and had a premonition of the dire events before the Iran-Contra scandal erupted. The former White House Chief of Staff revealed that in arranging the President's activities he had to take into account the zodiacal portents Mrs Reagan received from the astrologer—such as ensuring that the historic intermediate-range nuclear arms treaty be signed at precisely 2 p.m. on 8 December. Gorbachev's horoscope was closely studied to provide clues to his character and likely behaviour.

CHAPTER 8

The Blind Seer of Petrich—and Others

Mme de Thèbes, real name Anne Victoire Savary, had already made a reputation for herself before the twentieth century commenced, with her gloomy New Year prediction in 1899 that the French President, Felix Fauré, would die that year, which he did—on 16 February.

In her *Almanac* for 1905, Mme de Thèbes wrote: 'The future of Belgium is extraordinarily gloomy. As I have already predicted, a conflagration there will spread to the whole of Europe.' Then, eight years later, we read: 'Germany menaces all Europe and especially France...After the war that I foresee, Prussia and the Hohenzollerns will have lost their former power. As I have repeatedly stressed, the Kaiser's days are numbered, and after him conditions in Germany will be completely changed. I am referring to his reign and not to his life.' The Kaiser was deposed in 1918, but did not die until the 1930s.

Turning to Mme de Thèbes's *Almanac* for 1913, one finds her writing of Austria: 'The Prince who should have sat on the Imperial throne will not do so. His place will be taken by a younger man who at present does not expect this to happen.' The following year she reiterates: 'The tragedy in the Imperial House of Austria foretold a year ago will come to pass. No one can avoid his fate.'

Mme de Thèbes was also a palmist. Sir Osbert Sitwell in his book *Great Morning* has related how nearly all his brother officers of his own age had consulted her during the first half of 1914. In every case, just when she had started to read the outstretched hand, she had flung it away from her, exclaiming: 'I don't understand it! It's the same thing again!

After two or three months, the line of life stops short and I can read nothing.' Sir Osbert comments that the officers concerned were later killed in the First World War.

The German clairvoyant Mme de Ferriëm received her visions as if on a television screen, and would write down what she was foreseeing at the time, just like a commentator watching an actual event. For example, in 1899, her description of a mine disaster yet to occur was published in a German newspaper. This read:

All these people here at the entrance to the mine—how white they are—like corpses! Yes, that is what they are, corpses, every one. All being carried out. Everything is so black, nothing but little huts. The people here speak a different language. Now they are bringing out a body wearing a belt with a shining buckle on it. Soon it will be Christmas—how cold it is! Here comes a man carrying a lamp covered with wire mesh. Of course, this is a coal-mine. Now I understand what one of them is saying. It is—'The doctors are all from Brüx!' Ah, I know where we are—in Bohemia! The women and children all wear kerchiefs. Are those medical men giving first aid? Several have armbands with crosses on them... 'In the coal mines of Dux,' he is saying. But what I read is 'Brüx'. Why, I see it on his armband. Oh, they are from the hospital.

In September 1900, at Dux near Brüx in Bohemia, such a disaster occurred, and the details foreseen by Mme de Ferriëm proved remarkably accurate. Although it was not Christmas, the weather was unseasonably severe.

This century was only a few weeks old when Mme de Ferriëm had a vision of an immense fire on the other side of the Atlantic. She wrote:

Clouds of black smoke—coal-black smoke. How dense it is! The docks are burning. Oh, this is frightening. A colossal conflagration in New York. I see flames sweeping a ship in the harbour and I hear a fearful crash. So far as I can make out, it is not an American ship ...

The prediction came true on 30 June that year when the *Bremen*, the *Saale*, and the *Main*, all German ocean liners, were burned out and some 200 people died in the fire that raged through the docks at Hoboken, New Jersey, facing New York City on the other side of the Hudson River.

Mme de Ferriëm was a fiercely patriotic German, and it was when she allowed her prejudices to distort her visions that she failed by predicting victory for her country in the 1914–18 War.

Poland's most noted medium this century was probably Mme Przybylska, who claimed to receive predictions through voices speaking to her during seances. Fighting between her country and Russia continued after the First World War had ended in the West. In the early summer of 1920, the Poles were jubilant at their successes in driving back the enemy, but her controls were pessimistic and foretold reversals that would cause a complete change in the council ruling the country. A man named Witos would become Prime Minister, which was a surprising prophecy as he was unknown. In August, a great stranger from abroad would arrive and advise Pildsudki, with the result that the tide would at last turn from the middle of that month.

On 28 June, the Bolsheviks suddenly launched an offensive in the north, driving the Poles from Lida, Minsk, and Vilna. Then, on 12 July, when Warsaw itself seemed doomed, Mme Przybylska told anxious society leaders at a seance that the Russians would never cross the Vistula and that the capital would not be occupied. Her predictions were fulfilled. Witos became Prime Minister, and the military genius of General Weygand, who came from France to advise Pildsudski, proved invaluable in enabling the Poles to repulse the invaders.

Predictions also played a part in the fate of Finland according to the memoirs of Marshal Mannheim, who tells how, in 1917, at a tea party given in the Hotel London, Odessa, by Lady Muriel Paget, she provided the services of a clairvoyant to entertain the guests. The clairvoyant answered four questions written out on sheets of paper and handed over without disclosing the identities of the enquirers.

In reply to one of Mannheim's questions, the clairvoyant said that he would soon go on a long journey, become a commander of military forces, and win a battle gaining much acclaim for him and an important post which he would give up through dissatisfaction. Shortly after this, he would travel to the capitals of two major Western powers on urgent business which would have fortunate consequences. He would attain a higher position still, but only for a short while. However, several years later, he would be rewarded with the highest honour of all.

Mannheim acknowledges in his book that all of this happened as predicted. Leaving Odessa, he travelled via St Petersburg to Helsinki, where in January of the following year he took charge of the Finnish forces opposing the Communists and that May finally defeated them, becoming Commander-in-Chief. Owing to political intrigue, however, he resigned. Soon he went to France and England to urge their governments to recognize Finland as an independent nation, instead of making it a part of Sweden as had originally been proposed. He succeeded, and whilst in London visited Lady Muriel Paget and told her how the clairvoyant's predictions had so far come true.

In recognition of these achievements, Mannheim was appointed Regent of Finland in December 1918, but gave up the office when in the following August Stahlberg took over as President. The ultimate accolade came in 1944 when Mannheim himself was elected President without opposition.

Boriska Silbiger, the Hungarian psychic, gained international fame in 1934 when King Alexander I of Yugoslavia lost his life in Marseilles on 9 October of that year at the hands of an assassin. She had some months earlier predicted that a king whose name began with an A would be murdered—and had also predicted Ernst Roehm's execution on 30 June.

In December 1935, Boriska Silbiger wrote that the ruler of a great empire would die suddenly in the following month and be succeeded by his eldest son, who would abdicate within a year. King George V died on 20 January 1936, and his successor, Edward VIII, gave up the British throne on 10 December that year.

Boriska aroused the hostility of the Nazis by foretelling the defeat of Germany in a war and a violent death for Hitler, with the result that he had her arrested and sent to a concentration camp.

Mrs Eva Hellström, who founded the Swedish Society for Psychical Research, would write down accounts of her dreams in the mornings and get her daughter and her maid to add their signatures as witnesses of the details and the time. Eventually, she reached the conclusion that the first part of such dreams proved more accurate than the end, when the conscious mind started to take over and the vision became blurred.

During the night of 16 September 1950, Mrs Hellström dreamed that her husband, an engineer, had received a letter from Göteborg telling of some catastrophe at a dam-construction or similar site in which 16 people had lost their lives. Thirteen days later, what a newspaper described as the worst natural disaster in Swedish history happened when clay deposits crashed down upon a village near Göteborg destroying 35 houses and killing and injuring 20 people.

On 5 November of the following year, Mrs Hellström dreamed that on leaving a train at Saltsjöbaden she came across a crowd gathered round the scene of an accident. She was told that a labourer had been trapped in a kiln. She saw workmen carrying a stretcher on which lay the wounded man. It was dark and a red glow came from the kiln. Just over 12 months later, on 20 November 1952, she read the following headlines in the previous evening newspapers: 'Tunnel Disaster at Nacka. Labourer Trapped Behind the Rocks. Workmen Try to Save Doomed Man. Explosion in Rocks at Nacka. Labourer Killed in Tunnel. Severely Injured Men Crawl Out of Sea of Fire.'

Much of what Mrs Hellström read in these and the morning newspapers agreed with what she had previewed in her sleep.

That same year, 1952, on 5 August Mrs Hellström described in her diary how in a dream she had watched a man fall from the flat roof of a tall building. Four months later, on 8 September, this happened at the harbour of Värtan.

When she woke up on the morning of 26 March, 1954, Eva wrote down details of a dream in which a green railway car had crashed into the back of a blue number four tram. She felt sure that the accident would happen where the trains from the suburb of Djursholm and the number four trams met at Valhallavägen in Stockholm. Up till then, carriages had always been painted brown, but that June, when travelling, she noticed that one in her train was coloured green. She questioned the conductor and learned that a number of such carriages had been ordered as they were superior in design and more comfortably furnished than the older brown kind.

Almost two years later, on 4 March 1956, such a disaster took place. Eric Panzar, the stationmaster who had worked for the Stockholm–Djursholm Railway Company for 33 years, confirmed in a letter to Eva that such a collision had never happened before as far as he knew.

Apart from her account, Eva Hellström had drawn a sketch showing the green carriage driven to one side by the collision and ending up at right angles to the tram. After the accident, she obtained a sketch from the police similar to her own. This strengthened the case for regarding her dream as a precognitive one, especially as immediately after having had it she posted copies of her diary entry to Professor J.B. Rhine in America as well as to Swedish scientists.

As regards events of international significance, when visiting Aswan in Egypt Eva Hellström wrote in her diary:

February 17, 1952. Today after lunch I was so tired that I had a pain in the throat. I lay for half an hour trying in vain to sleep. Then I saw a vision. Not very clear—I believe it was a riot or turmoil of some kind. Then I saw a bridge that collapsed or went to pieces. People were hanging on the iron beams...amongst them was a Scotsman in a kilt, which I believe symbolizes that the English are involved.

Although Mrs Hellström was informed that such a violent incident had taken place in that locality, she had the strong impression that her vision applied to the future and to conflict between the British and Egypt, which four years later broke out.

Another Swede, Herr Berndt-Hollsten, managing director of the illustrated journal *Säningsmannen*, became celebrated in his country for his precognitive powers right from childhood. For instance, in June 1950, he dreamed that a large army bomber had crashed near his son, Ian-Ake, and himself when they were watching an air display. It was so vivid that he wrote down a detailed account and showed it to his family and friends. Three weeks later, Ian-Ake persuaded his father to take him to a display at Bromma, where a bomber crashed almost at their feet.

Elizabeth Steen, born in Holland, had a prevision of the floods that caused havoc there in 1952 and of her own house being inundated. When, later, she went to live in California, she foretold Martin Luther King's assassination, giving a date which proved to be only two days out. Her success led to Dr Charles Tart, a University of California parapsychologist, inviting her to undergo an ESP test, which she accepted. Handed a sealed envelope and asked to describe its contents, she said that it contained some hair from a black cat. It should have been human hair, but a student had substituted the other without Dr Tart's knowledge.

Influenced possibly by Edgar Cayce's earlier predictions, Mrs Steen had seven such frightening nightmares of earthquakes destroying California, where she was living, that her husband gave up his job and they moved to Washington. The catastrophe she had predicted would occur at the end of March 1969. She died suddenly on 28 March, aged only 29, possibly scared to death by her dreams.

Fortune-tellers usually avoid predicting deaths to those consulting them, but occasionally in the heat of the moment they have broken this rule. Sir William Barrett, FRS, once president of the Society for Psychical Research, reported to its members in 1924 his findings in the case of Nell St John Montague, a crystal-gazer then fashionable in London, and what she had predicted to a Mrs Holt whom she had met when visiting a Mr and Mrs R. Learning that Mrs Holt longed to have a reading, she agreed to try and discover what the future had in store for her. After getting the enquirer to hold the crystal in both hands, Miss Montague took it from her and, as she told Sir William later, was unable to hide her horror at what she saw in the crystal ball. Noticing this, Mrs Holt pressed her to reveal why she was so upset, and Miss Montague replied that she had witnessed a scene that, if it came about, would make Mrs Holt a widow within two days. Shock had led the clairvoyant into telling her client more than was wise, but Mrs Holt controlled her feelings and made light of it.

Nell St John Montague later showed Sir William the account which she claimed to have jotted down in pencil immediately after the consultation. This read:

I can see a tall, fair man, rather bald, pacing up and down a small room, evidently a smoking-room. Close beside the desk is a telephone, he is excitedly taking up the receiver and speaking into it. He opens a drawer in the desk and holds an object taken from it in his right hand—it is a revolver—again he speaks into the receiver excitedly and watches the closed door on the left eagerly. Once more he speaks into the receiver, and for a moment points the revolver in the direction of the door—apparently listening for someone to come—he makes a gesture of angry despair, and for the third time takes the receiver in his left hand, whilst his face, working with frenzied emotion, seems to shout into the telephone—he waits once more, pointing the revolver at the door. He turns his face and seems to stare out of the crystal—there is despair in his eyes. With a sudden gesture, he looks once more at the door and shakes his head as though giving up hope of it opening to admit someone for whom he seems to be waiting. He raises his right hand and staggers back, the revolver is now pointing at his own head—then I see blood everywhere gushing. A woman comes into the room, the same woman who is in the room with me now, only in the picture she wears a loose wrapper. She lifts his head—blood is everywhere.

Three days following this, Mr R. brought Nell St John Montague a message from his wife. He refused any refreshment, saying that he had to call on Mr Holt, who had phoned him three times in close succession, asking to see him at once and adding ambiguously: 'I want to take you with me.' Recalling her vision, Miss Montague begged Mr R. not to visit the man. Mr R. was mystified by her concern and was impatient to leave, but she kept on finding some excuse to delay him. After a quarter of an hour, he tried to phone Holt, but there was no reply so he refused to stay any longer and set off.

Nell St John Montague then left the house herself as she had an appointment with her doctor. Feeling very apprehensive, she told her maid that if anyone phoned urgently during her absence to let the caller know where she could be reached. Hardly had she entered the surgery than Mr R. rang. Later, he was to write to Sir William Barrett:

On April 17, 1920, when I called on Miss Montague, I told her I was going to see Mr Holt. She implored me not to go and kept me talking...Then I left and drove to Mr Holt's house. After ringing his front door bell, I heard the report of a pistol...I owe my life to Miss Montague's warning.

When Sir William investigated the case, he found that an account originally given in the *Daily Mail* for Monday 19 April

1920 was correct. Mr Holt had come out of the 1914–18 War
with shell-shock and was mentally unbalanced when he took
his life. In a crazed way, he had craved the company of
another man he knew to join him in death, and had chosen
Mr R.

Together with another member of the Society for Psychical Research, Sir William questioned Mrs Holt, who stated
that, after gazing into the crystal, Nell St John Montague had
said that she would be a widow 'within two days'. Several
people testified that Miss Montague had been extremely
upset on 17 April, and her doctor confirmed that someone
had phoned her when she was with him. Both she and Mr
R. agreed to be questioned by all members of the Society
for Psychical Research who wished to do so. A special meeting was held and those present were well satisfied with the
explicit and convincing answers to their questions. Whilst,
of course, Miss Montague was unable to produce any supporting independent evidence as to what she maintained she
saw in the crystal, she certainly did predict Mr Holt's death.

If we do not accept precognition as the explanation, then
psychometry may have played a part, as Mrs Holt held the
crystal before handing it to Nell St John Montague. Telepathy may also have played a part. Mr Holt had clearly been
contemplating suicide for some days, and when Miss Montague implanted in his wife's mind the idea that she would
be widowed within two days, Mrs Holt may unconsciously
have radiated thoughts that led to his taking the final step.

'Woody' was the sobriquet by which Mrs Vera Woodruff,
the clairvoyant popular in the twenties, was known to her
friends and clients. It was when she was earning her living
as a dressmaker in Kensal Rise, London, that her sixth sense
developed. As she fitted the clothes she had made in her
customers' homes, they would confide their problems to her
and she would find herself advising them and predicting
what would happen—just as if the words were being put
into her mouth by someone else, she claimed. She even
started going up to strangers in the street who looked
depressed and telling them that if they did what she said
all would turn out well.

As she had a large family and needed money, Woody
decided to become a professional fortune-teller. She bought

a pack of cards because she thought that would impress those consulting her. She would begin by reading the cards and giving them conventional interpretations and then, as if suddenly controlled by some invisible force, she would scoop them all up and the words would pour out of her as she made some remarkable predictions—these were the ones that usually came true.

Mrs Perry, wife of a former president of the Royal Society of Arts, has described how this happened at the end of a reading. Suddenly Woody cried: 'I've found her. I've found that child.' Mrs Perry could not follow what she was talking about. 'Not your family,' the other explained. 'It's that child who's missing. She's lying in three inches of water. They will find her tonight.'

This did not mean anything to Mrs Perry, but next morning she read in the newspapers that a child missing from home had been found drowned the previous night in three inches of water.

Five years before it occurred, Woody, when visiting the Perrys, predicted that the wealthy young socialite Elvira Barney would be tried for murder. Mr Perry was shocked and reproved her for saying such a thing, but over the following years she repeated her prediction from time to time. It seemed so absurd that Mrs Perry says it became a joke between her husband and herself. But one morning in the paper he read that Elvira had been arrested for murder.

Mrs Perry could not resist phoning Woody to point out that her prophecy had at last come true. The fortune-teller's response was unexepected: 'She'll get off. But not for long.' Again Woody was right. Elvira was acquitted, but died shortly afterwards.

Two years before King George V's reign ended, Woody predicted to Mrs Perry that the Prince of Wales would marry a commoner, and later, when Mrs Simpson asked Woody to the flat in Bryanston Court to tell her fortune, she predicted that Wallis would marry the Prince of Wales.

Woody helped the police unofficially in the detection of crime. In the Crumbles, Eastbourne, case in 1924, she told them correctly that part of the woman's body would be found at a London mainline station. Ten years later, in the investigation of the Brighton trunk murder, she asserted that the names of the girl whose body was discovered began with the initials V and K. The girl was eventually identified as Violette Kaye.

Reading the biography of this larger-than-life character of the 1920s and the 1930s by her equally famous son, Maurice Woodruff, one notices how superstitious the social butter-flies and the actors and acresses were. It would seem that there was hardly any celebrity living in London or visiting it who did not consult her. If one acts on a warning, it is not always possible to tell what would have occurred had one not heeded it. The Hollywood star Anna May Wong was told by Woody that she would cancel a trip to America and go to Scandinavia instead. Whilst there, she would be presented with a bouquet of white heather as she was about to board a train. This she must throw away. The change of plans transpired as foretold, and as Anna May Wong was handed such a bouquet, she remembered the warning and as soon as the train had left the station she pulled down a window and flung the bouquet out. One can speculate end-lessly as to what would have happened had she kept it.

There was a less pleasant side to Woody's fortune-telling. On occasion she cursed those who had offended her. In 1930, she spent a weekend as a guest of Air Marshal Sir Sefton Brancker, Director of Civil Aviation, and his wife. Lady Bran-cker, who was crippled from arthritis and was mostly con-fined to a wheelchair, had consulted Woody for many years. Among the guests was a young actress of whom Sir Sefton was obviously very fond. On the Saturday evening, Sir Sefton, who had been drinking heavily, called to Woody: 'Tell Poppy who she is going to marry.'

Laughing and not taking the question seriously, Woody retorted: 'One thing I can tell you, it won't be you!'

When dinner was over, Sir Sefton got up and said: 'I would like to propose a toast before the ladies leave us. Here's to the fortune-teller in our midst who doesn't know what she's talking about.'

Woody, who had a quick temper, was furious. She regarded his words as an insult to his wife, meaning that he would marry the actress once Lady Brancker had died. Jumping up and raising her glass, she glared at him and responded: 'And here's to you, Sir Sefton—may you descend in flames to hell.' Then she added in a whisper: 'As you will within three months of this night.'

Nearly three months later, Sir Sefton was burned to death in the R-101 airship disaster.

Woody had never liked the man, whom she believed to be a philanderer with no consideration for his wife's feelings. Nevertheless, the fulfilment of her curse upset her and she never uttered one again.

Maurice Woodruff wrote that his mother maintained that clairvoyants had a 'third eye'. She based this on an ancient Buddhist belief. According to her, in old Tibet any boy apparently able to see into the future would actually be given a third eye at the age of eight, but only on the Dalai Lama's authority. This was so as to strengthen the boy's prevision. A hole would be bored in the centre of the forehead just above the bridge of the nose, and a temporary wooden bung steeped in purifying herbs was inserted while the wound healed. During this period, the boy would be kept in a darkened room.

In the Inca museum in Lima, there are on display skulls of high priests with holes in the centre of the forehead that were made when they were alive to create third eyes which it was believed could see beyond the earth-plane dimension. Interestingly, some reptiles have a third eye or the evolutionary residue of one in the frontal area of the brain, and its role appears to be to spot low-energy radiation in the heat spectrum. Man has a seemingly useless organ, the pineal gland, in a similar position. This Descartes regarded as the place through which the spirit and the body interacted, and many spiritualists consider it to be the psychic centre.

Maurice Woodruff claimed that from an early age he showed signs of having inherited his mother's clairvoyance. When he was in his teens, she told him how she had noticed that even as a baby he would stick his fingers into a spot between his eyes and rub it, instead of his eyes as the average baby did. He had gone on doing this, which was why there was now what resembled a bruise mark over the bridge of his nose. 'That's your third eye,' she told him.

While serving in the army during the war, Maurice Woodruff's own clairvoyance sometimes came unexpectedly into operation. When stationed in Durham, he was drinking in a golf club and found himself walking over to a woman who was sitting on her own and saying to her: 'You may think

I'm barmy, but please don't worry. He will walk again.'

The woman recoiled as if he were intruding on some private grief. Tears welled into her eyes and, ignoring him, she hurried out. He felt that he had made a fool of himself and did not return there for some time. When he did, the barman passed him a pint of beer and explained that he had been paid by a lady to serve him with a tankard of the best every time he visited the club. The man explained that the last time Woodruff had come in, he had spoken to one of their lady members. 'You didn't know it but she had just had news that her husband's legs had been crushed and might have to be amputated. She badly needed the encouragement you gave her that night. By the way, sir, you were right.'

Soon after this, Woodruff warned his best friend in the army not to apply for a transfer overseas, but he insisted on doing so and was killed one week after reaching his new post. Then, when an officer commented that the war news was getting depressingly worse, Woodruff found himself saying: 'Don't worry, sir, Russia will be in with us by the 22nd of June, 1941.'

The other took it as a joke, but must have repeated it in the mess, for when Winston Churchill revealed on that very date that Russia had become an ally Woodruff became the talk of the regiment.

Woodruff wrote that much of his clairvoyance was sparked off by looking into his clients' eyes. When he did this, pictures, words, and feelings came immediately into his mind. It was like adjusting the focus of a highly sensitive camera. He achieved international fame thanks to his tireless exploiting of opportunities for publicity in the media. He had regular columns in the national press and in women's magazines. A single article in a British newspaper brought in some 8,000 letters. He thought that what helped to establish his reputation was accepting a challenge to demonstrate his clairvoyance on television. He was asked to identify before the cameras a cloaked figure whose eyes alone were visible through slits in the hood. He got the letters S and D, said the person had written a play, gave a date, which proved to be that on which the play had received its provincial première, said it would be presented in London and afterwards in America, and that the key letters in the title of the play were H and T.

The disguised woman was Shelagh Delaney, author of *A Taste of Honey*, which shortly afterwards was presented in the West End and later on Broadway. This could all be attributed to telepathy except for the last fact, for the American rights were not acquired until *after* the successful West End première.

Maurice Woodruff was destined to have a clientèle drawn largely from people in show business. Peter Sellers came to him when he was making a name for himself as a comedian on the radio. Woodruff told him he needed to embark on a new career that would bring him international acclaim. Later, Maurice predicted that Peter would soon start climbing to stardom in films, playing first a wide boy, followed by a second movie in which he would appear as five different characters and be directed by a man with an S or a Z in his name.

A fortnight later, Sellers was offered and accepted the wide-boy part in *The Ladykillers*. This was succeeded by the five-character role in Mario Zampi's *The Naked Truth*. Sellers was astonished. Woodruff then advised him to practise speaking with a slight Indian accent as he would be offered the chance to co-star with one of the world's most beautiful screen actresses. This would prove the turning point in his career. As predicted, Sellers played an Indian doctor opposite Sophia Loren in *The Millionairess*. And so it went on, with Woodruff proving right nine times out of 10, as Sellers acknowledged in a newspaper interview.

Other predictions that consolidated Woodruff's reputation were giving the exact date of birth and sex of Queen Elizabeth II's third son, Prince Edward, and of Princess Margaret's first child, Viscount Linley, and predicting that John F. Kennedy would be elected President—which Woodruff foretold long before the Democrats had chosen him as their candidate—and that Lyndon Johnson would succeed him. But Woodruff has also proved wrong on several occasions. In 1970, for example, there was no 'sensational discovery of a cure for cancer', Jackie Onassis did not give birth to a son, nor did Reagan lose the election in California.

Vanga Dimitrova, the blind seer who lived in the village of Petrich on the frontier between Bulgaria and Greece, has become a legend in her country. She was a simple peasant, dressed in black, which she wore ever since 7 April 1956, when her husband, Dimitri Georgeyev, died. She would describe him as a kindly man who had been driven to drink through the aggravation of having hundreds of people calling on them to tell her about their troubles and ask her advice. He obediently died on the day she had predicted. Vanga started losing her sight at the age of 13, and six years later went completely blind, but she gained instead the ability to trace missing persons, to solve crimes, to foretell the future and, in particular, to predict the dates of deaths.

One of Vanga's first successes concerned the younger brother of a local farmer, Nikola Gurov, who had vanished from home in 1923 at the age of 15, and whom for some 20 years no one had been able to trace. When Boris, the farmer, consulted her in the matter, she said that Nikola had run away to Russia, where he had become an engineer. He had fought with the Red Army in the war, and been captured by the Germans. She had a vision of him in a camp, but he would return to Petrich in the spring and could be recognized then by his grey uniform and the two suitcases he carried. She was right.

One day a woman called on Vanga seeking information about the circumstances of her sister's death, 15 years previously, and was told that she had been murdered by her own husband, who had faked an alibi by pretending to be in Sofia at the time. As a result, the case was reopened and the man's guilt was proved.

Vanga Dimitrova became the Bulgarian equivalent of Holland's Croiset and was regularly consulted by the police in difficult cases. One of her country's leading authors went to see her about a novel he had just finished and which no one but himself had read. To his astonishment, she began by telling the whole plot in some detail. She commented that it was a true story except for the end where he had made the chief character die. In real life, the woman had remained alive, and so she should in his book. He took Vanga's advice. She also predicted that he would go to Russia and narrowly escape being killed in an accident, which duly happened.

The blind seer's fame spread throughout Eastern Europe, and people flocked to Petrich. Sometimes she advised more than 50 enquirers a day. Following a nervous breakdown, she was taken under state protection, given the title of 'Assistant Professor', and paid a fixed salary, all fees going to the government. Applications for interviews were controlled by a small committee, and a hotel was built in Petrich to accommodate those permitted to consult her. On arrival, they would be handed a lump of sugar and instructed to place it under their pillows before going to sleep. Next day, on visiting Vanga, they had to hand it to her, and she would hold it against her forehead momentarily before starting with impressive accuracy to talk about the past and present of her clients and to foretell the future.

Bulgaria's leading parapsychologist, Dr Georgi Lozanov, director of the Institute of Suggestology in Sofia, spent over 20 years investigating Vanga Dimitrova's paranormal powers. Dragomir Simovet, a Yugoslavian researcher, interviewed him about her and published accounts in the Belgrade journal *Svet* in January and February 1967. Lozanov revealed that when he was in his twenties he went incognito to Petrich, together with Sasha Itrech, a friend from the University of Sofia. They left their car outside the village so that no one could have any clue to their identity and walked to Vanga's cottage, where they had to queue for three hours before their turn came. Sasha went in first, and the blind woman began by telling him both his names, his mother's name and the illness she had, and the date of his father's death and what had caused it. She told him where he had been born and described where he was living, then added that, though married for seven years, he had no children, but, she predicted, a child would be born to him and his wife one year from then. This occurred.

Dr Lozanov told his interviewer that when he entered the room where Vanga was seated, she startled him by saying: 'Georgi, you are a doctor who uses hypnosis to try and cure patients. You want to find out if I am genuine. But why now? You have come too soon. You will return in some years' time.' He thought she meant that more serious study on scientific lines would then be possible. He did not reply, but instead attempted an experiment. Employing all his willpower and hoping to communicate with her telepathically, he imagined that he was a close friend of his. Vanga started to predict, but Lozanov knew that none of it could possibly apply to himself. Suddenly she became aware of this herself and said: 'I can't tell you anything—please leave me.'

Lozanov told Simovet that his success in confusing Vanga supported his belief that she obtained her knowledge through somehow tapping the minds of her clients. The right time for his investigation came some 10 years later when he was established as a parapsychologist. In the next decade, according to him, he had spoken 'hundreds, probably thousands of times' to Vanga and had documented the future events she had foretold to those visiting her.

After Dr Lozanov had been testing Vanga for seven years, the authorities appointed a commission to judge whether or not his claims for her were justified. First he took them, one by one, to her. She proved astonishingly accurate in every case, and they reported favourably. It was arranged for questionnaires to be sent annually to all those consulting her, and her average success rate was never less than 80 per cent. She died in 1985.

In recent times, the Icelandic magazine *Vikan* has been publishing prophecies annually for the coming year sent to them by a Volva—a sage soothsayer. Reporting in the *Daily Telegraph* of 3 January 1987, Julian Isherwood wrote that Gudrn Alfredsdottir of *Vikan* told him that the oracle's identity remained a mystery even to them. He said: 'We get the prophecies from a middle woman. All we know is that there are two Volvas and we have been getting the prophecies from this one for several years now.' She was thought to be 'around forty and living outside Reykjavik'.

1986 proved a particularly successful year for the Volva. Her predictions published at the start of that year read:

An unexpected but highly publicised international event will take place in Iceland during the year. The world will not experience very much, peace in this international year of peace. A chemical catastrophe will take place in Eastern Europe which will cause major damage and widespread environmental debate... A world famous politician will be murdered in an event that will shake the world.

The three events thus correctly foretold were, of course, the Reagan-Gorbachev summit, the Chernobyl disaster, and the assassination of Sweden's Prime Minister Olof Palme.

For 1987, the Volva scored no 'hits' with her forecasts that scientists would, for the first time, register the presence of an intelligent life in space, and that an effective treatment for AIDS would be discovered by a Nordic scientist.

CHAPTER 9

Dame Edith Lyttelton's Case Book

Dame Edith Lyttelton, a member of a distinguished political and cricketing family, widow of a Colonial Secretary, herself a British delegate to the League of Nations, was for many years a prominent member of the Society for Psychical Research, and its president for 1933–4. She was also a medium, using automatic writing in which the fingers, loosely holding a pen or pencil, move involuntarily over a sheet of paper as if another intelligence has assumed control. In February 1914, her hand wrote: 'The terrible cry of the wounded ... the hot breath of the war ... the blending of many tears ... Now the trumpets blow, the bugles sound and all the world is at war.' That August, the First World War broke out.

Dame Edith continued: 'Lusitania—foam and fire—mest [*sic*] the funnel—in broken arcs.' Then that May, in another script, she again referred to this liner: 'Open your ear to the unknown—fear is the arch enemy, Lusitania.' In the same month of the following year, the *Lusitania* was sunk when a single torpedo fired by a German U-boat hit her on the starboard side, just behind the bridge, detonating the cargo of rifle ammunition and setting the ship ablaze so that the funnel was clouded with dense smoke.

On 31 January 1915, Dame Edith was a house guest of Lord Curzon at Hackwood in Hampshire, and early that morning as she sat alone, ready with pencil and paper, she found herself writing:

In the morning we are aware of the coming day ... The nemesis of Fate nearer and nearer—no respite now nearer much than you think and once it begins there is no stay—no one knows—the leaves of the autumn—they will fall in quiet—the fugitive armies—the overshadowing of fear—the price of peace. *Nolens volens.* ('Whether he will or not.') The Munich bond remember that—you will see strange things.

It was not until many years later that the meaning of this prediction became clear when on 31 January 1938 Neville Chamberlain, the British Prime Minister, and Hitler signed the Treaty of Munich.

At three o'clock on the afternoon of 24 May 1915, at Falconbridge in Kent, Dame Edith wrote:

In the western fields carnage—marching—the vines on the hills, the vintage—flight—now mark this—behind the curtains of blackness there is light never doubt it—be of good cheer. The hand stretched out to stay Bechtesgaden—markovitch.

This was taken at the time to refer to the future course of the 1914–18 War. Berchtesgaden is misspelt and, of course, it was to become best known as Hitler's mountain eyrie. What remains a puzzle is 'markovitch', which perhaps the future course of events will solve. From my examination of the script, the word begins with a small *m* and not a capital letter as some authors have given when quoting this.

Nearly 17 years later, on 2 March 1932, a script of Dame Edith's was concerned with a coming world war and contains this prediction:

I see a very curious looking instrument. At first I thought it was a miniature machine gun, but I think it is a very sharply pointed sort of telescope mounted on a sort of little carriage wheels and it has a great force—it is called 'the pencil of light'. It is manipulated from far away. I don't know what it means.

Today we know that 'the pencil of light' is most likely the laser beam which, intensified in power, may become the main weapon in the American 'Star Wars' arsenal.

Dame Edith's book *Our Superconscious Mind*, published in 1931, was mainly intended to give convincing examples of the unconscious mind's wider range of knowledge than the conscious mind—'such as knowledge of what is passing, or has passed, at a distance in time or space, what is about to happen; and the kind of vision which is either called prophecy or inspiration'.

During a broadcast in a series of talks called *Enquiry into the Unknown* in February 1934, Dame Edith Lyttelton invited listeners to write to her about their own experiences of prediction. There was an excellent response, and she personally investigated some of the cases for which she obtained corroborative evidence. These were later published in book form under the title *Some Cases of Prediction*. They were divided into four categories.

The first category consisted of cases which might possibly be attributed to coincidence. Included here are instances where the results of horse races were foreseen (with which I deal later in this book); the case of Mrs Edghill of Kenton, Middlesex, who, for three years running every January, while glancing down a list of football teams, would hear a sort of inner voice telling her correctly which team would win the Cup Tie and even in two instances the actual scores; of Mr T. Robinson of Birmingham, who foresaw his dog's being killed by a motor lorry; and of Mrs Thompson of Dartford who had 'a vision, or dream, as some would say of two ships in collision'. She also heard someone telling her she would see it announced in a newspaper in two weeks' time. 'In the *Daily Mail* about three weeks after the vision, there was a picture of the two ships exactly as I had seen.'

In Category II Dame Edith grouped cases which could be explained by telepathy. These included other instances where the names of horses winning races were foreseen, an account of a dream about chocolates being wrongly packed, and one from a Miss H.M. Mudie, joint principal with her friend Margaret Strachan of New Brighton High School near Birkenhead. One morning at the end of the Christmas term Miss Mudie told Miss Strachan that in a dream that night someone had said to her: 'There has been a murder in the Victoria Hotel and the murderer slept in your house.' This hotel was opposite where they lived.

As the two principals were then planning to go off on holiday and shut up their home, Miss Mudie wrote that she felt somewhat perturbed. Some three weeks later, when they were together in Eastbourne, Miss Strachan showed her a copy of the *Wallasey News* of 8 January 1913, which had been posted on to them, and exclaimed: 'Here is the explanation of your dream.'

Ruby Jones, a barmaid at the hotel, had been murdered

on 6 January by Harold Foster Farrar, the sweetheart she had jilted, who had then shot himself. However, the shooting did not take place in the hotel, but in the sandhills just below, and the killer had not slept in the two principals' house. Still, it was possible that he had hidden somewhere around it while waiting for the girl to come out.

In Category III Dame Edith included cases which she considered might be attributed to 'telepathy of an extended and complicated kind but would be more easily attributed to precognition'. A Mrs Wilkinson of Newton Abbot wrote how when her son was a baby his nurse used to take him out into the garden in his perambulator each day. One morning, the mother had a strong feeling of apprehension. She seemed to hear repeatedly a voice warning her: 'Don't put the baby near the shrubbery.' This had such an effect on her that she told the nurse to move the perambulator on to the lawn. Not long after this a bull escaped, tore into the next garden, jumped over the hedge, and would have crashed into the perambulator had this remained in the original spot.

In Category IV Dame Edith placed 16 cases she regarded as firm evidence for precognition. A Mrs Lloyd-Owen of Ickenham, wife of a commander in the Royal Navy, described how a few weeks before the Schneider Trophy Air Race was held on 13 September 1931, she went one evening to the cinema with her husband and a woman friend. The newsreel contained photographs of the British team, none of whom she knew. They were all RAF officers except for one from the Royal Navy. As his image appeared on the screen, she received 'a sudden terrific sensation of shock, the shock of violent physical impact. I started so violently in my seat that my friend sitting next to me whispered, "What's the matter?" I answered in great distress, "He's going to be killed, he's going to crash."'

During a trial, while practising for the race on 18 August 1931, the young man in question, Lieutenant Brinton, was drowned when G.6 plunged into the Solent.

Mr R.B. Calder, headmaster of Goole Grammar School, sent Dame Edith a detailed account of two dreams. In 1928, when they were living in Middlesex, his wife dreamed of an old house built of grey stone and situated in an attractive valley through which flowed a narrow stream of inky-black water. Soon after this, Mr Calder was appointed to the headship of Holmfirth Secondary School in Yorkshire, a county which his wife had never visited. When searching for a new home there, they inspected a house at Honley, three miles from Holmfirth, which she recognized as the one seen in her dream. It also had a stream nearby, the waters of which were often discoloured from the waste products of a dye-works. They liked the property and bought it.

In a letter to Dame Edith, Mrs Calder confirmed what her husband had written and added:

Only one detail was lacking—in my dream, I had seen that half of the house appeared to be occupied and outside the door was a barrel being used as a dog kennel for a black retriever. Certainly half the house was occupied, but the tenants had no kennel and no dog. A year or so later, new tenants arrived and my dream was recalled to me very vividly—when they brought with them a black Labrador retriever and placed a barrel by the door for its use.

The couple had to move a second time owing to Mr Calder's appointment as headmaster at Goole. After learning this on 28 December 1931, Mrs Calder dreamed of a dark red, square-shaped house situated on a corner of two streets. There was a fence over which she would see a low flat garden. She described the house to her husband next morning and said she felt convinced they would live there, and the idea depressed her.

On 31 December, the Calders went in search of a new house in Goole and failed to find anything suitable. Eventually the retiring headmaster, Mr C.J. Forth, took them to see a house which turned out to be exactly like the one she had foreseen in her dream. Circumstances forced them to buy the property and go to live in it.

A Mrs Gertrude M. Pritchard wrote from Herne Bay on 28 February 1934, describing how, in 1922, she had a very vivid dream concerning her husband, the Rev. James Pritchard, who had been Congregational minister there. In her dream, she had seen him die whilst preaching, and then, after making her way through a great crowd, she had come across his body placed behind velvet curtains. On 9 November 1924, the minister gave the address at the Armistice Service in the Pier Pavilion. There were 2,500 people present and Mrs Pritchard sat at the back of the hall. As she was turning to the last hymn, her husband fainted and she saw him being carried from the platform. When she reached it, she found him lying dead behind the green velvet curtains.

A Walsall policeman, Joseph F. Burrell, claimed that he had many prophetic visions which occurred in broad daylight whilst working. During the 1914–18 War, a friend of his, Jack Trench, served in the army as a machine gunner. One day while he was on leave from France he was walking along with Burrell when, according to the latter:

I distinctly saw Jack with a scar over his left eye. I had a strange feeling about it. I immediately told him to cut a button from off the bottom of my tunic, put it round his neck with his identity disc and told him he would come through the war with only a scar over his left eye.

Jack Trench, employed after the war as a railway police sergeant at Chester, confirmed in a letter to Dame Edith that this prediction had been fulfilled except that the scar was *under* his *right* eye.

Mr J.S. Wright of Liverpool wrote to Dame Edith that on two occasions some months before the R-101 disaster he dreamed that he had seen it plunge down in flames, followed by a terrific explosion. His friend, G. Coxon, confirmed that they discussed the dreams on several occasions before the airship crashed.

Another correspondent, R.W. Boyd of Enfield, stated in his letter that on 3 October 1930 he dreamed he saw 'a large airship crash, after some preliminary difficulties in manoeuvring, on to the top of a hill and burst into flames'. Many people were silhouetted against the yellow flames and were trying to escape, but none succeeded. While the wreck was still burning 'a small company of soldiers arrived under the command of an officer on horseback who was very excited and dashed about from place to place but was unable to help anybody'. Less than 48 hours later, Mr Boyd heard that the R-101 had crashed at Beauvais. He pointed out that when later photographs appeared in the press, an officer on horseback was conspicuous among those present.

Catherine Hare, Boyd's fiancée, confirmed that the contents of his letter agreed with what he had told her beforehand, and added that when they visited a cinema the following week and saw a newsreel film of the disaster, he was amazed to realize that 'the scene was almost identical with that of his dream, especially in the appearance of the French gendarmes who were shown examining the débris'.

When investigating this case, Dame Edith inspected a picture in *The Times* of 7 October 1930, which showed a mounted gendarme or soldier in the foreground.

The account that Mrs G.H.M. Holms of Cheltenham sent to Dame Edith of how she dreamed of the Meopham aeroplane crash is truly remarkable because of the amount of detail it contained. In July 1930, she and her husband and daughter were on holiday in Yorkshire and spent their days walking over the moors. During the night of the 18th, Mrs Holms dreamed that she was going along a path with a heather-covered hillside on her left, but on her right, where the ground fell away gradually, there was rough green grass dotted here and there with apple trees, and a short way ahead two labourers were working. Then, suddenly, out of the clouds, high up on her left, the body of a man came shooting down as if from a great height. He landed on his head a few yards from her 'with a sickening thud'. She heard something crack and said out loud: 'There goes his skull.' The body rebounded, and then rolled over once or twice and bumped into a tree. She saw the top of the mutilated head, which was towards her.

The labourers hurried down and carried the corpse up to the path behind Mrs Holms. She turned and saw a plastered, thatched cottage with gables to which the men went with their load. Then he woke up. 'As I dressed, the whole scene, instead of fading became more and more intensified. I told my husband and daughter, and could not shake it off. The words "There goes his skull" remained all day in my ears.' The dream obsessed her until 22 July, when *The Times* announced briefly that a terrible air crash had occurred at Meopham, Kent, in which Lord Dufferin, Lady Ednam, Mrs Loeffler, two other men, and a pilot had all been killed through falling from an aeroplane into the orchard of a private house on the previous day.

There were no further details, but Mrs Holms now became convinced that the scenery in her dream was Kent, but framed by the Yorkshire moors. The following morning a fuller report appeared in the papers. The chief witness was a farmer, and his description of the tragedy corresponded exactly with what she had foreseen, except that the first body had been followed by the others landing further down in the orchard.

Both Mrs Holms's husband and their daughter corroborated what she had written. All the deceased had been staying at Mrs Loeffler's house at Le Touquet for the weekend. Mrs Holms did come from the same part of Ireland as the Dufferins and her parents had met them but she had not. She told Dame Edith that she had had 'a fair number of personal psychic experiences'.

In the conclusion to *Some Cases of Prediction*, Dame Edith Lyttelton pointed out that science had discovered that our ideas about the world of matter founded upon the perception of our senses are a mass of inconsistencies. What we have called realities were largely constructs of our minds reared upon the illusory messages of these same senses. Telepathy revealed that our ideas of space are not final, and precognition revealed the same about our ideas of time.

Precognition, if it exists, must belong to an order of life different from that we think we know, Dame Edith thought. Just as observation of minute happenings in matter have heralded vast discoveries, so may the investigation and study of cases of precognition lead to stupendous philosophical developments. Certain questions obtruded themselves. Is everything that happens predestined? Or are we creatures restricted to certain boundaries yet, within these, allowed to exercise a measure of freedom and choice? Or again, do we create and shape our own futures, however unconsciously? If every case of precognition displayed a motive, it might be possible to postulate a guiding hand behind the phenomena. But many of the cases, even in her little collection, were trivial and seemed to reveal only a chance glimpse into the future.

The case of Mrs Calder, who foresaw the houses she and her husband were to occupy, is by no means unique. One of the most striking examples of this I have come across concerned a Surrey lady.

Some years ago my husband was attached to the Admiralty in a capacity which necessitated our moving from time to time to different parts of the country. Normally we would have no

knowledge of when to expect a transfer till about a week beforehand. Three months before our transfer would come through I
would begin to have a series of dreams. I would dream I was in
a certain town and could give a good description of the same but
could only say whether it was north, south, east or west—never
the name of the place. I would see the house both outside and
inside, and note all its characteristics and its vicinity so that by
the time our removal notice came we were quite ready and invariably found the new place to be exactly as I had described.

Some years ago when we were in North Wales I had a dream
of a town far north to which I felt we were going to be transferred.
I saw a castle and a bridge outside, guarded by two soldiers in
eighteenth century uniform. Through the archway I could see the
continuation of the road in which I stood. I went along this road
looking for our future house which I found to be a long way from
the town. It was an extremely pleasant road and ran alongside
a canal and through a glen, but I felt it held an element of danger.
I told my husband at breakfast. He said, 'Well, I shall soon scotch
that by putting in for a southern transfer, and I shall be certain
to have it granted after being North so long.'

I had the same dream again and again and went through a
harassing experience of being unable to find my way back to the
town. In the third dream, in the midst of the bad time I was having to find my way, I resolved that the next time I had the dream
(note here that I was well aware that I was dreaming) I would
find out the name of the road in which I became so confused.

In the fourth dream everything went as usual until I came to
my nightmare spot. I remembered my resolve of the third dream
and made my way down this road in order to ascertain the name.
I read 'King's Road' and thereafter all was well.

In the course of time, a reply was received from the Admiralty
in answer to my husband's request for a transfer to Southern
England. He opened it and to his amazement read out an order
to proceed to Inverness, Scotland. He was informed that he was
too skilled a man to be wasted at the location he had requested.

When we reached Inverness, I found everything to be as in my
dream except that the Castle bridge was no longer guarded by
soldiers. I even lost my way one evening, and on finding a road
named Queen's Road walked down it and found my way home.
On enquiring at the Public Library, I discovered that it had been
renamed in Victorian times and had been previously called King's
Road. Could I somehow have gone back in time in my dream?
Was that why the guards had been dressed in eighteenth century uniform? Why did that attractive route home past the canal
and through the glen have from the first in these repeated dreams

a sinister association? Another dream and subsequent events supplied the answer.

I dreamed one night that I was taking the two children to school as I always did. The road being long and lonely, it was my custom to take my cycle with me to ride back home. In this dream I seemed to be walking with a child on either side of me and my cycle when from some bushes stepped two men. I had time to notice one of these men whose legs were somewhat bandy. He was short and square. Across his middle he wore a gold chain. I saw him take off his coat and the next thing he had put it over my head and was dragging me towards the bushes. I called to the children to scream. I felt that I was suffocating and awakened in fright.

Two days later I was cycling through the glen with my two small dogs beside me, when I noticed two men come out from some bushes. At first I took no notice of them till both turned and looked at me and spoke about me. I dismounted and waited for them to go on. Instead, both men slipped back into the thicket again. I decided not to go on, but found that the path behind me was blocked by a herd of Highland cattle. Not a soul appeared to keep me company. For an hour, I remained where I was. Then I thought of a short cut across the fields, leading out of the bushes at one spot. I was just about to mount my cycle again, when out from the bushes stepped one of the men. He was facing in my direction and was in the act of putting on his coat. Across his middle was a large gold chain. I recognised the men as the same I had seen in my dream. In the present, I had two dogs instead of the two children of my dream.

I kept the men in front of me until clear of the canal, and rode home and told my husband of my experience. The following day I was able to point out the two men to my husband, who on enquiry discovered that they were strangers on a holiday from Liverpool. About a year passed, then one day I and my husband saw them again on the glen road. A few days later the wife of the local hairdresser was missing. She was never found, but her handbag and her hat and some flowers she had gathered were discovered on the canal bank near the spot of my experience.

This lady goes on to say that this undoubted murder in the glen broke her nerve. For the next three years, she did not dare to venture alone into any unfrequented spot. She concludes: 'I have never really recovered from the shock of what might have been but for the dream warning.'

CHAPTER 10

'An Experiment with Time'

Two years before the publication of Dame Edith Lyttelton's *Our Superconscious Mind*, much interest was roused by J.W. Dunne's *An Experiment with Time*, and innumerable people fascinated by the subject started keeping a notebook by their bedsides and recording their dreams immediately on awakening to discover whether they had seen into the future while asleep. His importance is that of a pioneer in this field, and any study of twentieth-century precognition should include some account of his contribution. As regards his own dreams, his accounts of them suffer from the disadvantage of not always having been independently witnessed immediately after occurrence.

J.B. Priestley was fascinated by the subject and based three of his plays partly on Dunne's conception of time, as well as writing a book, *Man and Time*, in which he referred to his meetings with Dunne and described him as being as far removed from the crank and crackpot as it was possible to imagine. He 'looked and behaved like the old regular officer type crossed with a mathematician and engineer'.

Dunne was in fact an aeronautics engineer who served with the British forces during the Boer War. In 1901, aged 26, he was on sick leave not far from Khartoum when he dreamed of three white men in travel-stained khaki arriving there, one of whom told him they had trekked from the Cape on foot. Next morning Dunne read these headlines in a newspaper: 'The Cape to Cairo. *Daily Telegraph* expedition arrives at Khartoum...'

The following year, Ferdinand Clere, a sugar planter who lived in St Pierre on the island of Martinique, at the base of Mont Pelée, dreamed that the volcano had erupted. However, the fact that no such disaster had occurred for years made him pay little attention to the dream. But when on 5 May 1902 lava suddenly shot out of the volcano crater and obliterated a sugar factory, killing 25 workers there, he recalled the nightmare, gathered together his family and his easily transportable valuables and, ignoring the derision of his neighbours who accused him of being superstitious, went off in a carriage as far away as he could from the danger zone. Three days later, his flight was justified when Mont Pelée like an enraged giant vomited its molten rock over St Pierre, burying all its inhabitants but one.

That same year, when in an army camp with the British Mounted Infantry near Lindley in the Orange Free State, Dunne dreamed that he was standing on the upper slopes of a hill or a mountain. The ground was of curious white formation. Here and there were little fissures from which jets of vapour were spouting upwards. He recognized the place as an island of which he had dreamed before—an island which was in imminent peril from a volcanic eruption. In his dream, he gasped: 'It's the island. Good Lord, the whole thing is going to *blow up!*' For he remembered reading about Krakatoa where, in 1883, the sea, infiltrating a volcano's heart through a submarine crevice, turned into steam and blew up the mountain. Recalling this, he was seized with a frantic desire 'to save the four thousand (I knew the number) unsuspecting inhabitants' of the present island.

The nightmare worsened as he found himself pleading in vain with the sceptical authorities to evacuate the inhabitants. He kept shouting: 'Four thousand will be killed! Four thousand!'

Some weeks later, newspapers from England reached the camp and among them was a copy of the *Daily Telegraph* in which Dunne read the headlines: 'VOLCANO DISASTER IN MARTINIQUE—TOWN SWEPT AWAY—AN AVALANCHE OF FLAME—PROBABLE LOSS OF OVER 40,000 LIVES.' The accounts by eyewitnesses agreed with Dunne's dream except for the number of dead. He did not notice this discrepancy at first. In fact, it was not until some time later as he copied out the details from the newspaper cutting when writing his book, *An Experiment with Time*, that he became aware of this.

This made him wonder whether the dream was not an

actual prevision of the disaster, but of his original reading of the *Daily Telegraph* in which he had misread 40,000 as 4,000. In fact, he had learned a few weeks after the catastrophe that the official number of dead was different from both numbers.

Dunne wrote in his book: 'So my wonderful clairvoyant vision had been wrong...But it was clear that its wrongness was likely to prove a matter just as important as its rightness. For whence in the dream did I get the idea of 4,000? Clearly it must have been in any case because of the newspaper paragraph.'

As there was also the possibility, however unlikely in the circumstances, that on reading the *Daily Telegraph* he had imagined he had dreamed about it previously, Dunne from now on carefully wrote down accounts of any unusual dreams as soon as he awoke. As a result no doubt of his army training, he ordered his conscious mind to remember what he had been dreaming. This device considerably improved his ability to recall dreams. When he first started doing this, nothing of a precognitive nature was produced until the eleventh day.

Dunne was out shooting when he noticed that he had wandered away from the area for which he held a permit. Hardly had he become aware of this than he heard the sound of two men bearing down on him from opposite directions and inciting a dog to go after him. He managed to escape before they reached him. He did not connect the incident with any dream until that evening when, leafing through his notebook, he read at the end of the previous night's entry the words: 'Hunted by two men and a dog.' He had no recollection of this, which demonstrated the importance of keeping records.

Following this experience, Dunne came to the conclusion that to obtain the best results from observation of our dreams we should reverse the way we think about time. We should pretend that the dreams occur after the events, the reason being that our minds are considerably more conditioned to take in dreams containing information from the past. Therefore we will be mentally more receptive if we employ this ruse.

It was in the autumn of 1913 that Dunne dreamed of a north-bound train plunging down the embankment on the other side of the Forth Bridge and that it would happen in the middle of the following April. Next morning, he related the dream to his sister, and they agreed to warn their friends against travelling to Scotland in the spring. Then, on 14 April 1914, the Flying Scotsman was wrecked on an embankment at Burntisland about 15 miles north of the Forth Bridge. The express left the permanent way, jumped a parapet, and dived on to the golf links below.

In another dream, Dunne found himself standing on a balcony crowded with young women and enveloped in dense suffocating smoke billowing through the shattered windows behind them. The hoses of firemen below were sending up streams of water in a vain attempt to put out the conflagration. Dunne could hear the shrieks of the girls as they collapsed around him. He awoke in great distress, and next day the nightmare became reality when he read in the papers accounts of a fire in a rubber factory near Paris.

Dunne dreamed before it happened of the Silvertown explosion of 1917, and also of trivial things like the exact time at which his watch would stop next day. He found himself in a sort of semi-trance able to read the time by his watch without looking at it—in other words he was able to foresee what he would see when he picked it up. Most of his previsions were of happenings in the immediate future. He mentions one, however, where fulfilment took 20 years.

'Why should I only be able to see into the future in dreams?' Dunne one day asked himself. Then he had an idea. Surely the simplest way to set about an experiment when awake would be to take a book just published of which he had not even read the review, sit down with it in an armchair in his study, concentrate on the title, so as to have associative links with whatever he might come across in his future reading of the book, and wait for odds and ends of images to come into his mind.

The experiment was a success, and he did write down words, phrases, and even whole sentences which corresponded remarkably accurately with what he came across when he read the book later.

One day Dunne had a vision of an umbrella standing on its handle with the ferrule in the air, and was disappointed to find no reference to one in the book on which he had fixed his attention. Then, a few days later out in the street, he came across an old lady tapping her away along in this fashion, which was an unusual occurrence but not convincing evidence for precognition. She might have been in the habit of using her umbrella thus, and Dunne could either have noticed her doing it unconsciously or have forgotten about it.

In his 1938 book, *The Serial Universe*, based on *What is the Fourth Dimension?* by C.H. Hinton, published in 1887, Dunne advanced his time displacement theory of Serial Time, which although much discussed is now regarded as no more than metaphysical conjecturing. Even his great admirer J.B. Priestley could not accept it as convincing.

Dunne believed that in the case of the Martinique disaster, he foresaw his reading of an account of it in the *Daily Telegraph*. Having heard that Clive Jenkins, the general secretary of the Association of Scientific, Technical and Managerial Staffs, had dreams which involved foreseeing the front page of the next day's *Times*, I wrote to him and he replied that it was true:

The story was always centre page and I was always accurate. The problem I have is that I know how news selection takes place and how page layout is done because I have watched it—particularly at the *Daily Mirror* where I was a columnist. So I *could* have anticipated it. Anyway, these dreams have stopped because I no longer read *The Times*.

CHAPTER 11

Warnings Affecting Travel

American mathematician William Cox conducted a fascinating survey in the 1960s to ascertain whether any travellers had a sixth sense that unconsciously warned them against taking a certain train in preference to any other on a particular day. Following an accident, he obtained from the authorities details of the numbers of people travelling on the same train on the six previous days and on the corresponding day in each of the four preceding weeks. This investigation was carried out at the same stations for a number of years, and the results showed in every case that far fewer passengers travelled in trains involved in accidents than might have been expected from the statistics.

For example, on 15 June 1952, a Chicago and Illinois train, known as the Georgian, carrying nine people was involved in an accident. On each of the six previous days, there had been 68, 60, 53, 48, 62, and 70 passengers aboard on this particular run. For 18 May, 25 May, 1 June and 8 June, the figures had been 54, 53, 55, and 35, respectively.

Later that same year, on 15 December, when a train on the Chicago, Milwaukee, and St Paul line was wrecked, there were 55 people travelling on it compared with an average of over 100 on the previous 10 days.

Cox concluded that his researches had proved the existence of an 'accident-avoidance' phenomenon, and that those concerned had avoided an accident thanks to 'subliminal premonitions'.

Dr Walter Franklin Prince, a graduate of Yale and a prominent member of the American Society for Psychical Research, kept written records of his dreams. In 1902, he had a nightmare in which he was looking at a train, the rear end of which was protruding from a railway tunnel. 'Suddenly, to my horror, another train dashed into it. I saw cars crumple and pull up, and out of the mass of wreckage arose the cries, sharp and agonised, of the wounded persons.' Then what appeared to be clouds of steam burst forth, and he found himself being awakened by his wife because she was concerned about his moans of distress.

A few hours after Dr Prince had gone back to sleep, the 8.15 Danbury to New York City express was standing some 75 miles away from him, half in and half out of the Park Avenue tunnel, when it was hit from the rear by the engine of a local train. Many passengers were killed. 'To add to the horror of it all,' an eye-witness was quoted in one newspaper as saying, 'the steam hissed out from the shattered engine upon the pinned down unfortunates and rose up in clouds from the tunnel opening.'

In 1917, Dr Prince had another grim excursion into the future. During the early hours of 28 November, he dreamed of a slender, willowy woman aged about 35 with blonde hair and rather pretty small, girlish features. She was holding out a sheet of paper. It was an order for her execution, printed in red ink. She said that she was willing to die if he would hold her hand.

Then the light went out and it was dark. I could not tell how she was put to death, but soon I felt her hand grip mine and knew that the deed was being done. Then, I felt one hand of mine in the hair of her head which was loose and severed from the body and felt the moisture of blood. The fingers of my other hand were caught in her teeth, and the mouth opened and shut several times as the teeth refastened on my hand and I was filled with horror at the thought of a severed but living head. Here the dream faded out.

On rising, Dr Prince told his wife about the nightmare, and, later that morning he reported the details to Gertrude Tubby, the secretary of the American Society for Psychical Research. The next day, the 29th, the *Evening Telegraph* published an account of how, many hours after his dream, a 31-year-old woman had lain down beside the track close to a Long Island station with her neck resting on the rail and had been beheaded by the wheels of a train. Her name was Sarah

A. Hand, which would explain why there were so many references to hands in Dr Prince's precognitive dream. But this was not the only extraordinary aspect of this macabre affair. It was disclosed at the inquest that Mrs Hand was mentally unbalanced, and in a letter left behind she wrote that, believing her head had an entirely separate life from the rest of her body, she was going to decapitate herself to demonstrate that she was right. The tragedy had occurred six miles away from Dr Prince's home, and like the woman in his dream, she was slender, pretty and blonde.

Joseph De Louise, who was born in Sicily and was brought to the United States as a child, first intended to become a priest, but changed his mind, took up hairdressing, and started his own salon. Soon the neighbourhood buzzed with tales of another talent of his, that of seeing into the future. On 25 November 1967, listeners to Radio WWCA heard him say: 'Before the end of this year, a major bridge—not as long as the Golden Gate or Brooklyn Bridge, but sizable—will collapse causing many deaths.' This was remembered when three weeks later, on 15 December, the Silver Bridge spanning the Ohio River at Point Pleasant, West Virginia, gave way during the busiest time of the day and there was a heavy toll of fatal casualties.

The fulfilment of the prediction gave De Louise nationwide publicity. Then, a year later, speaking on the radio at Gary, Indiana, he said that early in 1969 there would be a 'terrible train wreck on the Illinois Central line south of Chicago on a foggy night and involving two trains'. The bartender in a Chicago liquor saloon was puzzled when on the evening of 16 January 1969 De Louise, whom he did not know, came in and asked if he could have a look at a newspaper that gave an account of a head-on collision between two trains on the railroad south of the city. The man replied that there was nothing about any such disaster in the papers, neither had there been on the radio.

But De Louise insisted such a disaster had occurred and that thick fog was to blame. A few hours later, he was proved right when at 1 a.m. an Illinois Central passenger train, hampered by bad visibility, crashed into a freight train at Manteno, 45 miles south of Chicago, with the loss of three lives and severe injuries to 49.

The following month, on 25 February 1969, De Louise

described over the radio how he was witnessing in a vision an airliner hurtling down to earth south-west of Chicago. 'Seventy-nine passengers will die,' he went on, 'and I see the number 330—yes, 330. Only I'm not sure if that is the time or the flight number. I think it is the time.' His prediction was fulfilled with an impressive degree of accuracy when on 9 September of that year an Alleghany Airlines jet shot into a Piper sports plane some 135 miles south of Chicago. There were no survivors from either plane—83 people lost their lives. The collision occurred at 3.31 p.m. precisely.

De Louise's most remarkable vision took place when he was in the studio of a press photographer who got him to pose peering into his crystal ball. As the seer did so, he says he glimpsed a blurred newspaper headline. 'It said TED KENNEDY—blank—blank—DROWNS. The second thing I saw was a woman's face. Her hair was streaming in the water. I had my Predictions of the Year all written out ready to send to the Chicago *Sun-Times*, but after some thought I inserted this and sent it in.'

What appeared in the magazine section of the newspaper on 29 December 1967, however, was condensed by a sub-editor and read: 'I see tragedy involving water around the Kennedys.' This came to pass on 25 June 1969 when Mary Jo Kopechine was drowned after Senator Edward Kennedy's car dived over a bridge in Massachusetts.

De Louise compared his visions to 'the beam of a flash-light which—at odd moments—shines into a pitch-black vault, only to be flicked off again before the details of the interior have become clear'.

In 1967, the London *Evening Standard* set up its bureau to record people's premonitions independently and in advance of the events they foretell. A fascinating collection of 469 were logged during 1967. Some of the most impressive came from 53-year-old ballet and piano teacher, Lorna Middleton of Edmonton, and a 44-year-old Post Office switchboard operator from Dagenham, Alan Hencher. On 30 December, Miss Middleton had a vision of a bad crash involving a lorry with an 'exceptionally heavy load'. Seven days later, 12 people were killed when an express train hit a low loader carrying a giant transformer at Hixon level crossing.

Miss Middleton later sent accounts of her 'visions' to the Central Premonitions Registry of New York. These included one on 23 January 1970 of people from a holiday camp being killed 'in hundreds' through 'the worst crash I have ever known'. She saw 'blood gushing in the air like fountains'. On 2 February, in Buenos Aires, a passenger express train smashed into the rear of a parked commuter train filled with people returning from a weekend holiday, crushing two of the five cars and knocking the others off the track. The dead exceeded 150 and over twice that number were injured.

As regards Alan Hencher's submissions to the *Evening Standard* Premonitions Bureau, on 22 April 1967 he foresaw a train accident involving a narrow-gauge railway with flat-sided, wooden coaches and wooden seats for passengers. On 31 May, a 'Tom Thumb' miniature train crashed at Scarborough, injuring seven.

On 28 February 1975, a London tube train apparently out of control tore past the platform at Moorgate and the foremost two carriages were wrecked on striking the tunnel's dead end. Many passengers were seriously wounded and some died, while several hundreds were imprisoned in the blacked-out tunnel for hours. In his book *Science and the Supernatural*, Professor John Taylor includes an account received from a woman of a dream she had a few days earlier in which she was in a smoke-infested, ill-lit section of the Underground and could glimpse through the gloom jagged bits of debris and heard sobs and screams. On awakening, she roused her husband and described the nightmare to him. The details she gave agreed astonishingly with those of survivors of the Moorgate crash.

Sir Alec Guinness once told Arthur Koestler how after rehearsing for a new play in London on Saturday 3 July 1971 and dining with a friend, he went to bed at 11.30 p.m., having set his two alarm clocks to wake him at 7.20 a.m. It was his habit when thus working at the weekend to rise at that time on the Sunday and to leave his flat at 7.45 a.m. for the short walk to Westminster Cathedral to attend Mass at eight o'clock. On returning, he would have a light breakfast and catch the 9.50 a.m. Portsmouth train from Waterloo to Petersfield, near which was his country home.

Sir Alec said that he would normally wake up a few minutes before the alarm clocks went off, but on this particular morning when he glanced in the half-light at one of the clocks it appeared to him to read 7.40. Concluding that he had overslept, he dressed hurriedly and rushed to the cathedral. When Mass began, he noticed that the congregation was much larger than usual for eight o'clock. It was only when the sermon was under way that he glanced at his watch and realized that he was at the nine o'clock Mass instead of the eight o'clock one. On returning home, he saw that both his alarm clocks were correct and decided to catch the 10.50 train instead of the 9.50 one.

When Sir Alec arrived at Waterloo at 10.30, there was an announcement that all trains on the Portsmouth line were delayed. He learned that the 9.50 train had been derailed a few miles outside London. Subsequently, he discovered that it was the front coach of the train which had toppled on its side and that, although no one was killed, the occupants of that coach had been badly bruised and taken to hospital. When catching the 9.50 train on a Sunday morning, his habit had been to sit in the front compartment of the foremost coach because it was less likely to become crowded.

Arthur Koestler pointed out to the actor that he had not only overslept by an hour and 20 minutes, but had also misread the clock by an hour—and that had he not done so, he might have decided to miss Mass and catch the ill-fated 9.50 train after all. Sir Alec replied that he also thought his misreading of the clock was the oddest thing about the incident, especially as the two alarm clocks were almost side by side.

Was this an instance of unconscious precognition? If so, comments Koestler, one must also assume that the unconscious 'cunningly persuaded the conscious self to misread the clock'. Or it could have been just another coincidence, such as that which befell another actor, Anthony Hopkins, who sat down on a bench at a London Underground station in 1972 and, finding a package next to him, opened it. To his astonishment it contained a copy of a book, *The Girl from Petrovka*, by George Feifer. He was about to star in a film based on the book and had been trying without success to buy a copy—and a few days earlier its author had told him how he had lost his own on the London Underground. Feifer later identified Hopkins's find as the missing one through some pencilled jottings.

On one occasion, my friend Zelma Bramley-Moore was

about to board a train at Maida Vale tube station when she was overwhelmed by a feeling of impending disaster and stepped back on to the platform. The train crashed just before reaching Warwick Avenue station. Had she been on it, the consequences might have been fatal.

Zelma would not have travelled in the next train, for her sixth sense warned against doing it. However, as she was accompanied by a cynical friend, she did. Because of the accident to the other train, this one was pulled up in the tunnel before reaching Warwick Avenue. Out went the lights, and there they remained for a very long time in total darkness, with a distressing smell of burning adding to their ordeal. Eventually they had to leave their train by the rear exit, then, guided by a lantern held by an employee, and hand in hand forming a chain with those in front, they made their way through the darkness, and were at last helped on to the platform at Maida Vale station, having had to keep always to the right in the tunnel to avoid the live rail.

Jenny Randles, in her book *Beyond Explanation*, relates how in 1981 British Rail received a warning from a woman who had already sent them previous predictions about accidents that had proved correct. This time she claimed to have seen in a vision an engine bearing the number 47,216 being damaged in a crash. Two years later, a disaster occurred in the way she had described, but the engine's number was 47,279. However, British Rail had to admit that it was in fact the same engine which, in view of the woman's past reputation, they had renumbered as a precaution, hoping in that way to counteract her prediction.

Of all accidents involving travel, road accidents are the most numerous, so predictions concerning these need to be detailed to convince. Sir Alec Guinness relates how, when he was filming in Hollywood, James Dean, who had a passion for fast cars, proudly displayed to him his latest acquisition and boasted that it could speed up to 140 miles an hour. A premonition of disaster came over Guinness and he found himself pleading with Dean never to drive the car. 'I have a feeling that if you do, you will be dead within a week,' he said. Dean ignored the warning, to his cost.

Among the many letters describing precognitive dreams that were received by the distinguished parapsychologist

Professor W.H.C. Tenhaeff in Utrecht, and published in the *Journal of the Society for Psychical Research* in 1939, was one in which the correspondent related how she had dreamed of a car travelling at speed along a road. As it accelerated to try and reach the other side of a level crossing, a tyre exploded and the vehicle crashed into a gate and a lorry. She saw a body lying on the ground and recognized it as that of Prince Bernhardt.

Two days after receiving this letter, Professor Tenhaeff heard on the radio that the Prince had been injured in a motor accident, and the details reported corresponded in many ways with those Mrs O. had given in her letter. A lorry had been loading sand in the meadow by a level crossing and the car had collided with it. After being extricated from the wreck, the Prince had been placed on a blanket by the roadside.

Reality differed from the dream in that there was no level crossing and no tyre had burst. The lorry had driven so suddenly out of the meadow that Prince Bernhardt had been unable to brake in time to avoid a collision.

Sir Winston Churchill consulted fortune-tellers on several occasions as well as having premonitions of which he always took notice. Once, during the Second World War, he made all his domestic staff take cover in the air-raid shelter just a few minutes before a bomb fell. Lady Churchill in her autobiography relates how, on finishing a tour of inspection during the blitz, he refused to return to Downing Street in the armoured car in which he had been driven because he found it very uncomfortable. He took over a staff car instead, but as he was on the point of getting in on the near side, which he invariably did, he changed his mind and went round and, opening the door himself, sat on the other side. On the way back, a bomb fell so close to the car that the blast forced it on to its near-side wheels. Had Churchill been seated on that side, the vehicle would have toppled over. Only his extra weight on the opposite side had averted a catastrophe. Later he told his wife that some sixth sense had warned him against sitting where he usually did. He once revealed at a public meeting: 'I sometimes have a very strong feeling of providential interference.'

J.B. Priestley told of a neighbour and friend of his, a university lecturer whom he described as both intelligent and scrupulously truthful, who had a vision suddenly when out of doors of the name of the film star, Bonar Colleano, written above the 'picture' of a very violent car smash-up. Two days later, Colleano died in a such a crash.

In his *Man and Time*, J.B. Priestley includes an account of a bizarre dream sent him by an Irish lady. She was driving her car along a road near her home when suddenly—out of nowhere it seemed to her—a little girl about three years of age appeared right in front of the car and was hit by it and killed. The writer continued that, on awakening, she realized with dismay that she had to drive down that road that very morning on her way to lunch with her youngest daughter, so she decided to be more careful than usual. On approaching the spot, she was relieved to see no children, only about five women waiting at a bus stop. She glanced down at her speedometer, then, on raising her eyes, she was horrified to see, standing still in the middle of the road, the little girl of her dream, 'correct in every detail, even to the dark curly hair and the bright blue cardigan she was wearing'.

Priestley's correspondent wrote that she was afraid to use her horn in case she startled the child and caused what she felt was going to be a fatal accident, so she slowly brought the car to a halt just beside her. The girl never moved, but stood staring at the driver.

Meanwhile, the women in the bus queue showed no interest and made no attempt to get the child off the busy road. In fact, they seemed more interested in the fact that the driver had stopped. Feeling very shaky, she continued on her way, and looking in the mirror, she saw that the girl was still standing there and nobody was bothering about her. By the time the motorist had reached her destination, she was over half an hour late. Her daughter looked very worried on opening the door and explained that it was because the previous night in a terribly vivid dream she had witnessed her mother run over and kill a little girl with dark curly hair, wearing a bright blue cardigan.

Priestley comments that this story sounded highly improbable, so he asked for confirmation and received it from the lady's husband and the daughter. He concluded that the child was a phantasm out of a double dream, and that either the daughter picked up the fatal accident episode telepathically from her mother's mind, or the mother from the daughter's. Some might argue that the mother's dream was precognitive, based on what her daughter would tell her later. But such an explanation seemed to him far-fetched.

After a matinée at the Palace Theatre, Zelma Bramley-Moore and a woman friend strolled along to a taxi-rank and were about to get into a cab when Zelma suddenly felt that, if they did, it would be involved in an accident. She told her companion about this premonition and that it would be better to wait and take the next taxi, but Annette was not impressed. Seizing Zelma by the arm and muttering 'I'll put a stop to this nonsense of yours,' she bundled her into the taxi and climbed in after her. They were travelling down Charing Cross Road when off came the cab's near-side front wheel, throwing them together on the floor, while a bus pushed into them from behind. Fortunately, no bones were broken—and Zelma could not resist saying to her friend 'I told you so!'

Louise Rhine mentions the case of a girl named Rosemary who had a premonition of disaster when her younger sister was leaving for a dance and was about to get into a car. She found herself shouting 'Don't go in that car, Frances! Take the other one.' But the girl did not like driving in the second car, and went off in the first. Later that night, she was killed in an accident.

Most bizarre is the case of New York script writer Danny Davis, author of a new television situation comedy series set in a store, who insisted on each episode opening with a shot of the proprietor arriving in his automobile and driving through a plate glass window. The producer, Peter George, thought this a quite unnecessary opening and one expensive to stage, but Davis, normally placid and submissive, was unyieldingly stubborn and so had his way. He rarely left his apartment until mid-afternoon and had made an appointment to meet a comedian there at 11.30 one morning. But, acting on some impulse, Davis left home at 11.15 and walked west towards Third Avenue, then he turned southwards in the direction of 59th Street. Meanwhile, his friend had called at the apartment and was surprised to find that Danny was out.

At the time when Danny Davis ought to have opened the door of his apartment to admit his guest, he was standing before the window of a store in 59th Street. Suddenly, a car out of control, after felling a lamp-post, knocking down a woman, and tearing on to the sidewalk, propelled Danny through the plate glass front and halted inside the store with his body trapped under the wheels. He never recovered.

Was it precognition that influenced Davis and made him insist on that opening to the episodes in his television series? Or was it psychokinesis that attracted the death-dealing automobile to him? Or was it just a coincidence?

Disasters occurring on water have also been foreseen sometimes. The evening before Donald Campbell tried to break the world speed record in his motorboat, *Bluebird*, on Coniston Water in the English Lake District in 1967, he said to a reporter from the *Daily Express*: 'I have the most awful premonition that I'm going to get the chop—I've had the feeling for days.' He decided to consult the cards, so shuffling a pack he drew two, then blenched on seeing that they were the Ace and Queen of Spades. 'These are the same cards that Mary, Queen of Scots, turned over on the night before her execution,' he commented. 'I think that someone in my family will die soon.'

Next morning, 4 January, *Bluebird* reared up on her tail while skimming over the water, turned a back somersault at nearly 300 m.p.h., and plunged to the bottom. Campbell's body was never recovered. Was he scared to death?

Often mentioned when discussing the tragic sinking of the *Titanic* in 1912 are the strangely similar events described in Morgan Robertson's novel *Futility*, which was first published in 1898 and republished in a revised form under the new title *The Wreck of the Titan* in 1912, a short while before the disaster. Robertson had been a sailor, and though of limited education was the author of several novels and 200 short stories. He was an alcoholic, always poor and impoverished, and, according to what H.W. Francis, a journalist friend, wrote in the 28 March 1914 issue of the *Saturday Evening Post*, he 'implicitly believed that some discarnate soul, some spirit entity with literary ability, denied physical expression, had commandeered his body and brain'. Robertson regarded himself 'as a mere amanuensis, the tool of a "real writer". For months at a time, however, although mentally alert, he would be incapable of writing a single sentence.'

Another friend, J. O'Neill, also wrote in the *Post* that at

such times Robertson would lie on his lounge bed, sometimes for hours at a time, in a semi-sleeping state. 'His ideas
would marshal themselves into a coherent, consecutive narrative up to a certain point, and then they would stop,
whether he liked it or not, and that stopping, sometimes in
the middle of an exciting situation, was the plague of his
literary existence. He would then sit at the typewriter and
pound out his story in a steady stream of words until he had
finished what he had gotten in his somnolent state. Then
he would be obliged to wait for the rest of the narrative,
which sometimes would not come for days, sometimes not
for weeks.' That was because 'this discarnate man, a writer,
who used Robertson as a channel for his literary talents and
output on a physical plane', was apparently busy doing
something elsewhere.

One day in 1898, in a room on 24th Street in New York
City that was furnished like a ship's cabin, Morgan Robertson relaxed until he fell into a trance, when he believed his
'actual writing partner' would take over. It was in this state
that he wrote *Futility*. Suddenly he saw himself in the Atlantic, the horizon curtained by fog, then through it cut the bows
of a ship whose size and beauty delighted him. It must be
almost 1,000 feet long, with three propellers, but was travelling too fast—at a speed of at least 23 knots. It came nearer
and he was astonished to see so many people walking about
on its decks. Must be at least 2,000, he told himself—never
had he known a ship to carry so many. Then he read 'THE
TITAN' in large letters on its side. A voice reached him that
boasted: 'Unsinkable—unsinkable!'

This drew Robertson's attention to the lifeboats. He
counted 24, not enough for so many passengers should an
emergency arise. And now ahead of the liner, partly
shrouded by the fog, he glimpsed an iceberg. His fingers
started to pound the keys of the typewriter and on the paper
appeared: 'She was the largest craft afloat and the greatest
of the works of man...spacious cabins...decks like broad
promenades...Unsinkable, indestructible, she carried as few
boats as would satisfy the laws...' Her 19 watertight compartments 'would close automatically in the presence of
water. With some compartments flooded, the ship would
still float, and...no known accident of the sea could possibly fill this many...'

And now, Robertson found himself typing of how on the *Titan's* third voyage from New York to England 'Seventy-five thousand tons—deadweight—rushing through the fog . . . hurtled itself at an iceberg . . . Nearly three thousand voices, raised in agonized screams.'

At 11.40 p.m. on 14 April 1912, the 'largest craft afloat' in the real world, the *Titanic*, on her maiden voyage from England to New York, was to collide at speed with an iceberg off Cape Race, Newfoundland, and out of 2,207 passengers on board 1,517 were to die. The liner of 66,000 tonnage was 882 feet in length, had three propellers, a top speed of 25 knots, carried 20 lifeboats, and its owners, the White Star Line, had stressed before it sailed that the 15 bulkheads were 'absolutely watertight'.

These similarities were remarkable enough. Furthermore, J.W. Hannah in his book *The Futility God* (1975) has pointed out that under the article 'Ship' in the 1911 edition of the *Encyclopaedia Britannica* a table gave dimensions and other data for 60 Atlantic liners from 1819 to 1910. None approached those of the *Titan* except the *Titanic*. And names of mythical deities were extremely rare for ships.

Several individuals had premonitions of the calamity. W.T. Stead (1849–1912), the newspaper editor, had a lifelong interest in spiritualism. He himself was a medium with a girl control, Julia, and obtained messages through automatic writing. He was also intensely interested in everything to do with the sea. In 1880, he published a story in the *Pall Mall Gazette* about an enormous ship that sank with few survivors in mid-Atlantic, and he added an editorial comment: 'This is exactly what might take place and what will take place if liners are sent to sea short of boats.'

For the Christmas 1893 issue of the *Review of Reviews*, W.T. Stead wrote a story, 'From the Old World to the New', about a ship colliding with an iceberg in the Atlantic and the sole survivor being taken aboard the White Star liner *Majestic*, which in fact existed and whose captain, Edward J. Smith, was in 1912 to become captain of the *Titanic*. Next, in 1909, lecturing in London, Stead depicted himself, shipwrecked and drowning as he called desperately for help.

From time to time, Stead had consulted the palmist and seer Cheiro because he was haunted by a fear that he might die through mob violence on account of his political opinions. Cheiro wrote to him on 11 June 1911 to say that he had studied the latest impressions he had made of Stead's hand and

judging from them and from your date of birth in the sign of Cancer, otherwise known as the First House of Water, in my humble opinion, any danger of violent death to you must be by water and nothing else. Very critical and dangerous for you should be April, 1912, especially about the middle of the month. So don't travel by water then if you can help it. If you do, you will be liable to meet with such danger to your life that the very worst may happen. I know I am not wrong about this 'water' danger; I only hope I am, or at least that you won't be travelling somewhere about that period.

Not long after this, Stead consulted another clairvoyant, W. de Kerlor, who, looking into a crystal, said that he saw him travelling to America 'on a huge black ship, but I can only see half of the ship—when one will be able to see it in its whole length, it is perhaps then that you will go on your journey'.

That winter, de Kerlor claimed to have dreamed of a shipwreck with over 1,000 people struggling in the water whose calls for help he could hear. He caught sight of Stead among them and warned him. Two similar warnings followed. The first came from an American who wrote to the periodical *Light* that a voice had announced to her that Stead would be 'called home in the first half of 1912'. Then, early in the New Year, Stead received a letter from Archdeacon Colley saying that he had a terrible feeling that the *Titanic* would sink that year. But Stead had been invited by President Taft to speak at a peace conference and felt obliged to attend.

At least 19 people had premonitions about the dangers of travelling on the great liner. Colin Macdonald turned down the offer of a post as its Second Engineer because of a presentiment that the *Titanic* would have a short life. At the end of March Connon Middleton of London dreamed on two successive nights that he was floating in the air just above the wrecked giantess, which had her keel turned upwards with the passengers and crew swimming around her.

Middleton was in a dilemma. He was not superstitious and it was vitally important for him to go to New York to attend a business meeting, and then to his relief he received a cable postponing this, so he cancelled his passage. Later, he was to speculate on whether floating in the air in the dream meant that he would have survived had he travelled.

There was a dramatic last-minute warning on 10 April, the day the *Titanic* was due to leave Southampton, when a clairvoyant, V.N. Turvey, declared that if the liner sailed she would sink in two days' time. But the White Star Line officials were not impressed, and the maiden voyage began as scheduled on a morning radiant with spring sunshine and with the sea invitingly calm.

The premonitory albatross had not, however, been put to flight, for as the *Titanic* came into the view of one Jack Marshall and his family, watching from their house on the coast of the Isle of Wight, Mrs Marshall seized her husband's arm and cried: 'It's going to sink! That ship is going to sink before she reaches America.'

Jack and the others did their best to calm her, but her excitement grew. As they watched, his wife explained, the sky had darkened, shrouding the liner, and she had seen it sinking miles away in the Atlantic and hundreds of people struggling in the ocean beset by ice floes. 'Don't let them drown!' she screamed. 'Save them! Save them!'

On board the *Titanic*, a young fireman also had a foreboding of peril ahead and, losing his nerve, he deserted when the ship picked up passengers at Queenstown.

On the disastrous night of 14 April, a 14-year-old English girl dreamed twice that she was out walking in Stoke-on-Trent where she lived when ahead of her in Trentham Park she saw a huge ship with people moving about on deck. Suddenly it tipped downwards at the stern and she heard a terrified scream. Later she was to learn that her uncle, Leonard Hodgkinson, the *Titanic*'s Fourth Engineer, was among the missing.

Four days after the liner sailed, when the Rev. Charles Morgan of the Rosedale Methodist Church in Winnipeg was considering what hymns to choose for the evening service, he fell into a kind of trance. The words of one that he had never included in a service before started repeating themselves to him to the exclusion of everything else: 'Hear, Father, while we pray to Thee, for those in peril on the sea.' So he searched for the music. Later, about the same time as his congregation were singing this hymn, another group of worshippers, gathered in the second-class dining-room of the *Titanic*, were uttering the same words led by the Rev. Carter. Two hours after this strange coincidence, peril in shape of an iceberg was to destroy the liner.

As passengers fought frantically to stay alive in the hostile ocean, there were instances of telepathic communication between a few of them and those dear to them from whom they were separated by thousands of miles. Colonel Archibald Gracie recalled later how he prayed that somehow he could contact his wife and children and let them know that his last thoughts were of them. His wife in New York City was suddenly roused from her sleep by a voice bidding her to get down on her knees and pray. Alarmed and apprehensive, she found herself searching for a prayer book, and as she opened it the first words she saw were: 'For those in peril on the sea.'

Elsewhere in New York City, a woman whose mother was a passenger on the liner dreamed she was with her in a packed lifeboat while, close at hand, an enormous liner sank and hysterical people struggled as they drowned. Awakening, she described the nightmare to her husband, who tried to calm her by pointing out that her mother's letters had not mentioned any plans to visit them. But he was wrong. She had been in a lifeboat at the time of the dream thinking only of her daughter and regretting that her decision to pay her a surprise visit had ended in this way. Fortunately, she was among the survivors.

A thorough investigation into all these apparently precognitive experiences was carried out by Dr Ian Stevenson Carlson, Professor of Psychiatry at the University of Virginia and once president of the Parapsychological Association. His findings, entitled respectively 'A Review and Analysis of Paranormal Experiences Connected with the Sinking of the *Titanic*' and 'Seven more Paranormal Experiences Connected with the Sinking of the *Titanic*', were published in 1960 and 1965 in the *Journal of the American Society for Psychical Resarch*.

Dr Stevenson was doubtful whether Morgan Robertson's account in his novel about the wrecking of the *Titan* could be regarded as precognition of the *Titanic*'s fate. At first glance, it might, he admitted, but he points out that at the end of the nineteenth century confidence in engineering skills knew no limits. The novels of Jules Verne and H.G. Wells predicted extraordinary future developments:

A writer of the 1890s familiar with man's repeated *hubris* might reasonably infer that he would overreach himself in the construction of ocean liners which then ... were man's greatest engineering marvels ... A large ship would probably have great power and speed; the name *Titan* has connoted power and security for several thousand years; overconfidence would neglect the importance of lifeboats; recklessness would race the ship through the areas of the Atlantic icebergs; these drift south in the spring, making April a likely month for collision ... Having reached the general conclusion of the probability of such a disaster, inferences, such as those I have suggested, might fill in details to provide correspondences which would have an appearance of precognition, but which we should, I believe, consider only successful inferences.

Disaster almost befell another ship with a similar name. One night in April 1935, aboard the *Titanian*, a ship carrying coal from the Tyne to Canada, one of the crew, William Reeves, experienced a feeling of approaching peril that grew in intensity as the vessel neared the area where the *Titanic* had sunk. Would he be justified in stopping the *Titanian* on account of this? he wondered. The matter was settled for him by another coincidence. He had been born on the day when the earlier catastrophe had occurred. 'Danger ahead!' he shouted to the bridge. Hardly had he done so than an iceberg became visible in the darkness. The *Titanian* steered clear of it just in time.

In many prophetic dreams, events do not correspond in every respect with what the dreamer has described. It may be because on awakening we forget our dreams very quickly. Some details are lost in rising from the deep unconscious to the conscious, and the latter then plays tricks, filling in with assumptions.

Take the case of 17-year-old Sandra MacDonald, who had gone out dancing with two sailors, Doug and Taffy, when the submarine HMS *Artemis* had visited Grimsby in 1971. Three nights after it had sailed away, Sandra dreamed she saw it sinking and that her two friends were trapped in a compartment with another man and that one of them died. She told her mother and several other people about her nightmare, and then a week later the *Artemis* sank at her

Gosport moorings and the three men were trapped in the watertight compartment in which they had taken refuge. They were eventually rescued and no one died.

Dennis Elwell, author of *Cosmic Loom* (1987), is an astrologer of international repute who has spent his life studying the subject, and its rehabilitation has become his chief interest. He corresponded with me at length about his remarkable unheeded early warnings of the several shipping disasters in 1987.

In April 1912, two major planets, Neptune and Jupiter, became stationary in the sky and were in biquintile (at an angle of 144°). This could be interpreted as man mastering, even defying, nature with a great ship. This might not have been ominous had not two eclipses taken place, that of the moon on 1 April and that of the sun on 17 April. As Dennis Elwell stresses, one finds that an aspect formed at the time of an eclipse is increased in intensity and not always for the best, and he adds: 'Other, more technical considerations, involving the Jupiter–Neptune configuration were also operating negatively.'

Early in 1987, Mr Elwell noticed that Jupiter and Neptune would soon be coming into square aspect (a 90° angle capable of generating many conflicting energies), which would not normally attract much notice except for the fact that in this case an eclipse of the sun fell on the Jupiter arm. The eclipse would raise the whole temperature of that square.

There were a few technical add-ons, which made the negative side of this configuration more acute. The date of the eclipse was March 29. It is an astrological commonplace that an eclipse can make itself felt several weeks before it actually takes place—which ought to convince astrologers, if nothing else does, that we are not dealing with any kind of mechanical causation here—and that its 'effects' can appear for months afterwards, perhaps even up to a year.

Because people are so often accused of being wise after the event, on 18 February Dennis Elwell sent identical letters to the two leading shipping lines, P&O and Cunard, stating that the approaching eclipse figuration was reminiscent of April 1912. Since both companies specialized in cruises, and since the configuration appeared to indicate large ships, he warned that the least to be expected was some sudden

upset of liner schedules and the like, but that there had to
be a risk of more serious occurrences. He offered, with their
co-operation, to try and pinpoint the danger. At that time,
Elwell had not realized that P&O, through their recent acquisition of Townsend Thoresen, owned the *Herald of Free Enterprise*. It was the first time in 40 years devoted to astrology
that he had issued such a warning, so, as he puts it, he 'cannot be accused of casting them around like confetti in the
hope that some day one of them might turn out to be significant.'

Cunard replied to Elwell on 20 February stating that the
contents of his letter had been passed on to their fleet com-
modore, who was on board the *Queen Elizabeth II*, their flag-
ship, which was making her much-publicized trip after refit
to New York. He wonders whether this may have influenced
the decision to make a 250-mile diversion in fog to avoid icebergs in the area where the *Titanic* sank. The prior publicity
had promised 'truly gracious sailing.' Instead, cabins flooded;
at one point the ship was listing 15° to port so that passengers
could not eat their meals in comfort; the air conditioning
failed, and so on.

In the case of the *Herald of Free Enterprise*, Dennis Elwell,
writing to me on 27 March 1987, said that what astonished
him was the ferry's name:

Because, according to the rules of astrological symbolism, it had
jumped straight out of the eclipse formation. Jupiter was in Aries,
and as the first sign of the zodiac, Aries has to do with 'firsts',
forerunners, precursors—and hence heralds. Again, Aries is the
most enterprising sign of the lot. As for Jupiter, since classical
times this planet has been associated with the ideal of liberty, freedom. So a ship (Neptune) named the *Herald of Free Enterprise*
(Jupiter in Aries) belonged so completely to this eclipse configuration that I am bound to say, had I arrived at the quayside and
seen that name, I personally should have been reluctant to board
her. At the very moment the ferry capsized, Jupiter in Aries was
on the horizon at Zeebrugge, thus confirming the identification.

Nine days before the disaster, P&O in reply to Dennis
Elwell's letter of 18 February had assured him that their
procedures could deal with the unexpected from whatever
quarter.

Mr Elwell told me that he was always on the look-out for
coincidences because, if astrology were true, then events that

are alike must tend to converge. Thus, on 15 April, the anniversary of the *Titanic* sinking, the memorial service for those lost on the *Herald of Free Enterprise* was held, and that same day memorabilia of the *Titanic* herself went under the hammer. Also on 15 April, it was revealed in the *Daily Telegraph* for the first time that seven weeks after the loss of the *Titanic* her sister ship, the *Olympic*, almost met the same fate when an extraordinary steering error nearly put her aground off Land's End—an incident hushed up by the White Star Line. And again, seven weeks after the *Herald* disaster, there was nearly another on 24 April, when the *Hengist* collided with a French trawler, which like the *Herald* suddenly capsized. Next, on 1 May, two ferries collided in fog, and two days later there was yet another collision involving a sister ship of the *Herald of Free Enterprise*, in Calais harbour. Such coincidences, Dennis Elwell says, are unremarkable to anyone who habitually monitors events against their astrological background.

Mr Elwell gave me futher examples:

Another stricken P&O ship, the torpedoed liner *Medina*, was back in the news (March 19) after seventy years because attempts were to be made to salvage treasure said to be worth £20 million. On March 30, it was announced that the remains of the Confederate cruiser *Alabama* were to be retrieved from the sea-bed off the French coast. On March 31, the captains of two Soviet ships that collided in the Black Sea, with large loss of life, were jailed...

This experienced astrologer continued:

I ought to make it absolutely clear that noting 'straws in the wind' about upcoming ocean voyages is in no sense a prediction ... Astrology at this level is like a spy satellite: if you spot something interesting in the broad picture you can zoom in on the detail. But for that one would need information I do not possess, like the birth data of those most affected, sailing times, and so forth. And the time to process it. It is only through a spread of data that a confident statement can be made.

Denis Elwell also stressed that a warning on the basis of past experience differs from the oracular type of prophecy which implies that 'the future is already set in concrete'.

The number of precognitive dreams involving air crashes is considerable. The sceptic's explanation is that there are so many thousands of flights taking place that it is only to be expected that someone somewhere should dream of a disaster, and that one does not hear of the dreams that do not come true. Nevertheless, at times, such specific details are dreamed about that the case for genuine precognition is a strong one. An alternative hypothesis is that, having dreamed of a catastrophe involving a particular plane on which one has arranged to travel, one may by the power of thought and through psychokinesis cause it to happen.

Such an explanation might account for the case reported in French newspapers in October 1961, when Cuisseau, a gymnastics instructor, predicted that an airliner in which he was due to fly from Paris to the Ivory Coast would make three abortive attempts in succession to reach Marseilles.

The chapter of accidents commenced when he was seated in the plane at Orly Airport awaiting take-off and he remarked to a stewardess that on arriving at Lyons they would have to return to Paris because of mechanical trouble. He was right. Next morning, no sooner had the passengers begun to file on board than they were told that the rescheduled flight had been postponed until next day, 4 October, at noon, on account of another defect. The following morning, Cuisseau was so confident that he was going to be proved correct again that he remained in his hotel bedroom. When his prediction was finally fulfilled, he was questioned by the airport officials and told them that he had lived for some years in India, where he had studied yoga. Such premonitions came to him when he was tired.

Instant fulfilment occurred in the case of Raymond Massey, the actor, who had a vision of a plane hurtling down towards him and his wife. Shaken, he told her about it and insisted on their walking rapidly away. A few minutes later, a plane came crashing down on the very spot where they had been standing.

Several remarkable precognitive dreams involving air disasters were received by the *Evening Standard* Premonitions Bureau after it was set up in 1967. On 20 September, Mr S. Nichol of Leigh-on-Sea, Essex, telephoned them at 6 p.m. to say:

Last night I had a dream in colour of a Boeing 707 taking off. The right wing dipped down. Then it flew on again. I thought it was OK. But then it suddenly dipped and burst into flames. The countryside was rolling uplands—not mountainous. I have no idea where this will be.

On 6 November, 37 days later, a Boeing 707 slewed off the runway during take-off at Greater Cincinnati Airport, Ohio, where the countryside is 'rolling uplands'. Its right wing dipped and caught fire, and the airliner crashed.

Alan Hencher of Dagenham explained that his head would usually ache before precognition of a disaster. It was as if a metal band were being tightened round it. Then he would see, as it were, a flash photograph of the event. On 21 March 1967, he foretold in great detail an early morning air crash in mountains near a church encircled by statuary and on an island. He thought that it would be in Nicosia and that 124 people would die.

On 20 April, a Britannia crashed into a hill in Cyprus, exactly as predicted except that an injured passenger died later, making the total losing their lives 125.

On 1 May, Alan Hencher had a detailed vision of an air disaster in the near future in which more than 60 people would be killed, including children, but from which there would be a number of miraculous escapes. On 4 June, a plane crashed at Stockport when 72 people, including 10 children, died. The tail fin stood out from the wreckage, as he had described, and there were some incredible escapes.

In October of that same year, Hencher had a vision of himself flying off in a plane from Spain with four little girls sitting beside him, then being buffeted by a storm as it reached England. An engine exploded and a wing hit a hill. There were many fatal casualties. This would happen early in November. On the 4th of that month, a Caravelle flew off from Málaga and came into a storm over Surrey, where it crashed into a hillside. Among the 37 who died were two little girls (not four as in Hencher's vision).

Lorna Middleton of Edmonton, London, was the most successful of those sending accounts of predictions to the *Evening Standard* Premonitions Bureau in 1967. On 9 July, she had a vision of a plane crash in a swamp. Ten days later, there was such a disaster in Madagascar. On 11 January 1968, she wrote of an aircraft crashing in the snow, probably in Canada. On the 23rd, a B-52 bomber dived through the ice in Greenland Bay off eastern Canada. On 1 December 1969, the Central Premonitions Registry of New York were sent a prediction by her of a plane crashing into a mountain. She had a vision of 'heavily clothed' people climbing through mud up its side. On the 7th of that month, an Olympic Airways DC–6B smashed itself against Mount Panteion as it struggled through a storm. It took almost an hour for men to climb up through the blizzard to the rescue. Ninety of those aboard were killed.

In 1972, three days before Prince William of Gloucester died in an air crash, Lorna Middleton wrote to her friend Michael Jefferies: 'The Queen may receive bad news.' She was about to stick a postage stamp on the envelope when, in her words: 'The stamp seemed to jump out of my hand and spiralled to the floor landing with the Queen's head downwards. From my previous experience, I knew that it was linked with bad news for the Queen and the Royal Family.'

Not all Mrs Middleton's experiences were accompanied by deaths when they were fulfilled. On 29 July 1969, she wrote to the Central Premonitions Registry enclosing a sketch of what she had seen in a vision. It was of a plane half-submerged in a lake surrounded by woods. The accident would take place in the evening. On 3 August, at Marseilles Airport, a plane overshot the runway and sank into a lake. Fortunately, all the 45 people aboard were rescued.

The files of the Central Premonitions Registry are well stocked with accounts of air disasters sent in before they happened. An Eastern Airlines stewardess employed on the New York–Miami route dreamed in mid-December 1972 of a jumbo jet hurtling down at night, left wing foremost, into water. She woke with a feeling that this would happen about New Year's Day. On 29 December, owing to a sudden alteration in her rota of duties, she did not fly on the night service between New York and Miami. At 11.42 p.m. the plane in question plummeted, left wing foremost, into the Florida Everglades and 79 of those aboard lost their lives.

In his *Riddle of the Future* Andrew Mackenzie includes an account sent to him by the family of a Mrs Monica Clarke of Letchworth. During the night of 17 June 1972, she dreamed that she was sitting on a bench in what seemed to be the country, although not far away were tall buildings. The sky suddenly became dark and threatening. Suddenly there was a flash of lightning, and an aircraft fell from out of the sky into a field close to where she was seated and almost immediately burst into flames. 'Prior to this there had been no sound of an aircraft's engine,' Mrs Clarke told her husband and daughter.

Next day, the worst disaster up till then in British air travel history occurred when the engines of a BEA Trident jet, destination Brussels, cut out and the plane stalled during ascent from London Airport, then fell without a sound, as in Mrs Clarke's dream, until it crashed killing every one of the 118 aboard.

Mr Mackenzie carefully checked the account published in the *Evening Standard* of Mrs Marian Warren living in the Somerset village of Churchill Green, who dreamed that she saw an aeroplane skim over trees and crash into the snow. This farmer's wife said that she watched the bodies of her friends being laid out. It was all so vividly horrible that she felt cold all day after waking up, despite sitting before a big fire. With other local housewives she had booked to go three weeks later on a day trip to Switzerland by plane, but was so scared by her nightmare that she sold her ticket to someone else through the organizer, thereby losing half its cost. She kept her dream a secret, however, apart from telling her best friend, because she thought no one would believe her.

Then, on the day Mrs Warren should have been one of its passengers, 10 April 1973, a chartered Vanguard plane struck the side of a mountain during a snowstorm, killing 107 women from Churchill Green and three other nearby villages.

For 10 successive nights, starting on Tuesday 15 May 1979, David Booth, a car rental company's office manager in his early twenties living in Cincinnati, had identical nightmares in which he saw a three-engined jet with American Airlines markings take off. Then he heard the sound of stuttering engines as it tilted perilously to one side before turning over and plunging to the ground in flames. He saw it explode and even felt the heat given out. He awoke in a cold sweat and all day the nightmare haunted him, then next night, to his dismay, he dreamed it all over again. After having had the same experience for the seventh time, he felt on the verge of a nervous breakdown, and in desperation he telephoned American Airlines, the Federal Aviation Administration Offices at the Greater Cincinnati Airport, as well as a university psychiatrist. Talking to them had only a temporary calming effect, for he went through mental torture for three more nights.

Then, on Friday 25 May, Booth heard on the television news that on taking off from Chicago's International Airport an American Airlines DC-10 had crashed killing 273 passengers in what was up to then the worst disaster in North American aviation history. The FAA personnel who had spoken to him three days earlier were astounded, for they now realized that his description of the site of the catastrophe in his dream fitted that at Chicago.

The *Evening Standard* Premonitions Bureau was not the first organized attempt to record precognitive dreams and visions. Twenty years earlier a similar investigation was begun by Dr Alice Buck, the London psychiatrist. In 1945, she dreamed of some terrifying upheaval of the elements; on July 16, the first atomic test took place at Los Alamos. In early August, she had two even more violent dreams, then, on the 6th of that month, the Hiroshima bomb was dropped. In 1947, she interested a number of her professional colleagues in a project. They agreed that, immediately on awakening in the morning for six days a week, they would write down accounts of any dreams and post these to the Jung Institute in Zurich. If they felt that what they had dreamed was of especial significance, they were to lodge an additional copy with a bank so that the time could be established beyond all doubt. These records were then centrally examined by experts, and soon it was found that whilst the dream of one participant might vaguely foretell some disaster, if the dreams received from all over the world were carefully studied quite an impressive pool of information might be assembled, giving a strong indication of what might be expected to happen.

For example, on 2 and 3 September 1954, Dr Alice Buck dreamed of an impending aircraft disaster in which the time, 3 a.m., seemed important. At 3.40 a.m. on 4 September a KLM Super-Constellation airliner crashed within sight of Shannon Airport. Meanwhile, during the night just before this disaster, a member of the research unit dreamed of people acting *Pilgrim's Progress* in twentieth-century dress. Men and women were battling on a journey against severe climatic conditions. They were passing through a ford when water engulfed them. The dreamer summed it up by saying that it was like Christian and Faithful going through the River of Death. This dream is remarkable when one compares it with the following description of the actual disaster in a newspaper:

Men and women died yesterday, trapped in darkness in the cabin of a crashed airliner slowly filled with the muddy waters of the river Shannon. One man had clung for three hours to the tail of the almost submerged airliner waiting for rescue. The plane crashed at 3.40 a.m. but it was not until nearly 2½ hours later that warning was given to the airport, and that was given by the Second Officer who swam to a mudflat and then crawled painfully through two miles of mud and slime to reach the airport. The first rescue party arrived 3½ hours after the crash.

On 12 March 1954, another member of this group dreamed of a bird like a duck on the ground amid tropical vegetation. Immediately on awakening, she drew a picture of what she remembered. In this drawing, the duck looks remarkably like the outline of a modern airliner. That same night, Dr Alice Buck in London awoke with a feeling of great distress. Next day, there was a Constellation crash in Singapore with the loss of 33 lives.

These researchers came to the conclusion that any connection between the dreamer and the persons likely to be involved in a disaster might produce a warning dream. For this reason, after the Comets had been grounded as a result of the Elba disaster of 10 January 1954, Dr Buck decided to travel herself in the first plane directly the service was resumed on 23 March. But from the beginning of February, accounts of dreams accompanied by drawings submitted began to suggest that some new disaster was impending. Dr Buck therefore did not proceed with her plan to travel on the Comet. In early April, more and more dreams were collected which gave details of the site, altitude, cause, number of passengers, and amount of wreckage likely to be found in the next Comet crash, which occurred as predicted off Naples on 8 April with a death toll of 28. The full story of this group's work was told in a book, *The Clothes of God*, by Dr Alice Buck and F. Claude Palmer.

So far none of these cases have included in vision or dream the actual name of any traveller on the doomed aircraft. A Dutch clairvoyant, Tholen, claimed to have had a curious experience. He was studying a book of music when the print faded and he saw instead the misty face of the Virgin Mary, which slowly turned into that of Queen Juliana, and over it appeared the words '*Ave Maria*'. Then this faded and he had a vision of a plane followed by a procession of motor-hearses. He counted 41, and at the end walked a woman dressed in black.

The dream's meaning became clear when a week later an airliner named *Queen Juliana* crashed in Frankfurt killing 41 people aboard. Only the stewardess survived.

J.B. Priestley has related how he had a friend who three weeks before the Duke of Kent lost his life in a Second World War air disaster had a prevision of its happening and saw over the wreckage the words 'Duke of Kent'. He had similar experiences with other celebrities who met with violent ends.

In January 1946, after the end of the war, Air Marshal Sir Victor Goddard broke his journey in Shanghai on the way to Tokyo, and in the evening he went to a cocktail party given in his honour by the British Consul, George Alwynne Ogden. Goddard was talking to Brigadier John McConnell when he overheard his name being mentioned. A naval officer, later Admiral Sir Gerald Gladstone, was telling another man how he had dreamed the previous night of Goddard's dying in an air crash. Suddenly, an incredulous look come over Gladstone's face and he became extremely embarrassed as he noticed Goddard standing by him. He explained to the Air Marshal that the dream had made a great impression on him because of its vivid realism. It was evening and he had watched a plane come across the mountains in a snowstorm and hurtle down on to 'a rocky, shingly shore'. The aircraft had been a Dakota transport and so was the *Sister Ann*, the one in which Goddard was about to fly. Gladstone urged him to delay his departure for a few days.

But the dream Dakota, apart from half a dozen airmen, had carried three civilians, two men and a girl, whilst the real-life plane had only the crew on board, so Goddard refused to postpone his departure. Then, in the short time before take-off, Lord Camrose's son, the Hon. Seymour Berry, and George Alwynne Ogden asked if they could be given a lift to Tokyo, together with an Englishwoman, Dorita Breakspear.

Goddard could hardly object, but he was now feeling somewhat uneasy. However, not wishing to upset the others, he allowed events to take their course. At least the weather reports were favourable, but these proved wrong. The Dakota was beset by threatening clouds and was forced to climb to 17,000 feet. Ice formed on the wings and the plane was buffeted by a gale and it started snowing heavily. There were mountains below, and through a gap Goddard spotted the 'rocky shingly shore' of the dream. Then the pilot reported that he was short of fuel and could not possibly reach Tokyo. The Dakota circled, searching in vain for somewhere to land in safety. Life jackets were donned and they prepared for a crash landing. Was he about to die and fulfil the dream? Goddard wondered, but although badly shaken as the plane made a wheels-up landing, they managed to clamber out on to the beach.

Why had the nightmare proved correct in every detail except that he was still alive? Goddard wondered. He was so intrigued that, some time after being rescued, he wrote to Gladstone to ask if in the dream he had seen him dead or had just assumed it from the way in which the Dakota had grounded. Gladstone replied that with the passage of time the dream had become vague, but he had not seen Goddard actually dead. It could be that he had assumed this was so.

Goddard wrote an article about his experience which was published in the Saturday *Evening Post* of 26 May 1951, and four years later a film based on it was made—*The Night My Number Came Up*.

Sir Victor Goddard himself had a precognitive experience before the Second World War in 1935 when, as a young RAF officer, he flew over the abandoned airfield at Drem in Scotland which had been allowed to revert to farmland. As he looked down through the driving rain, the scene was suddenly lit with brilliant light and he saw an airfield in full working order. The nearest hangar doors were open, and on the tarmac apron stood three biplanes and a monoplane of a type he had never seen before. Emerging through the hangar doors was a second monoplane being pushed by two mechanics. They were painted yellow instead of the then regulation silver, whilst the men wore blue instead of the then customary brown dungarees.

On returning to base, Goddard described what he had seen to his wing commander, who suggested that he had been suffering from a hallucination. Then, four years later, just before the war, Goddard visited Drem and found that it had been rebuilt and was exactly as in his prevision with mechanics dressed in blue, busy round yellow Avro 504s and Magisters. The latter, trainer monoplanes, had not existed in 1935, yet they were in every detail like the ones he had previously seen.

It was at the home of Lady Muriel Dowding, at Tunbridge Wells, that I first met Sir Victor and heard from him about his Drem prevision. She herself described to me her own extraordinary precognitive experiences on various occasions. Max Whiting, her first husband, served in the RAF during the Second World War as the co-pilot of a Lancaster bomber. On the night of 22 May 1944, he was reported missing. The BBC news bulletin had announced that 70 Lancasters had failed to return from attacking Duisburg, so when the dreaded telegram arrived from the Air Ministry she assumed that he had been on that raid.

As the months dragged by, the tension of not knowing whether Max was alive or dead became unendurable. Eventually, his father persuaded her to write to Air Marshal (then) Sir Hugh Dowding, who was trying to communicate with the spirits of young Spitfire and Hurricane airmen through a medium. He replied advising her to consult one at the College of Psychic Science, which she did. There she had a sitting with a Miss Topcott, who began by accurately describing Max and asking: 'Why is he holding two wedding rings over your head, one of which glitters?'

A week before their marriage, Muriel and Max had visited Mappin and Webb's to buy the wedding ring, and, because of the superstition that it is unlucky for a bride to see it before the ceremony, he had left her in a waiting-room whilst he went to choose the ring. The assistant showed him plain gold and platinum hoops and also some encircled with small diamonds. Max thought she would prefer the latter, so he bought one. That night, however, he was beset by doubts as to whether it would look like a real wedding ring, so next morning he rushed back to the jewellers, who suggested that he should buy a platinum ring as well and they would then wire up the two together in time for the occasion.

Miss Topcott then went on to say that the man contacting her had been flying in a bomber over Denmark when German fighters came in pursuit and shot it down heading for Norway. This conflicted with the BBC news bulletin statement that the Lancasters had been destroyed in the vicinity of Dresden.

The last thing the medium told Muriel was: 'Your husband's name began with D. She replied that there wasn't a D in any of his names. Miss Topcott returned: 'Well, your name does.'

Muriel explained that even her maiden name had no such letter in it, but she did have a son, David. The other shook her head. 'Oh, no, it isn't that. It is either your name or your husband's name. There is a big D enveloping you. It has a little crown or coronet on top of it.'

The future Lady Dowding then left, regarding the whole sitting as unsatisfactory except for the description of Max. Then, two years later, she received a telegram from the Air Ministry stating Max must be presumed killed.

Soon after this, in 1946, Muriel's stepfather, when travelling by train from Tunbridge Wells to London, got into conversation with a Dane who told him he owned a farm near the sea and that a Lancaster had flown over it and was making for Norway when German fighters brought it down. The local people were able to carry some of the wreckage and the bodies to his farm. The Dane took out of his wallet and showed his railway companion a photograph of the memorial they had erected to 'our gallant English allies, May 22, 1944'.

When he heard this date mentioned, Muriel's stepfather asked the Dane if he had reported the incident to the British Air Ministry. The man said he hadn't, and was asked to do so. The remains of the wreckage were then examined, and the plane was identified as the Lancaster in which Max had been flying.

CHAPTER 12

War and Natural Disasters

Arthur Ford, the American Nonconformist minister, and later a spiritualist medium, who died in 1976, became aware of his sixth sense during the First World War when serving as a newly-commissioned second lieutenant in the US army at Camp Grant, Illinois, during the 1918 influenza epidemic. Awakening in the morning, he would have a vision of the names of soldiers who had died during the night in the base hospital. It was his duty to pick up the roster of their names from the adjutant's office, and when he did so he found that not only were they the same as he had foreseen but they were in exactly the same order.

This happened three days in succession before Ford mentioned the matter to two of his friends. They would not believe him, so immediately on awakening he wrote down the names that he had glimpsed and told them that they would appear on the list of deaths to be issued that day, which again proved to be the case. After this had gone on for a whole week, Ford felt he ought to consult the chaplain or the doctor, but on reflection he decided it would be unwise and might lead to his being demoted or sent to a mental hospital. He prayed that his daily ordeal would cease, but instead it took on another form.

One morning, Ford learned that the names he had foreseen were no longer those of men who had died from influenza but those of men who had lost their lives miles away fighting in France. On any day up to a week after he had dreamed of these names, they would appear in the same order in the casualty lists printed in the newspapers. What puzzled him was that he would foresee certain sections of the lists and not the rest, and that he had known none of the men. He came to the conclusion that he was foreseeing what he would read in the newspapers.

During the Second World War, Michael Bentine had a somewhat similar but more horrific experience. At the height of the 1943–4 winter bombing operations he was posted to the Polish squadrons at Wickenby in Lincolnshire. He revealed in his *Doors of the Mind* how on every raid they made, as soon as he saw the air crews having their meal before departure, he knew which men would die that night. He would have a vision in which the face of the man he was watching would change into a skull as though he were suddenly staring through skin and flesh.

This upset Bentine so much that he went to see the chaplain. The chaplain did not seem surprised, and he disclosed that he knew of others who had had similar experiences. They knelt down and prayed, and the visions ceased.

Arthur Ford's First World War extrasensory perception led to his joining the American Society for Psychical Research and later becoming a trance medium with a control called Fletcher. Ford continued to receive precognitive impressions, chiefly in dreams. In 1927, he visited London and attended a spiritualist meeting at the Grotrian Hall. After Sir Arthur Conan Doyle had spoken, on the spur of the moment he invited Ford to come up on to the platform and demonstrate his clairvoyance. Ford did so with striking success, causing Conan Doyle to tell the press that it was one of the most convincing exhibitions of paranormal powers he had witnessed in 41 years.

Apart from professional fortune-tellers like Mme de Thèbes who predicted the 1914–18 War, many relatives and friends of the combatants had precognitive dreams concerning their fate. A curious case was reported in the *Journal for Psychical Research* of December 1920. Mrs M.E. Munro wrote:

On the night of October 26, 1917, I had a dream about my son who was in Palestine. I thought I saw him in what appeared to be a tent, when suddenly he jumped up and put both hands to his forehead. I realized at once that he was hit, and looked around for a doctor. At the same time, I felt it was hopeless. When I turned to him again, I saw him as he was at the age of eleven or twelve. Someone called out, 'It's the ice cream he has eaten which has caused congestion of the forehead.'

A few days later, the Munros received a telegram from the War Office stating that their son had been killed in action on 2 November. It told them: 'He was hit through the forehead with a rifle bullet while crossing over our parapet at the head of his men . . . He lived for an hour, but was totally unconscious.' In a later statement, Mrs Munro wrote:

My boy when quite small could never properly enjoy ice-cream because he always said it gave him a pain in the forehead. Dragging this story into my dream seemed to me to be a clever subterfuge on the part of the unconscious, for even in my dream it was quite unconvincing.

In the *Journal of the Society for Psychical Research* in 1961, the Dutch parapsychologist George Zorab described how on 3 June 1939 a friend of his, Mrs N. Hekke, told him that she had consulted a clairvoyant at The Hague to try and discover what was going to happen to her 26-year-old nephew, Fritz Hekke, who was extremely lazy and not very good at his job. After fingering the nephew's photograph, the clairvoyant declared that he was going to be a soldier. The aunt retorted that this was impossible as he had already done his full military service some years previously.

The fortune-teller insisted that she would be proved right and added: 'Mark my words. On the 29th August, he will be walking about in uniform.'

All this Mrs Hekke told Zorab, ending that she was convinced the woman had been talking nonsense. Zorab states that as a conscientious parapsychologist he noted down the particulars, not imagining for a moment that he had become a witness to a case of precognition.

On 28 August 1939, the Dutch government proclaimed a General Mobilization of all its military forces. Fritz was unable to reach his destination, Den Bosch, on the 28th, but arrived the next morning—and walked about in his uniform on the 29th.

Germany's great parapsychologist Professor Hans Bender of the University of Freiburg, collected several precognitive experiences concerning the Second World War. A mother told him how, shortly following the birth of her youngest son in 1919, she dreamed that he was missing and that she was walking frantically over a strange seashore, stopping here and there to kneel and scoop up the sand as she searched for the boy's body. Suddenly she woke up and shook her husband, crying that Hans was missing and that something terrible had happened to him. Then she realized that it was a nightmare, for the baby was safe in his cot. But it proved a recurring dream that was to disturb her sleep periodically in the years ahead.

When Hans was 20, he was conscripted into the German army, and in 1946 his mother was told that he had died in a French prison camp and lay buried in the dunes near Fort Mahon, some 800 metres from the sea.

Professor Bender's collection includes two examples of premonitions that led to a happier outcome. Ever since her soldier son was a boy, another mother had been troubled by a recurring nightmare in which she saw him kneeling in a neglected field with a bullet wound in his neck and an imploring, desperate look in his eyes, which were fixed on her. Then, during the night of 8 February 1945, when he was away with the German army in the Ukraine, the nightmare recurred with such intensity that she felt sure he was in the utmost peril, so she spent the rest of the night in prayer. Meanwhile, in a field in the Ukraine, the Russians were shooting prisoners one by one as a searchlight picked them out as targets. It reached a youth with a bullet wound in his neck and terror in his eyes. An appeal to his mother to save him burst from his lips. Acting on some impulse, the Russian officer in charge took pity on him and ordered his life to be spared. Two years later, he returned home.

The other case concerned a mother who saw in a dream her daughter in a stationary train during an air-raid. The scared girl commenced to climb out of the carriage with the intention of lying down on the verge of the embankment. Overcome by a premonition of death if her daughter did this, the mother called to her in the dream to go back to the compartment.

When, some weeks later, the girl returned home, she told her mother how on the night of 30 January 1945 she had been on a train when it was dive-bombed by a plane. In a panic, she had left the carriage. Then all at once she had felt herself drawn back. A woman passenger who sought safety in the spot the girl was making for lost her life when the bomb fell.

As the year 1939 grew older, the outbreak of another world war appeared increasingly likely. The editor of *Prediction* tried to gain foreknowledge by consulting a number of well-known mediums and astrologers. They all said that there would be no war that year. In the October issue, he was faced with the problem of explaining to his readers what had gone wrong. He did so by quoting the distinguished psychic researcher H.F. Saltmarsh, who had once written that a prophecy might be frustrated by human intervention. In his book, *Foreknowledge*, he stated that his investigations had led him to the conclusion: 'There is a future which is now determined by the present and past, but ... it is, to some extent at least plastic and can be modified. Human beings have some degree of freedom of choice.'

From the age of six Kenneth More, the actor, had a recurring dream which never varied in its details. He would be lying in naval uniform on the deck of a ship, listening to the sound of approaching aircraft. A plane would appear above him and, as he watched, it would release a bomb which dropped towards him, becoming larger and larger until it filled the whole sky. Then, just as it was about to explode, he would wake up trembling and sweating.

In 1944, during the Second World War, More was serving as an officer on the cruiser HMS *Aurora*. He had just been moved from the anti-aircraft guns to the lower bridge with orders that, in the event of an attack, he was to give a running commentary over the ship's tannoy system because the Captain thought it was bad for morale if the men below decks did not know what was happening above. Soon afterwards they were raided by 18 Stukas and opened up against them with their main armament of six-inch guns, but hit nothing. Speaking into the microphone, More kept nothing back because he realized that this was a time of life or death. 'Diving now,' he said. 'Fourth plane diving. Third plane's bombs have gone to starboard. Wait ... ' Suddenly his voice failed him, for there up in the sky he spotted the exact shape of the plane seen so often in his dreams. He told me:

There it hung directly above, and as I looked I saw the bomb leave the Stuka as I knew it would and grow larger and larger—and

I knew this one would hit us. It landed square on the four-inch gun deck aft—exactly where I would have been standing had I not been moved to the lower bridge to do my commentary. By a miracle I wasn't killed. I never had that dream again.

Ena Twigg, the British medium, claimed that she received her precognitive visions as if looking at a miniature movie in full colour on a borderless screen and often accompanied by warning voices. She said that in the quiet of the night before D-Day, she had a prevision of the entire landing that was to take place a few hours later and heard a voice telling her that her husband would be aboard one of the first cruisers to go into action, that it would be hit fore and aft, but that at eight o'clock on a Tuesday morning, a fortnight from then, he would knock on the front door.

All this came about, and so, too, did the reliably witnessed prediction that Mrs Twigg made in a trance that her husband would embark for the Far East on a ship called the *Maloja*, but that the war would be over by the time they reached 83° east longitude and 5° north latitude on 6 August 1945. Harry did sail on the *Maloja*, and on the date mentioned the first A-bomb was dropped on Hiroshima. At the time of this prediction no one, not even the American President, knew when or where the bomb would be used—if ever.

One of the oddest occurrences involving apparent precognition took place on the morning of 7 December 1939, when the children reaching their primary school in Owensville, Indiana, found painted on the sidewalk before the entrance the words, 'REMEMBER PEARL HARBOR'. There seemed to be no logical explanation for such a peculiar form of graffiti until exactly two years later the Japanese attacked Pearl Harbor.

In her book *Out of the Mouths of Babes*, Aileen H. Cooke gives several examples of children with precognitive powers. When, in 1942, the Japanese invaders were bearing down on Singapore, a Mrs Phyliss Morris was on the point of boarding an aeroplane to take her children out of danger when her little girl drew back crying that the plane would be bombed and crash into the sea. She was so terrified that Mrs Morris let others take their places on board. Next day, she arranged to leave on a ship instead, but no sooner had they stepped on the gangway than her daughter begged not to go, saying that the vessel would be bombed and sink, so once more they remained ashore. To her relief, when they boarded another steamer the girl raised no objections and went on deck quite happily. When they reached Australia, Mrs Morris learned that both the plane and the ship that had been anathema to the child had been attacked and destroyed by the enemy.

In November 1918, a London schoolboy named Cyril Macklin, on hearing that the Kaiser had abdicated, told his history master: 'Another man will rule Germany who will raise Hell.' Nine years later, when he saw a group photograph of some members of the National Socialist German Workers' Party reproduced in a newspaper, Macklin pointed at the figure of Hitler and said: 'That's the man who will cause a world war in 1939.' The following year, Macklin had a vision of London in flames being bombed from the air, and he wrote down the names of streets in the City which would be razed to the ground during the hostilities. This, he claimed later, proved correct.

When the blitz on London began, Macklin was working in an aircraft factory in a south-western suburb, and one day in the canteen, seated talking to other employees, he suddenly felt that he was going to pass out. A noise like that from an X-ray machine sounded in his ears. He saw the canteen wrecked and his fellow workers mutilated and dying. It was all so realistic that he threw in his job and left. Hardly had he done so than a direct hit destroyed the machine shops and an oil tank, and killed everybody in the canteen.

Macklin next found employment in an Acton factory manufacturing components for lorries and tanks, where he also acted as a warden organizing air-raid drills. Sitting in a deep shelter with some fellow workers following a practice, he had a vision of an aerial torpedo piercing the machine shop's roof, then shooting down the steps into the shelter and cutting off the legs of a woman taking refuge there. Once more he gave himself the sack, and hardly had he departed than everything happened just as he had predicted.

A factory in Wimbledon was where Macklin worked after this, but not for long. As he was about to leave home for the nightshift, he obeyed a voice telling him not to go, and next morning he learned that the division of the factory where he should have been toiling was now rubble.

All those at Hoover's factory making parts for aircraft were extremely apprehensive when Macklin was engaged, for his fame as a successful forecaster of disaster had spread. He had worked scarcely half a day there when he told his foreman that the Luftwaffe would attempt to obliterate the factory that very night. Two or three bombs would land in a lane a short distance away, a couple more in the coke dump, and another near the canteen, but that one would not explode. Again he was right.

After the war, Cyril Macklin did not rest on his laurels, but predicted two more great wars, followed by the whole world becoming united under one government.

The date and details of the Allied invasion of Europe in 1944 were kept the closest secret, and code names were used—'Overlord' for the operation, 'Neptune' for the naval spearhead, 'Utah' and 'Omaha' for the beaches chosen for the landing, and 'Mulberry' for the artificial harbours. Astonishingly, every one of these highly secret words appeared as answers to clues in the *Daily Telegraph*'s crossword puzzles in the month prior to D-Day. Was there a mole at the offices of that newspaper who was relaying vital information to the enemy? Security investigators found that the innocent cause of the scare was schoolmaster Leonard Dawe, who had been responsible for preparing crossword puzzles for some 20 years and had no links with those planning the campaign. If not a mere coincidence, telepathy would seem the most likely explanation in this case.

In his book *Thirty Seconds in Quetta*, Robert Jackson tells how on 30 May 1935 Field-Marshal Lord Montgomery, then an officer at the Quetta Staff College, and his wife Betty entertained some friends to dinner. Before it was served, they were all seated in the lounge and she was holding some embroidery on which she had been working. Suddenly, she looked in amazement at the skein of silk and displayed it enquiringly before her husband, for every strand was erect like a guardsman on parade. A Colonel Hawes who was present wondered if it were caused by the electricity in the air.

The same night, far away at Farnborough in Kent, Colonel Hawes's wife had a dream in which she was perched high up peering down on a plain. It was just as if she were in an identical location to that of the college and Quetta itself.

The sky was threateningly dark. Then the plain cracked open in innumerable places revealing black and white faces and a voice said: 'He's going to be all right.' Hardly had she heard this than Mrs Hawes woke up and found herself shaking uncontrollably.

Dawn had barely broken next morning when an earthquake destroyed every building in Quetta and in 30 seconds some 30,000 of its people died. Meanwhile, in the Staff College secure on its rocky heights above the disaster zone, the Montgomerys, Colonel Hawes, and the rest of the staff slumbered on, oblivious of the horror so close to them.

Shortly after nine o'clock on the morning of 21 October 1966, a rain-soaked slag tip on the mountainside above the mining village of Aberfan in Wales suddenly slipped and engulfed the Pantglas Junior School, a row of terraced houses, and a farm, killing 144 people, of whom 128 were children. A psychiatrist, Dr J.C. Barker of the Shelton Hospital, Shrewsbury, was at the time engaged in research for a book, published later under the title of *Scared to Death*, the theme of which was that predictions were often self-fulfilling. Interested in investigating cases of apparent genuine precognition, he appealed in the London *Evening Standard* for those who might have had premonitions of this appalling disaster to send him particulars. Within a fortnight, he received 76 replies, out of which he judged 60 worth following up with requests for supporting statements from people who might have been told of the premonitions before the event. Interviews were also arranged.

After careful consideration of all the evidence, Dr Barker decided that 35 of his correspondents had proved that they had foreseen the catastrophe in remarkably convincing detail. Most of these lived in the vicinity of London and had no links with Aberfan. Nearly all the previsions had been in dreams.

Some 50 miles away across the Bristol Channel at Barnstaple in North Devon, Mrs Mary Hennessy dreamed the night before the disaster of many children in two rooms. After a while some of them joined others in an oblong-shaped one, at the end of which there were wooden bars:

The children were trying somehow to get over the top or through the bars. I tried to warn someone by calling out, but before I could do so one little child just slipped out of sight. I myself was not in either of the rooms, but was watching from the corridor. The next thing in my dream was hundreds of people all running to the same place. The look on their faces was terrible. Some were crying and others holding handkerchiefs to their faces. It frightened me so much that it woke me up.

Mrs Hennessy had two granddaughters, but they were too young to attend school so she felt sure the nightmare did not involve them. Nevertheless, she phoned her son and told him about it, then that afternoon on the five o'clock radio news she heard abut the Aberfan tragedy.

Further away, in Kent, Mrs Grace Eagleton of Sidcup wrote to Dr Barker:

I have never been to Wales nor do I possess a television set. On the night of Friday, October 14, I had a vivid horrible dream of a terrible disaster in a coal mining village. It was in a valley with a big building filled with young children. Mountains of coal and water were rushing down upon the valley, burying the building. The screams of those children were so vivid that I screamed myself. It all happened so quickly. Then everything went black.

A nine-year-old girl, Eryl Mai, on waking one morning told her mother how in a dream she had seen slag from the tip tumbling down and burying her school. She added: 'I'm not afraid of dying. I shall be with Peter and June.' Her mother, Mrs Jones, was shocked by this. Then, on the eve of the disaster, Eryl Mai said that in a second dream she had approached the school and had found it covered in a black mist. Next morning Eryl Mai and her friends Peter and June died in the disaster.

In other dreams, one woman found herself being 'smothered in deep blackness'; another saw a screaming child in a telephone booth with 'a black billowing mass' following a second child outside; and a man living in the north-west of England saw in the early hours of the fatal day in huge illuminated capital letters the word 'Aberfan'.

On the evening before, Mrs Constance Milder of Plymouth, one of seven in a private spiritualist circle, had a waking vision:

First I 'saw' an old school house nestling in a valley, then a Welsh miner, then an avalanche of coal hurtling down a mountainside. At the bottom of the mountain of hurtling coal was a little boy with a long fringe looking absolutely terrified to death. Then for a quite a while I 'saw' rescue operations taking place. I had an impression that the little boy was left behind and saved. He looked so grief-stricken. I could never forget him, and also with him was one of the rescuers wearing an unusual peaked cap.

Mrs Milder went on to state that when on the Sunday evening after the disaster she watched on television the programme *The Mountain That Moved*, she was astonished to see both the terrified little boy talking to a reporter and also the rescuer with the peaked cap whom she had seen in her vision.

Everything to do with the occult has always fascinated the Chinese. In the early 1960s, a book entitled *Heavenly Prophecy* was published in Tibet and became popular there. One prediction was that in 1981 there would be widespread drought and floods causing famine, and that this would grow worse, culminating in the end of the world. As a result, the Tibetans started hoarding food and clothes, thus emptying the shops. The state-controlled radio denounced the work as superstitious rubbish. But in March 1981, the authorities in Peking were seeking international aid to the tune of $7 million to feed the 23 million people starving in Hebei province as a result of drought, as well as 20 million more in Hubei province in distress from floods. In the last week of that month, over 100 junks crowded with some 4,000 distraught people reached Hong Kong and begged for refuge until 10 April, as astrologers and Taoist monks had foretold that an earthquake would devastate the southern province of Guangdong before that date. The sceptical immigration controllers refused landing permission and forced the junks to leave.

On 9 April, a minor earth tremor shook Guangdong for 10 seconds. Although it did no damage, merely rattling windows, doors, and dishes, this lent some credence to the predictions, and deliverance from disaster was attributed to the prayers of the priests. Rumours of strange phenomena, reported that February in the *Shansi Daily*, had contributed to the panic, for the paper stated that shrieks for help had been heard coming from a rock that was a prominent feature of the Dongting Lake in Hunan province. It was suggested that the rock had somehow recorded the screams of the drowning and released the sounds when physical conditions permitted.

CHAPTER 13

Auguries of Assassination

Apart from the much-discussed predictions of the violent deaths of the Kennedy brothers, there have been others equally extraordinary involving public figures in this century. Hardly had it dawned than King Umberto I of Italy met such a fate. On 29 July 1900, he was to be present at an athletics meeting in Monza. When accompanied by his aide, he dined at a restaurant the previous evening, they were astonished to find that its owner so resembled the monarch that he might have been his twin brother, and they also learned that his Christian name was Umberto, that he had been born on the same day and in the same town, Turin, that both had wed brides called Margherita on identical dates—and that the restaurant had opened on the occasion of Umberto's coronation.

The King invited his *doppio* to be his guest at the athletics meeting, but he failed to arrive, having lost his life that morning in a strange shooting accident. No sooner had Umberto I been told this than he himself was shot dead by the anarchist Bresci, thus fulfilling almost to the day a prediction made three months earlier to the King by Cheiro, the palmist.

Colin Wilson in *The Occult* claims that Rasputin was stabbed at Pokrovskoe and the Archduke Franz Ferdinand of Austria was assassinated at Sarajevo probably at the same time. Rasputin, however, recovered from the knife wounds in his stomach. Then, some two and a half years later, on 29 December 1916, Prince Youssoupoff killed him and another prophecy of Cheiro's was realized. According to the palmist, during a dramatic encounter with the 'Mad Monk' in January 1905, he told him: 'You will be menaced by poison, by knife, and by bullet. Finally, I see the icy waters of the Neva closing above you.' Rasputin proved immune to the poisoned cakes and wine served him by Youssoupoff, and even when shot several times might have survived had he not been drowned. He himself must have been affected by Cheiro's forecast, for he wrote in a letter that he had strong feelings that he would no longer be alive by the end of 1916, and that if he were murdered by aristocrats they would be destroyed as a class in Russia and the Tsar and Tsarina and their children killed within two years.

On 28 June 1914, Dr Joseph de Lanyi, the Archduke Franz Ferdinand's tutor and Bishop of Grosswardein in Hungary, was in his residence there whilst the Archduke was some 300 miles away. At a quarter past three that morning, the Bishop awoke from a distressing dream. It had such an effect on him that he sat down and wrote a full account which he posted to his brother, Professor Edouard de Lanyi. This read:

I had dreamed that I had gone to my desk early in the morning to look through the post that had come in. On top of all the other letters there lay one with a black border, a black seal, and the arms of the Archduke. I immediately recognised his writing. I opened it and saw at the head of the notepaper in blue colouring a picture like those on picture postcards. This showed a street and a narrow side-street. Their Highnesses sat in a car, opposite them sat a General, and an officer next to the chauffeur. On both sides of the station there was a large crowd. Two young lads sprang forward and shot at their Highnesses. The text of the letter was: 'Dear Dr. de Lanyi, your Excellency, I wish to inform you that my wife and I were the victims of a political assassination. We recommend ourselves to your prayers. Cordial greetings from your Archduke Franz, Sarajevo, June 28, 3.15 a.m.' Trembling and in tears, I sprang out of bed and I looked at the clock which showed 3.15. I immediately hurried to my desk and wrote down what I had read and seen in my dream. In doing so, I even retained the form of certain letters just as the Archduke had written them. My servant entered my study at a quarter to six that morning and saw me there pale and saying my rosary. He asked me whether I was ill. I said, 'Call my mother and the guest at once. I will say Mass immediately for their Highnesses, for I have had a terrible dream.' My mother and the guest came at a quarter to seven. I told my mother the dream in the presence of the guest and of my servant. Then I went into the house chapel. The day passed in fear and apprehension.

Shortly before 11 o'clock that morning, the Archduke and his wife were assassinated in their car. The dream was correct in showing the place where the shots were fired and that a general sat facing the Archduke, but there was only one assassin not two and there was no officer next to the chauffeur.

Two years previously at a seance held in the Archduchess Isabella of Austria's home, the medium Madame Sylvia had told her: 'Your Royal Highness, I beg you to be less hostile to the Archduke Franz Ferdinand and his wife. We must be kind to them. They haven't long to live. In two years' time, they will die from the same bullet.'

It is possible that the Bishop might have heard of the medium's prediction and that this would have made him always apprehensive whenever he knew his charge was undertaking public duties, that he picked up telepathically the thoughts of the plotters, and that his subconscious then 'dramatized' them. There was nothing haphazard about the spot chosen for the assassination. The junction of Appel Quai and the narrow street into which the royal cavalcade turned forced the Archduke's car to slow down and made him a perfect target. The variations between events in the dream and what really happened imply that the Bishop was experiencing telepathy rather than precognition.

On 22 June 1922, Field-Marshal Sir Henry Wilson was shot dead by Irish nationalists in London. Ten days previously, his friend Lady Londonderry dreamed that she had witnessed two men commit the crime outside a cottage on a moor. Next morning she told two people about it, and they were able to confirm after the murder had been committed that the dream had come true in detail, except for the location. It is possible that the outrage was planned in a moorland cottage, and that Lady Londonderry, like the Bishop, picked up the terrorists' thoughts.

Spain's most noted seer was Tomas Menes, who, on 23 May 1934, predicted in a Madrid newspaper that Chancellor Dolfuss of Austria would be murdered within three months. During a meeting with his ministers on 25 July, Dolfuss was assassinated.

A number of astrologers foretold a cruel end for Mussolini. 'Raphael' published his commentary on the Duce's horoscope as early as 1932, in which he prophesied the outbreak of a European war leading to an ignominious death for him.

One of Michael Bentine's many precognitive experiences related in his *Doors of the Mind* occurred in 1979. After performing his cabaret act at a country club in Gloucestershire, he went to bed and had hardly put out the light when a deep voice, which seemed to come from the centre of the room, intoned two words: 'Blood sacrifice.' He switched on the lamp but there was no one there, so he tried to go to sleep again. A few minutes later, the words were repeated, and this time the voice sounded nearer. The same thing happened a third time. He could not sleep and spent the rest of the night reading in an armchair. In the morning, he questioned the manager as to whether the room was haunted, and he was assured that no one had ever complained of being disturbed in this way before.

But no sooner had Bentine lain down in the darkened bedroom the next night than the voice spoke again, and the words 'Blood sacrifice' were louder than ever. This time, he did not give the invisible entity a chance to speak again and, leaving the light on, he read until dawn.

On his way home by car next day, Bentine paused outside the gates leading to Blenheim Palace, and this time in broad daylight he heard the words 'Blood sacrifice' again. There was no one in sight. Back home, he told his wife about it, then went to relax in the sitting-room. He had been there only a short while when suddenly the occasional table facing him shook violently and a resounding explosion came from inside the wood, and he heard the words 'Blood sacrifice'—but now they were spoken within his head.

As Bentine jumped up, the phone rang in the hall. His wife answered it, then she entered and told him that Airey Neave had been murdered in a bomb outrage at the House of Commons. Horrified by the news, Bentine prayed for his close friend, and as he did so a noise like a pistol shot burst from the coffee table and the voice uttered the words: 'And all the trumpets sounded for him on the other side.' The words were so loud and clear to Bentine that he was surprised his wife did not hear them.

Michael Bentine attended the Memorial Service for Airey Neave at St Martin-in-the-Fields. He sat behind the organ loft and was deep in reflection when suddenly he heard these words from Bunyan's *Pilgrim's Progress* again: 'And all the trumpets sounded for him on the other side.' But this time it was a woman's voice. The words came from the lips of Margaret Thatcher.

It was the Sri Lankan astrologer Cyrus D.F. Abayaikoon who, whilst in El Paso, Texas, was reported in the *National Enquirer* of 18 May 1975 as predicting that Mrs Thatcher would become Prime Minister of the United Kingdom some time between 28 Novembr 1977 and 22 April 1980. He also predicted danger if not actual assassination for another woman Prime Minister, Indira Gandhi, in *Weekend* on 4 April 1984:

As a Cancer subject running Saturn-Mars till July 18, 1985, and with Jupiter the 9th lord in the 6th, dissension and revolution cannot contribute towards a stable existence after June 9, 1984. She should pay more attention to her personal safety between September 25 and November 6, 1984.

Can astrology aid terrorists to select a precise time favourable for them to perpetrate their crimes? Dennis Elwell, the astrologer mentioned earlier, claims to have found remarkable links between planetary positions and IRA outrages such as the assassination of Lord Mountbatten and the Brighton hotel bomb which almost killed Margaret Thatcher and most of her Cabinet. Earlier evidence supporting his argument that this might be so could be found in the choice of day and hour for the Maze prison coup when the break-out occurred almost to the minute of a conjunction of Jupiter and Uranus on the cusp of the twelfth house (imprisonment) at that locality! Mr Elwell points out that such a conjunction takes place only once every 14 years and he comments that though sceptics might scoff at the suggestion that the IRA were guided by some expert astrologer, it was a known fact that the Israeli secret service, the Mossad, had been so influenced in deciding when to launch the astonishingly successful rescue of the hostages at Entebbe Airport.

Dennis Elwell wondered whether the IRA, aware of the Mossad's tactics, might be copying them. Regarding it as his duty to convey his suspicions to the British Prime Minister as head of the security services, he sent her a detailed letter which was merely acknowledged. Then when they attacked target after target at times lending credence to his belief, he again wrote to Mrs Thatcher drawing her attention to how events were proving him right, and he also posted a similar warning to the Home Secretary. At last, 10 months after sending his first warning, he received a brief communication from the Home Office stating that 'as far as we are aware there is no evidence to support your theory'.

Fourteen months after the Home Office's curt rejection, five IRA men went on trial for bomb offences. It was stated in evidence that when they were arrested, a piece of paper had been found listing exact times and dates in 16 named seaside towns where bombs were to be planted during the summer of 1985. The violence was to begin at 1 p.m. on 19 July with bombs exploding almost daily until 5 August. Elwell writes in his book *Cosmic Loom* that at noon on 19 July, the moon in Leo was opposing Jupiter in Aquarius, both squaring the point of a previous lunar eclipse. 'Leo, like the corresponding fifth house, has to do with holiday-makers, and Aquarius is said to rule Brighton, picked as the scene of the first bomb.' Elwell stresses the destabilizing potentialities of this configuration. It was also around midday on 19 July that hundreds died in the dam disaster at Stava in Italy, and that there was panic on the Italian exchanges with the lira diving. 'Leo is regarded as ruling Italy. At Brighton a violent conjunction of the Sun and Mars would have been in the mid-heaven at 1 p.m.'

According to Dennis Elwell, the IRA campaign of terror's 'launch' chart would also have an exact opposition between 'Venus, planet of leisure and pleasure, peace and quiet, and the explosively disruptive Uranus'. The reason why such a blitz on British holiday hotels was crowded into three weeks could he thought, be best explained by the new moon figure of 18 July.

The new moon was conjunction Mars, and opposed to the mid-heaven at Westminster. Saturn in the tragic Scorpio opposed the ascendant, and exactly squared Mercury in Leo in the fifth house—holidays. Not too complicated a set of aspects for the average astrologer, and it would be no surprise to learn that the aborted campaign had been planned with them in mind.

Dennis Elwell maintains that his warnings might not have been disregarded if Sir Maurice Oldfield of MI6 had still been head of the British secret service, for he had a deep interest in Chinese astrology—or if Maxwell Knight, 'M' of MI5, had

been around, for he had recruited Aleister Crowley as an
agent and had been introduced to the occult by him.

CHAPTER 14

Radio, Television, and Film Precognition

If one can, in dreams, see passsages in newspapers that have yet to be printed, it would be even more extraodinary when awake to hear voices on the radio describing events that have not yet taken place. Both phenomena were experienced by the late Juliet, Lady Rhys-Williams, once a governor of the BBC and vice-president of the Economic Research Council. Waking up at 4 a.m. on 17 January 1964, while staying in her country house in Wales, and switching on her radio to Voice of America, she heard the announcer reporting riots caused through blacks being attacked by Ku Klux Klan supporters in Atlanta, Georgia. After rising and having breakfast, she told her daughter about it, but was surprised not to find the affair reported in any newspapers, day after day.

Then, during the evening of 26 January, Lady Rhys-Williams, back in her Belgravia home in London, heard on the BBC World Service a report about race riots in Atlanta the previous day, and she read accounts in the papers next morning. Puzzled, she wrote to Voice of America in Washington, and they confirmed that there had been earlier rioting but said they had not broadcast anything about it until 48 hours after she had 'heard' their news flash.

Lady Rhys-Williams claimed to have had several similar experiences. Turning on the radio by her bedside on the morning of 24 February 1964, she heard the newscaster saying that Archbishop Makarios had called on General de Gaulle to mediate between him and the British in Cyprus, and this time she told both her daughter and her chauffeur about it. Once again there was not a word regarding the matter in the newspapers or any further radio reports until, on the 27th, *The Times'* political correspondent reported that, in an interview that had appeared in a Paris newspaper the day before, Makarios had said he would like the French leader to act as arbitrator.

About 6.30 a.m. on 3 June 1964, Lady Rhys-Williams heard on the radio a commentator announcing that Senator Barry Goldwater had defeated Governor Nelson Rockefeller in the Californian presidential primary and that Governor Rockefeller had conceded defeat before going home. She told her two daughters over breakfast at 8.30 a.m. The first radio broadcast giving this news was on the American CBS network at 10.39 a.m. New York time—3.30 p.m. London time, seven hours later. The first BBC broadcast was at 5.30 p.m., and this said that Rockefeller had *not* conceded defeat.

The following year, on opening *The Times* first thing one morning, she 'read' an article about the hardships small farmers were enduring through a steep fall in their income. Much concerned about this, she went straight to her desk and wrote to the Prime Minister urging him to help them, but when she leafed through the newspaper with the intention of cutting out the item it was nowhere to be seen. Nevertheless, having written the letter, she posted it. Next day, the article she had foreseen was published in the paper.

The same thing happened the following year, also in *The Times*. It was a description, together with photograph, of a three-bedroomed house with a sloping roof on one side costing only £1,000 to build. As chairman of the housing committee of a town council and disturbed by rising prices, Lady Rhys-Williams told her secretary to cut out the feature and send it to the municipal architect, but the girl searched the paper in vain. Next day, article and picture appeared just as her ladyship had 'seen' them.

A Mrs Lesley Brennan of Cleethorpes had a similar experience to Lady Rhys-Williams, except that in this case it was on television. On the morning of Saturday 1 June 1974, she was at home taking her ease on a sofa while she watched an old film, *The Nevadan*. Suddenly, she later claimed, there was a news flash reporting many casualties through an explosion in the huge Flixborough Nypro plant, 20 miles away. Towards midday, her friends, Janice and Peter East called, and she told them about it.

That evening, the television news covered the disaster, stating that it had happened at five o'clock in the afternoon, and this was confirmed by the details next day in the newspapers. The explosion had occurred at 4.53 p.m. It seems that Mrs Brennan had had a prevision of the catastrophe that cost 28 lives and wrecked nearly 2,000 buildings on the 60-acre site.

Mrs Brennan's strange experience led to her and the Easts being interviewed by Robin Furman, and the whole story was then published in the *Grimsby Evening Telegraph*.

In a competition for the person having had the most number of precognitive dreams, actress Mrs Christine Mylius might well prove the winner. For about 20 years, she sent accounts of her dreams to Professor Hans Bender, the German parapsychologist. Out of over 2,000, a tenth have corresponded in many respects with future events. Reporting on these in the *International Journal of Psychiatry* of October 1966, the professor describes how Mrs Mylius dreamed in advance of scenes in which she was to appear in the film *Night Fell Upon Gotenhafen*, which started being shot in the latter part of 1959.

The script did not exist on 15 September 1957, when Mrs Mylius dreamed of a scene in which she and other refugee farm women were swimming out to a ship in the harbour of Gotenhafen in the Baltic during the Second World War. Then, on 10 October, she dreamed that a cameraman attempted to film her as she ploughed her way through water, but in the dream she soon gave up, telling herself that it would prove not to be worth it. Both these scenes were shot when the film was made, and in the case of the first this happened exactly two years later. But the second one was cut from the finished film, so she was right in what she had told herself.

Mrs Mylius dreamed in February and July 1958 of a 'gigantic lobster' which she and several other people were eating at a party. Later, during the filming, such a lobster was caught and she prepared a lobster dinner for the film unit. On 29 April 1958, in another dream, she was sitting on the deck of a small steamer, talking to a very friendly ship's cook. In September a year later, she remembered this when shooting was taking place at sea and such a man would fuss round her while she rested after returning on board exhausted from swimming in a shipwreck sequence.

On 22 May 1959, Mrs Mylius dreamed at length about the

steamer. It was a very old and dirty fishing-boat that had been chartered, which moved slowly and unsteadily and had a grimy and tipsy crew. This turned out to be an accurate prevision of the boat on which they sailed from Bremerhaven.

Earlier, on 3 January of that year, Mrs Mylius dreamed of a girl with flowing hair, of several people in asbestos suits, and a crater full of a white chalky substance. When, some nine months later, the unit was on location in Heligoland, the actors were given protective asbestos suits as a safeguard against drowning, a crater lake as described was prepared for a scene, and Mrs Mylius recognized a diver as being the double of the one she had seen in the dream.

Professor Bender verified that the film script had not been written when Mrs Mylius began having her dreams, and also that when she had those about the fishing-boat, the producer had no intention of chartering one.

In 1965, just before *Gemini VI* was to be launched into space, Mrs Mylius dreamed that her daughter, Bella, was dressed as an astronaut, and next to her was a man similarly attired who was dying, choked by a plastic cup that had stuck fast in his throat. On awakening, Mrs Mylius wondered if this presaged some disaster for the spacecraft. It was only just before *Gemini VI* was due to be launched that a possible catastrophe was avoided when a plastic cup blocking the fuel line was discovered and removed.

But why had Mrs Mylius's daughter been clad as an astronaut in that dream? She too was an actress, and some months later was cast in such a role in a television drama. It was first screened on 27 January 1967, and when Mrs Mylius went to bed that night, she dreamed of disaster for another countdown. That same night at Cape Kennedy three astronauts perished in the Apollo VI capsule when fire broke out.

Peter Fairley, former science editor of the London *Evening Standard* and the *TV Times*, who for a while ran the Premonitions Bureau, related a few years ago on a BBC Radio 4 programme a remarkable series of coincidences. His mother-in-law had given him an old Chinese picture showing the waterfront at Canton. After two visitors had both mistaken it for Venice, his wife said: 'Isn't it strange, but I'm reading a book about Venice and the charlady has just told me that her next door neighbour has had to fly back from Venice because her daughter had to have her appendix out and the surgeon then discovered that the appendix was on the wrong side of her body.'

Fairley says he was even more astonished than his wife on hearing this and told her: 'My dear, this really is incredible, because in my office today I opened a letter from a woman who said her son wanted to get married and she was worried because his appendix was on the wrong side of his body, and now you're telling me the charlady's friend has had exactly the same thing—and it's in the book you're reading. What is the book you're reading?'

Mrs Fairley replied that the book was upstairs and that she would go and fetch it. Her husband experienced a feeling that this was going to prove to be the most amazing series of coincidences he had come across. He pulled out two tickets and placed them face downwards on the table as she returned with a paperback and said: 'It's called *Don't Look Now*.' Peter Fairley turned over the two tickets, and they were for the première of the film *Don't Look Now*.

CHAPTER 15

Forseeing Winners

Once at Longchamps Gerard Croiset foresaw the names of the winners of the first four races, but feeling the loss of his gift might ensue if he exploited it for such purposes, he never again attended a race meeting. There have been some remarkable instances in the course of this century of people dreaming of the results of classic and other races. For instance, readers of the *Sunday Graphic* turning to the column of the much-read journalist Hannen Swaffer one morning in 1921 might have made a great deal of money had they placed bets on a horse in tartan colours—Shaun Spadah. Swaffer reported that Dennis Bradley, a friend of his, had dreamed that it would win the Grand National that afternoon—and that only three out of the 35 runners would not fall in the race, which also came true.

Forty-six years later, George Cranmer, an Australian, saw in a dream the colours on the jockey winning the Grand National, and the horse he rode, Foinavon, did so at 100–1. Cranmer next dreamed of Ribocco being acclaimed after the Derby. When it came second at Epsom, it looked as if those precognitive powers had failed—but Cranmer was consoled later when Ribocco won the *Irish* Derby.

Lord Kilbracken, better known as John Godley the well-known journalist, wrote in his autobiography how in 1947 the whole of the rest of his life was changed by a dream. He was then aged 24 and had served in the Fleet Air Arm during the Second World War, reaching the rank of lieutenant commander. In January 1946, he returned as an undergraduate to Balliol College, Oxford, where he had studied for some nine months prior to joining up in 1940. On Friday 8 March, he read until midnight before going to bed. He dreamed that he had next day's evening paper open before him at the racing results. On awakening he could recall only the names of two winners, Bindal and Juladin, which he found on looking at the morning paper over breakfast were both running that afternoon. In his dream they had both started at 7–1.

Godley told a dozen or so undergraduate friends he knew about this. He was asked to place £5 on each horse for them, and he himself wagered 50s. to win on Bindal, 50s. to win on Juladin, and a 50s. win double, which was all he could afford. Delighted when Bindal won at odds of 5–4, earning him £3, he increased his stake on Juladin by that amount, but he did not ring his bookmaker that afternoon to learn the result, feeling superstitiously that, as in his dream he had read the names of the winners in a newspaper, it would prove unlucky to find them out in any other way. So he waited patiently another hour until he could buy a copy of the *Evening Standard*, and then he read that Juladin had won at odds of 5–2, making him richer by £34. The two horses having started at 5–4 and 5–2, the odds for the double were $7^7/_8$–1, very close to the 7–1 of his dream.

In the next few weeks, Godley kept pencil and paper by his bedside every night. He knew that he had seen the names of all the winning horses in that lucky dream, and that his poor memory was to blame for his remembering only two of them. He did not want the same to happen again. Immediately on awakening, therefore, he carefully made detailed notes of everything he had experienced in his dreams, but not one had anything to do with racing. In fact, they were all so ordinary that his enthusiasm swiftly petered out. He came to the conclusion that the dream had been a fluke never to be repeated.

In the early hours of 4 April, however, when on holiday in Ireland, Godley dreamed again that he was reading the names of winners in a newspaper, but on waking he could recall only one name, Tubermore. The nearest village was five miles away. The postman called once a day and the London *Times* which he brought with him was always two days old, so Godley drove to the village to collect a copy of the current *Irish Times*, but to his disgust could find no such horse mentioned.

Perhaps Tubermore might be running the following day, Godley eventually decided, so next morning he telephoned a friendly postmistress in another village and asked her help. She could find no Tubermore, listed but there was a Tuberose running in the first race at Aintree, so he bet on it and so did his sister and brother-in-law. This outsider won at 100–6 and Godley collected £62.

The land of leprechauns failed to induce any more significant dreams, but that summer vacation, when Godley was staying in his brother's Oxford rooms, he dreamed during the night of 28 July that he was in a telephone box asking his bookmaker's clerk the result of the last race. The clerk replied: 'Certainly, sir—Monumentor at 5–4.' Then Godley woke up. It was three a.m. and, reaching for a pencil, he made a note of what the clerk had said.

Next morning, Godley hurried out to buy a newspaper. In the last race at Worcester, the favourite at 5–4 was named Mentores. It was not exactly the same name, but near enough. Godley told seven other undergraduates before putting £4 on the horse, which won at 6–4—not 5–4 as in the dream.

There was another long gap, this time of 11 months, before any more racing tips came to Godley in his dreams. It seemed that thinking so much about the subject had quite the opposite effect to what he had hoped. In fact, it was only when he had given up doing this that he dreamed of his next winner. This was also in Oxford, during the night of Friday 13 June 1947. He saw a horse well ahead of the rest of the field which carried the colours of the Gaekwar of Baroda. The jockey Godley recognized as Edgar Britt, an Australian, who rode most of the mounts in the potentate's stable. Then the scene swiftly changed to the next race. As it ended, Godley heard the onlookers all shouting: 'The favourite wins! It's the Bogie.' There was such an uproar that it woke him.

As soon as *The Times* was delivered, Godley turned at once to the racing section. There was only one race meeting taking place that day. It was at Lingfield Park and the Gaekwar's Baroda Squadron, ridden by Edgar Britt, was running. In the following race, the 4.30, the favourite was not The Bogie but The Brogue. However, the name was sufficiently similar for Godley to risk his solitary fiver on it. And then he wondered whether there might be some further way in which he could turn his strange gift to financial gain. So he telephoned the *Daily Mirror* and offered if the two horses won to sell them his story for £25. They agreed. Baroda Squadron and The Brogue romped home, and the *Mirror* devoted its centre pages to 'The Strange Dream of Mr. John Godley'.

The dream tipster had sat all the examinations for the Foreign Office and had come top. Despite this, when the *Daily Mirror* made him an offer to become one of their journalists for a trial eight weeks, Godley accepted and gave up the chance of possibly becoming an ambassador. The job suited him, and he worked on the paper for one and a half years before transferring to the *Sunday Express*. As might be expected, his post at the *Mirror* attracted hundreds of letters from readers, many offering him a percentage of their winnings if he would tell them exclusively his racing predictions. He refused in every case.

Four months after his double win, Godley suffered his first failure. Through studying form he had concluded that Claro ought to win the Cambridgeshire. A fortnight beforehand he backed his choice with a fiver at odds of 16–1. During the early hours of the day on which the event was to take place, he dreamed he was going down a busy street in Oxford when he enquired of a passer-by which horse had won. 'Claro' was the reply.

On awakening, Godley promptly doubled his stake on Claro, which came nowhere. He tried to find a reason for this fiasco. Unlike previously, he had known a great deal about the horse before dreaming, and was keen that it should win. The dream was therefore more wish fulfilment than precognitive.

But worse was to follow. In December Godley started work at the *Mirror* and for a whole year horses were absent from his dreams. At last, on 15 January 1949, as he slept, he visualized that he was attending the preparation of the racing page in the newspaper and that another journalist was typing out a winner's name—Timocrat.

Godley had arranged to go next day to the Cheltenham races, and he was delighted to find that Timocrat was entered for the fifth race. He passed his dream tip on to various friends, but after his failure with Claro they had lost faith in his forecasts. Nevertheless, he himself backed Timocrat, which won easily at odds of 4–1.

It had been Godley's rule to bet only small amounts in these instances, both because he was always short of money and also because he felt if he took too great an advantage of the information thus received he might one day lose a lot. His winnings to date were therefore a mere £87. Nevertheless, when a seventh dream livened his sleep less than a month after his success with Timocrat, he jettisoned caution and made up his mind to wager as much as his bank balance permitted.

This time, as on the first occasion, he dreamed that he was looking at the results in the following day's papers. Pretence and Monk's Mistake were the names of the two winners that he remembered on awakening. He found that only the second horse was running that afternoon, and then just before the race in which Monk's Mistake was listed as a winner it was scratched. The day following this, both horses were competing at separate meetings, so he wrote down on a sheet of paper exactly what he had dreamed, sealed it in an envelope, and handed it to another journalist for him to keep as indisputable evidence.

Monk's Mistake was running in the three o'clock at Taunton, and Pretence in the last race at Lingfield. Godley's bets were: £20 win double, Monk's Mistake and Pretence; if Monk's Mistake lost, £8 to win on Pretence; if Pretence lost, £8 to win on Monk's Mistake. This meant a maximum possible loss of £36, and a win of £1,240 should the dream come true. He paid the bookmaker £28 in cash and was allowed credit for the rest. This left him with only one shilling in his pocket.

Godley went to Lingfield knowing that he would learn the result at Taunton by ten past three. It so happened that Monk's Mistake was ridden by Attic Corbett, a friend of his, who told him later exactly what occurred.

Monk's Mistake had started well reaching second place, three jumps from the finish, and only two lengths behind the favourite, Morning Cross. Both were far ahead of the rest. Gradually but surely Monk's Mistake narrowed the gap between it and Morning Cross. They were neck and neck. Attic believed he would win by six lengths. Then his mount blundered for the first and only time. Taking off a little too early and catching the very top of the last fence, it stumbled and Attic tried in vain to get going again. Morning Cross

won and Monk's Mistake was third, six and three-quarter
lengths behind.

It was a bitter disappointment for Godley. His only con-
solation was that Pretence won by five lengths at Lingfield,
so with odds of 8–1 he gained £44. This proved the end of
his career as a dreaming tipster—except in 1958 when he foresaw the name of the winner of the Grand National, Mr What,
on which the odds were 18–1.

A stranger experience than Godley's was that of Douglas
Jerram. He was serving as British Ambassador in Sweden,
and was very friendly with King Gustavus V. One Saturday night, the diplomat dreamed that he was at a race meeting the following afternoon and was struggling through a
dense crowd to reach the Tote. Next to him stood the King.
In desperation both climbed over some railings and managed
to reach the box where bets were made. Jerram did not even
know the names of the runners, but the monarch told him:
'Put your money on Mandalay. He's an outsider, but I am
sure he will win.'

Next day, Jerram was sitting among the other diplomats
at the races when he read in huge letters on the front page
of a neighbour's newspaper, 'DEATH OF THE KING'. Jerram
knew he must hurry away to perform all the duties now
required of him. Before doing so, as there was an outsider
in a race named not Mandalay but Manderley, he impulsively
entrusted all the money on him, almost the equivalent of
£100, to a close friend with instructions to place it at once
on the horse. Manderley won, making the Ambassador richer
by almost £1,000. He related all this to the husband of Ann
Bridge, who included an account of it in her book *Moments
of Knowing*.

Several cases of people foreseeing winners in dreams are
described in the *Proceedings of the Society for Psychical Research*.
In volume XIV, page 251, Professor Haslam tells how when
half asleep he was thinking about an imminent race meeting when there flashed before his eyes a vision of a jockey
in scarlet who, after pulling on his horse, won. Haslam was
telling himself that scarlet was a common colour when the
vision was repeated. The following day, he told some friends
about it, then went to the meeting, where to his surprise
he came across a jockey in scarlet in the saddling paddock.
This encouraged him to place a modest bet on the man's

mount, which he pulled on hard during the race and in the end won.

In volume XXVIII of the Society's *Journal*, page 216, the case was reported of an octogenarian Quaker, strongly opposed to betting, who on 31 May 1933 awoke at 8.35 a.m. after dreaming that he had been listening to a running radio commentary on the Derby due to take place that afternoon in which he had heard names of the first four horses but could only remember those of the winner, Hyperion, and the runner up, King Salmon. Intrigued by this, he overcame his disapproval of racing sufficiently to switch on the radio at 2 p.m., and as he listened it seemed to him that the very expressions the commentator was using were the same as in the dream, and the result was as foreseen.

Sir Edward Marshall-Hall, the famous barrister, once related how he dreamed the winner of two races. He said that he awoke with a name impressed upon his mind which consisted of two syllables. The first he could not remember, the second remained in his memory, probably because it was his own—Hall—together with the fact that a horse, 'something' hall, would win both events. The following day he took steps to find out if there was a horse bearing a name of two syllables, the second being 'hall'. If there was, was it decided that this horse should run in two races? Sir Edward discovered that Foxhall was entered for the Cesarewitch and also for the Cambridgeshire at Newmarket. The dream occurred in July and the races were run in the following October. On both occasions, Foxhall was the winner.

Dame Ethel Lyttelton was president of the Society for Psychical Research for 1933–4, and among the experiences of predictions sent to her by listeners following her broadcast on the subject were a number concerning the sport of kings. In February 1934, she received a letter from a Mr W.L. Freeman of South Wepton near Leicester describing how in November 1913, though he had no interest at all in horse racing, he dreamed one night that he had travelled to Lincoln to attend the spring meeting but had spent so much time inside the cathedral that he arrived late at the course and learned that the big event, the Lincoln Handicap, was over and that Outram had won it. Upon waking, he related the dream to several friends. It was not until then that he discovered there was a horse so named. The list of entrants for the Handicap was not issued until January 1914, and to his surprise he saw the name Outram included. That March, though an outsider with long odds laid against it, Outram won the race.

Dame Ethel also heard from a Mrs G. Ling of Cromer that a week before the 1932 Derby she was awakened early in the morning by a voice saying: 'April the Fifth will win the Derby.' She roused her husband and they both put a modest bet of one shilling on the horse, which won. Over 20 people were told about the dream before the race. Mrs Ling claimed to have had two other dreams with the same voice waking her. 'The one four years ago proved true, the other one has not had time to prove itself and they were over private matters,' she wrote.

Miss Edith L. Willis of Norwich wrote to Dame Ethel that on 4 June 1929, being interested in psychic matters and remembering that the next day was the Derby, she thought she would try and get the name of the winner through automatic writing. So she took up a pencil and waited. Presently, she wrote 'Trigo'. On looking through the list of runners in a newspaper she found that Trigo was entered and had odds of 32–1 against it. She told the rest of the household and got a friend to put five shillings on Trigo—and won £8.

Dame Ethel commented that as there are a limited number of horses running in a race this increases the case for regarding these three cases as possible coincidences. Neither Miss Willis nor Mr Freeman knew the names of any racehorses, so they may have picked them up from other minds through telepathy.

Mr G.N.M. Tyrrell, the psychic researcher, said these dreams could be explained rationally. He maintained that people had such a vast number of dreams that there must be a few chance hits. These only were remembered while the rest were forgotten, and 'so you get a set of cases which you falsely imagine to be precognitive, but which are really only the cream of coincidences which are due to natural chance'.

This explanation, Dame Ethel claimed, could hardly hold in other cases she went on to quote. Some might, on the other hand, be instances of telepathy rather than precognition.

According to Miss Emily Isherwood of Southport, the

evening before the Grand National was run on 27 March 1907, she was sitting in her house near Aintree thinking about the famous steeplechase when in her 'mind's eye' she saw a horse's head which was black and decorated with red ribbon. As Rubio's jockey carried these colours, she backed the horse, which won.

Later Miss Isherwood wondered if she could find the winner of the Manchester Cup race and, concentrating on this, she had a 'mind' picture of the grandstand and the winning jockey, who wore blue and white check colours and a cerise cap. These proved to be Colonel Hall Walker's racing colours, and his Polar Star won the Manchester Cup on 12 June 1908. Following this, she got a 'mind' picture of a horse swimming which had a bright star on its forehead, and she read a short time afterwards the Polar Star had been sent to South America.

Miss Isherwood wrote that four years previously she had had the impression that a horse whose name was something like Murphy would win the Grand National, but she could not find any horse entered with that name. Afterwards she learned that the winner's name, Moifaa, when correctly pronounced sounded very much like Murphy.

Dame Ethel regarded Mrs Phyllis Richard's dream about Kellsboro Jack winning the 1933 Grand National as definitely precognitive. This lady was asleep on a ship crossing from Belfast to Liverpool on her way to attend the race meeting next day when she dreamed that she was at Aintree, and that a horse whose name began with K and ended with Jack had won, although he was not the first horse past the winning post. Next day, over lunch, she told some friends about her dream. They looked up the list of runners and suggested Pellorus Jack, but she insisted that the name began with a K. They read on and found Kellsboro Jack, and she told them that was the horse. He won but, as in her dream, a riderless horse was the first past the post.

Fortunately for the bookmakers, when most people dream of winners this does not continue for long. A typesetter on a London newspaper dreamed that he had been handed a last-minute item to set which read: 'The winner of the Derby has now received a name. It is Kisber.' So vivid was the dream that next morning the man hunted through the racing pages for a horse of that name, but without success.

However, he did come across an entry so far without a name, owned by an Hungarian aristocrat, Alexander Baltazzi, so he bet as heavily as he could on this runner, which to his delight became Kisber shortly before the race and finished several lengths ahead of the favourite. But the typesetter did not dream of any further winners.

On the other hand the mother of my friend Zelma Bramley-Moore often dreamed of winners for her husband. It always began in the same way. Mrs Grierson would see a stage with heavy black curtains which would then be pulled back and some act would be performed which she knew represented the name of a horse. 'Harry,' she once said to Captain Grierson, 'I had one of my dreams last night. I've got a winner for you. When the curtains were drawn aside, there was an an acrobat on a trapeze.' Zelma's father searched through the racing papers and found a horse called Acrobat entered for a race in a few days' time. It was an outsider, but he backed it and won.

Three or four times in the season, Mrs Grierson would have these dreams, but in spite of her never having made a mistake, her husband lacked the courage to put more than a small sum on the horse. Only once, to Zelma's knowledge, did something appear to go wrong. Her mother dreamed that when the curtains parted she saw there on the stage a huge placard on which was written in enormous letters LIMELIGHT. Then she felt she had dreamed the winner, and so, highly elated at the thought, she roused her husband and told him.

Captain Grierson jumped out of bed and consulted the racing guide and sporting papers, but no Limelight was entered for the race—in fact, there was no racehorse with such a name mentioned anywhere. So he backed his fancy, which came in last. But imagine his annoyance later when he found, on reading the name of the winner in the paper, in brackets after it the words: 'Renamed—formerly, Limelight'.

Like Captain Grierson, Archie Jarman failed to interpret correctly a dream when, for the only time in his life, he foresaw the name of a winner. It was during the night of 10 November 1947. He appeared to be standing between the beach at Brighton where he lived and a race track. As the horses approached, all except one, ridden by a man wearing dark colours, turned away and vanished into the sea.

Facing the stands, Jarman saw an outsize white board on posts bearing the figures '2-0-20'. The jockey and his mount were no longer in view, but they had obviously won the event. All around him, Jarman heard excited voices indicating that it was a popular win.

Next morning, Jarman called on business at the Richmond office of a firm of builders and in the course of conversation told its managing director, Mr M.B. Campbell, about the dream. They looked through the racing pages of a newspaper to see if the figures '2-0-20' corresponded with the statistical details of any runner that day, but found nothing.

What the two men had omitted to take into account was the horses' names. The 3.45 at Leicester was won by Twenty-Twenty ridden by Gordon Richards.

Peter Fairley, who was responsible for setting up the London Premonitions Bureau after the Aberfan disaster, obtains his racing foreknowledge not through dreams but through coincidences. In 1967, the morning of the Oaks, he unexpectedly received a letter from a lady named Pia, then he settled down with a book of short stories and found that the first one he read was about a Pia Linstrom. Until that day he had never heard the name Pia, so he took this as an omen and backed a filly of that name on which the odds were 100–7. It won.

Two years later, on the morning before the Derby, Blakeney, the surname of the Scarlet Pimpernel, was spoken by different people quite unconnectedly in Fairley's presence, so he backed a horse similarly named which won at 15–2. This made him watch out for other coincidences that he might turn into a loss for the bookmaker. Lunching at L'Escargot in Soho, he noticed that a horse bearing the same name as the restaurant was running in a race that afternoon, so he backed it and won at 33–1. For some time, he went on winning in this way until suddenly, for no apparent reason, he lost this gift.

Every year, the results of the Royal Ascot meeting in June were scanned by Wilfred Hyde White, the famous actor, to see if the vision that he had had there in 1935 had come true. One afternoon in 1935, a week before the traditional opening by the King, he and a friend visited the course. It should have been deserted, but to their surprise, on nearing the stands, they heard a murmur of voices, and from the Heath came hurdy-gurdy music and the shouting of tipsters. This was followed by the National Anthem announcing the arrival in the distance of the royal procession, and they heard a child cry out: 'Look, the lady isn't wearing a crown.'

Then, according to Wilfred Hyde White, something happened which made what they were experiencing distinctly uncanny. To quote his words:

A disembodied voice began to announce the runners and riders for the first race. I can't remember when this system was first introduced in Britain, but it was unheard of in 1935, and we listened in shocked amazement. More surprising still, the names of the horses were completely unfamiliar to us. I, who find it hard to memorize lines I have to speak in a play or film, can recall the name of every good horse which has run in England since I was a boy.

There was nothing to be seen—not a soul on the race course. Yet the voice called out: 'They're off!' and as the two men approached the rails they heard the thunder of hooves, the comments of an invisible crowd, and the voice giving the names of first, second, and third. The actor and his companion remained where they were, writing down the results of all the other races, and even heard the daily double, £183, announced. Then rain forced them to retreat to the cover of the stands and everything was quiet again.

When describing this experience Wilfred Hyde White stressed that both he and his friend afterwards compared their notes, which corresponded in every detail. They later reached the conclusion that they had somehow attended a race meeting of the future at which Queen Elizabeth II was present. The actor would never reveal the names of the horses, but he has left them behind in safe hands so that a watch can be kept to see whether his pre-audition ever turns into reality.

Wilfred Hyde White was deeply interested in the turf, but that is not essential to success in predicting winners. Maurice Woodruff, the clairvoyant, stressed that he had no interest at all in racing, yet he correctly foretold the Epsom Derby winners in 1962, 1963, and 1964. Once in America he was challenged by a reporter to forecast the result of the Kentucky Derby. Not knowing the names of any of the runners, he had no idea what to reply for a minute. Then, suddenly, he smelt a perfume. He looked around. There were no flowers in the room and no woman who could have been wearing perfume. He had to say something, so he said simply: 'I smell flowers.'

The reporter smiled and ran out of the room. Shortly afterwards, he reappeared and announced: 'I have put my shirt on Rosebowl.' Woodruff commented later: 'Rosebowl won...fortunately for me.'

Foretelling not merely the winner of the 1959 Kentucky Derby but also the names of the horses coming second and third, and doing this under the most stringent test conditions, was the crowning achievement of Spencer Thornton, the Nashville physician who became a reluctant predictor through studying the art of the illusionist with the intention of exposing fradulent mediums. The tricks he performed were so brilliant that many in his audiences believed him to be psychic despite all his denials. Then he was disconcerted to find that he and his wife could read each other's minds over a distance. If she willed him to telephone her, he automatically responded by doing so. When she went out shopping, he could telepathically persuade her to buy something he needed.

As part of Dr Thornton's demonstration of faked magic, he attempted to forecast a week in advance what headlines would be in the local papers on the day of his advertised show. At first he was wrong most of the time, but then, to his own astonishment, he started really seeing them, as if an illuminated shop sign were suddenly being switched on and off momentarily. He would glimpse a few words or see the actual event. He found that this happened when he was especially interested in the subject. Soon he was making predictions on the radio and on television with increasing accuracy.

Despite Spencer Thornton's successes, there remained a hard core of sceptics among the local people, so it was arranged for him to predict, under strict supervision, the first three horses in the Kentucky Derby to be run on Saturday 2 May 1959. Four days previously, he wrote down the names on a sheet of paper and this was sealed, unread, in an envelope and placed in a vault of the Third National Bank which could be unlocked only by a combination of three keys, kept by two vice-presidents and its custodian.

On Monday 4 May, the three men unlocked the vault, while Dr Thornton remained in the room leading to it, together with reporters and a press photographer. Bank Vice-President Granville Bourne tore open the envelope and read: 'Tommy Lee in a photo finish—Sword Dancer, Second—First Landing, Third.'

Pressed by the incredulous newsmen to explain how he had achieved so accurate a forecast, Dr Thornton told them that normally predictions occurred to him as thoughts but that now and again he saw a picture. In the case of the Kentucky Derby he did see 'some sort of a horse race in progress'. Then, half-way, the thought came to him that Tommy Lee would win. 'Immediately after, I got another thought—Sword Dancer. I couldn't figure out what it meant at first, but decided it would be Tommy Lee over Sword Dancer in a close one, and I made it a photo because that's as close as they came.'

Spencer Thornton's spectacular racing hat trick aroused tremendous interest, and it was not long before readers of the *Nashville Tennessean* learned over breakfast on Tuesday 23 June 1959 that Dr Thornton had agreed to predict what the front-page headline would be in the Thursday edition. That morning he wrote down his forecast, folded the paper, and handed it to Tim Dawson, a prominent member of the local Lions Club, who covered it in aluminium foil and put it in one envelope and then in another, both of which were sealed before being locked in the safe of another Lion.

On the Thursday, at a packed Club luncheon, the envelopes were opened by the chairman, who read out: 'I predict the biggest news on June 25 will be about a steel industry ultimatum to the union. This will overshadow all international news. I predict the *Tennessean*'s main headline will read: "STEEL THREATENS TO CLOSE."' Once again, the reluctant psychic was right.

Next morning on the paper's back page the editor, in paying tribute to Dr Thornton's remarkable achievement, described how the headline had been chosen just before the presses started to roll, and after an alternative one on quite another subject had been discarded.

But Dr Thornton's main interest in life was medicine, and ultimately he refused to make any more public predictions so as to concentrate on his practice.

Jeane Dixon claims to have foreseen the results of horse races on several occasions. She does not approve of using her gift for such a purpose, but feels it is excusable if the winnings are donated to a good cause. Visiting the Bowie race track in Maryland in May 1967 for the first time, as a guest, with her husband, Jimmy, of the chairman of the board of directors of the track and his wife, she was pressed to pick a winner and heard a soft soothing voice that seemed to come from above whispering in succession: 'Summer Sunshine.'

A horse of that name was running in the sixth event but it had never won a race in its life. The odds were 20–1. Jeane put all the money she had with her on Summer Sunshine. She spent her winnings on providing tuition, room, and board at Beckley College for a young black boy she was helping with his education.

Texan tycoon, H.L. Hunt relates how he first met Jeane Dixon in 1967 and accompanied her when she spoke to army officers' wives at Fort Myer, Virginia. Asked if she could predict which horse would win the Kentucky Derby the following Saturday, she replied: 'It will be Prince Clarion in the post position seven.' At the time this had not been decided, so the odds against the horse getting such a position were 13–1 since there were 14 runners.

Mr Hunt says that he watched the race on television and learned that a horse called Proud Clarion had been allotted post position seven. The horse won at odds of 30–1, so these multiplied by the 13–1 made the odds against the completion of the prediction — 390–1. Regretting that he had not backed Jeane's choice, Hunt phoned her in the New Year to ask who would win the Kentucky Derby in 1968.

'Wish I could tell you,' Jeane replied, 'but I can't. It's all so fuzzy...I can't get a thing. Something is wrong this year...there will be a mix-up of some sort.'

There was. The winner, Dancer's Image, was disqualified when it came out that he had been drugged to ease the pain in his ankle.

There is quite a case for believing that successful gamblers owe their success to their possessing, without realizing it, a precognitive gift. Dr Robert Brier of Professor Rhine's Parapsychology Laboratory at Duke University, North Carolina, was able to finance his researches with his regular winnings at roulette, according to Professor Thelma Moss of the psychology division of the UCLA Medical School. He explained to her that he tested students to discover whether any could predict when red or black would turn up on the roulette wheel. He found that some were lucky more often than not and others were just the opposite. Then he would take a few of each type at a time to Las Vegas and bet with the lucky ones and against the unlucky ones. The venture proved a success and Dr Brier found himself consistently in profit.

Professor Moss herself investigated the claims of a woman who, it seemed, could pick winners by passing a finger over the names of the horses running in races printed in newspapers although she had never studied form. Thelma Moss compared this woman's selections for a fortnight with those of a student who maintained that he had supported himself at college through his knowledge of racing, and also those of a graduate assistant who was neither precognitively gifted nor at home on the turf. The woman had won most by the end of the period, with the student and the graduate assistant trailing behind.

Elisabeth Tarb and her friend Janice Boughton, both medical students with an excellent record of success in precognitive experiments at Stanford Research Institute, tried in 1980 to foresee the result of the sixth race at Bay Meadows, which had six runners. Janice asked another person to select six objects as the targets for Elisabeth's remote viewing lest as questioner she might telepathically influence Elisabeth into choosing an object which she herself preferred to the others.

The experiment took place the evening prior to the race. The objects were numbered linking them with the six horses. It was impressed upon Elisabeth that at the finish of the race she would be asked to hold the object bearing the winner's number. She was then asked to describe what this would be. Concentrating on her task, she said that she saw something that was hard and spherical, resembling an apple in shape, and that she could see right through it. This was a very good description of a spherical apple-juice bottle, embossed round its edge with the design of an apple leaf and used to contain juice. It represented a horse named Shamgo running in the sixth race. This so excited the other students that they all bet on Shamgo, which won at 6–1.

It was the year of the American Presidential election, so Elisabeth Tarb and Janice Boughton decided to attempt an experiment on the same lines. Four objects were chosen, one representing a victory for Anderson, one for Carter, one for Reagan, and one for none of them winning. These were placed in separate boxes without Elisabeth being allowed to see them, and she was asked to describe which one she would be handed at midnight on election night. She predicted that it would be white, shaped like a cone, and hollow, with a string fixed to its tip, and looking as if made of shell.

This was easily identified by Janice as a description of a whistle in the Reagan box, and six weeks later, when voting was completed, Elisabeth was given the whistle to hold.

Charlie Chaplin in *My Autobiography* related how on many occasions he had premonitions that were fulfilled. Once he went into a bar at Biarritz with two companions, one of whom was the great tennis player Henri Cochet. There were gambling machines with three wheels, numbered from one to ten. Suddenly, the foretelling mood came over Chaplin, who announced that when he spun the three wheels, the first would stop at nine, the second at four, and the third at seven. They did—a million-to-one chance.

During the 1914–18 War some American lawyers in St Louis would meet to play poker. They included the well-known attorney L.C. Johnson, who dreamed one Wednesday night that the weekly game was in full swing and he had been losing all evening. Eventually on one deal he picked up his hand and found it to contain three kings, a knave, and an ace. This made him open the pot, and the betting was brisk. Finally came the draw. He discarded the ace and asked for one card. Picking up what was given him, he found it to be an ace, but as he looked at it the image gradually changed and finally became a jack, thus giving him a full house—three kings and a pair of knaves. In his dream he had won the pot, and it was a very good one.

On awakening from this vivid dream, Johnson immediately wrote down a detailed account of what he had experienced in his sleep and took it with him the following Saturday. Much to his astonished delight, all went as foreseen. Towards the end, he picked up his own hand, and the betting, too, conformed. But he did not see how the ace could possibly turn into a knave. All the same, when the time came for the draw, he discarded the ace and asked for one card. The rules of American poker state that a card falling on the table face upwards without being touched by the drawer is regarded as dead. The drawer then proceeds in regular order, and finally the player of the dead card is given another in its place. When Johnson asked for one, it was faced on being dealt to him and was an ace. The draw continued and at the finish he received a card in exchange for the faced card. It was a knave, fulfilling his dream. He then showed the other players the notes he had made on awakening.

Johnson later related his tale to Rodolphe Megroz, who included it in his collection *The Dream World*. The attorney added that for a long time following the episode none of his fellow poker players would bet against him on a hand unless he swore that he had not had another precognitive dream.

A New York researcher, Douglas Dean, suspected in the 1970s that certain top businessmen owed their prosperity to unconsciously foreseeing market trends, so he persuaded some of them to take part in an experiment. He asked them to predict what symbols would appear next as they operated one-armed bandits. He then compared their scores with the profits recorded on the previous year's balance sheets of their businesses. Dean found that those who correctly guessed the most symbols on the machines ran the most profitable concerns.

CHAPTER 16

Papal Prophecies

Malachy O'Morgair, better known as St Malachy, was born in Armagh in 1094 or 1095, became its Archbishop in 1132, and died at Clairvaux on All Souls Day, 1148 in the arms of St Bernard, who was his closest friend, and who wrote a book about him describing his miracles of healing the sick and the prophecies he made which were fulfilled, including the date of his own death. On an earlier visit to Clairvaux, St Malachy is reputed to have recorded in a state of semi-trance his predictions concerning future popes and to have given the manuscript to Pope Innocent II (1130–43) on a visit to the Vatican, where it lay forgotten in the archives until discovered in the sixteenth century. This consisted of 112 Latin mottoes meant to identify in turn the popes from Celestine II (1143–4) to the last pope of all.

The fact that these mottoes applied so aptly to the Popes prior to the discovery of the manuscript led to accusations that it was a forgery. The seventeenth-century Jesuit Father Menestrier suggested that the person responsible might have been a supporter of Cardinal Simoncelli who invented the motto *Ex antiquitate* as most applicable to Simoncelli of all the candidates at the conclave of 1590, as a result of which he was elected Pope Gregory XIV. But Menestrier's case was based only on rumours.

Certainly, since the sixteenth century, many of the 'tags' can be regarded as apposite, starting with Leo XI (1605) for whom the phrase translated from the original Latin goes: 'Like the wind he came and like the water he went', which sums up the reign of a pontiff lasting only 22 days. Apt, too, were 'Perverse people' for his successor, Paul V (1605–21), who had trouble with the Protestants; 'Guardian of the hills' for Alexander VII (1655–67), whose family's coat of arms depicted three hills with a star casting its rays over them; 'Of a good religious background' for Innocent XIII (1721–4), from the ranks of whose family had come several previous popes; 'Rose of Umbria' for Clement XIII (1758–69), who had been governor of Umbria, the emblem of which was a rose; 'Running bear' for Clement XIV (1769–75), whose coat of arms already bore one; 'Apostolic wanderer' sums up the latter days of Pius VI (1775–99), rendered a fugitive through the wars caused by the French Revolution; 'Rapacious eagle' has been regarded as referring to Napoleon's harassment of Pius VII (1800–23); and 'From Balnea in Etruria' is remarkably apt for Gregory XVI (1832–46), who prior to his election was a monk in a monastery there.

Several of the emblems on family coats of arms of popes correspond so faithfully with Malachy's mottoes that one wonders whether the Cardinals may have been unconsciously influenced into electing them popes. Leo XIII (1878–1903) bore on his shield a golden comet on an azure field, which agrees with the prophetic 'the light in the sky'. Clement XI (1700–21) was born in Urbino and its badge was a garland of flowers. As Malachy's suggestive phrase in his case was 'encircled by flowers', Clement adopted it for his motto as pope.

In this century *Religio depopulata* ('religion depopulated') was cruelly correct for Benedict XV, elected pontiff in 1914, but how could *Pastor et nauta* ('shepherd and sailor') apply to John XXIII? The ingenious have interpreted this as references to his shepherding his flock into new doctrinal pastures and to his links with the sea as Patriarch of Venice. Incidentally, whilst the conclave was being held which resulted in his election, someone started up the story that Cardinal Spellman of New York, influenced by the prophecies, had hired a boat, filled it with sheep, and sailed with them up and down the Tiber.

St Malachy's 'flower of flowers' has been regarded as alluding to the fleur-de-lis on the shield of the next pope, Paul VI, whilst the cryptic *De medietate lunae* ('from the half moon') was considered a prediction of his death on 28 September 1978, almost midway between the full moons of 16 September and 16 October. Others have pointed out that his surname, Luciano, means 'pale light', perhaps 'moonlight', and that he was born in Belluno—'beautiful moon'.

For the present pope, John Paul II, the Malachy motto is *De labore solis* ('from the toil of the sun'), which some have regarded as a reference to the hard physical work he did as a young man in his native Poland, when he was a labourer, and as one who never tired of climbing, hiking, canoeing, and skiing. Another translation of this motto could be 'of the eclipse of the sun'. Consulting the ephemiris for the date of his birth, 18 May 1920, we find that there was a total eclipse of the sun on that day and he was born at the exact hour of the eclipse. The moon having completed its conjunction with the sun at 27°, Taurus moved into Gemini next day.

The tag given to the next pope, *Gloria olivae* ('the glory of the olive'), suggests that he might prove to be a great peace-maker. Or there is an alternative interpretation. The Benedictines are also known as the Olivetans, and their founder, St Benedict, prophesised that before the end of the world one of his order will lead all Catholics to a great victory over the forces of evil. In 1976, a monk of this order, Basil Hume, Archbishop of Westminster, was elected a cardinal. Might he succeed the present pope?

The prophecies then cease with these words: 'During the final persecution of the Holy Roman Church there shall sit *Petrus Romanus* who shall feed the sheep amid great tribulations, and when these are past, the City of the Seven Hills shall be utterly destroyed and the awful judge will judge the people.' It should be noted that the Latin *Petrus Romanus* can be translated as either 'Peter of Rome' or the 'Roman rock'.

However, controversy has arisen over this prediction. There are grounds for believing that it may have been added later. Others maintain that St Malachy does not specifically state that no further popes will reign between 'The glory of the olive' and *Petrus Romanus*.

There have been popes, too, who have apparently possessed the gifts of clairvoyance and of prophecy. During the proceedings in 1928 for the canonization of Pope Pius IX (1846–78) it was proved that he had on many occasions predicted that Cardinal Pieri would succeed him, which came about. Once when a religious ceremony was taking place and a large candle was lit, Pius rose from his chair and ordered it to be put out at once. Afterwards they found that a terrorist had hidden an explosive cartridge in the handle which, had it exploded, would have caused havoc.

Another time, a woman appealing for an immediate audience with the Pope was admitted to his antechamber. Told about her plea, he said: 'I do not speak with the dead.' Taken aback by this unexpected response, and thinking that the Pope might have misheard, the chamberlain on duty repeated the message. But once again Pius answered: 'I do not speak with the dead.' When the chamberlain withdrew, he learned that in the interim the woman had collapsed and died from a heart attack. Later it was discovered that she had come with false credentials, planning to assassinate the Pope.

In support of the case for Pius IX's canonization, evidence was also produced of how, when two ladies begged him to bless a deaf and dumb child in the hope that it might restore those lost faculties, the Pope replied: 'Why ask me for this favour, the child is already cured.' The supplicants withdrew and found their charge happily chatting away with an attendant outside.

In 1909, when the General Chapter of the Franciscans were having a solemn audience with Pope Pius X, he suddenly seemed to go into a semi-trance and his head sank on to his chest for a few minutes. When he opened his eyes again there was horror in them, and he stood up crying: 'What I have seen was terrible. Will it be me or my successor? I don't know but I saw the Pope fleeing from the Vatican and priests carrying his body. Do not tell anyone while I am alive.' Then, five years later, just before he died, Pius X is supposed to have had another vision and to have told those with him at the time: 'I saw the Russians in Genoa.'

This pope was probably obsessed with the prophecies of the nineteenth-century monk and mystic Don Bosco, who had predicted: 'The horses of the Cossacks will drink at the fountain at St. Peter's.' It is therefore not surprising that since then the religious in Italy should have been influenced by such forecasts, especially after the revolution in Russia and the Communist take-over. In 1959, the superstitious were awed by Sister Elena Aiello when she predicted that armies from the Eastern bloc would sweep over Europe with Italy as their main target, and that the hammer and sickle would fly over the dome of St Peter's. Earlier she had warned Mussolini that Italy would be ignominiously defeated if it entered the war on Hitler's side.

CHAPTER 17

Prophecies from the Madonna

On 13 May 1917, three children, ten-year-old Lucia, nine-year-old Francisco, and seven-year-old Jacinta, were looking after sheep in a natural hollow known as the Cova da Iria near the village of Fatima, some 80 miles north of Lisbon. The previous year they had claimed to have enjoyed visions of an angel, but today, a Sunday and the Feast of the Ascension, something stranger was to happen. They reported that suddenly there was a startling flash of light. They gazed up into the unclouded blue sky, but could detect no signs of an approaching storm. A second flash drew their attention to a dazzling light coming from a sapling oak, and there stood a beautiful Lady wearing a white mantle and holding a rosary of diamond-like brilliance. She told them not to be afraid for she would not harm them, and when asked where she came from she replied: 'I am from Heaven.'

'What do you want of us?' Lucia stammered, and the vision replied: 'I came to ask you to come here on the thirteenth day of the next six months at this same time, and then I will tell you who I am and what I want.' Later, the Lady rose into a globe of light which disappeared, into the eastern sky.

When the children told their parents about their experience, they were met with disbelief, while the neighbours ridiculed and even spat upon them. On the morning of 13 June, only a few curious villagers accompanied the trio to the small holm oak. At noon, the onlookers were astonished to see a small white cloud of light float down from the sky and hover over the tree where the children were kneeling, who alone were able to see the apparition. The Lady asked Lucia to learn to read as she would remain on earth for some time, but Francisco and Jacinta were not to be there much longer—a prediction that was fulfilled.

When the Lady departed, it was as on the previous occasion, and the villagers present claimed to have heard a sound like a rocket and to have seen a little cloud of light vanish into the sky. They also told their friends on returning home that the leaves of the holm oak were bent in the direction that the Lady had taken, as if what she had been wearing had brushed against them.

The news spread, of course, with the result that some 5,000 people gathered round the holm oak on 13 July, when the little white cloud phenomenon was repeated. Lucia was emboldened to ask the Lady who she was, and if she would perform a miracle so that others would believe that she was appearing to her. The Lady replied: 'Continue to come here every month. In October, I will tell you who I am and what I want. And I will perform a miracle so that everyone may see and believe.' She went on to predict that the World War then in progress would end soon. 'But if people do not stop offending God, another, even worse, will begin in the reign of Pius XI. When you see a night illuminated by an unknown light, know that it is the great sign that God gives you that He is going to punish the world by means of war, hunger and persecution of the Church.' Lucia went white and cried out in fear at what the Lady told her next. Afterwards, when questioned as to why she had reacted in this way, Lucia replied that it was a close secret, 'good for some, but bad for others', which she must not disclose.

Regarding the prediction of a Second World War breaking out when Pius XI would be pope, it was pointed out to Lucia in later life that he died on 10 February 1939, and that Pius XII was reigning when England and France declared war on Germany on 3 September 1939. Lucia, however, took the view that the war dated from the invasion of Austria in 1938 and claimed that Pius XI had said so. The 'unknown light' that was to be 'the great sign' occurred on the night of 25 January 1938, when the skies in the northern hemisphere were filled with a crimson light like, as one newspaper put it, 'a reflection of the fires of hell'. The superstitious were terrified, expecting the end of the world. The *New York Times* devoted nearly a page to the strange light with the headlines 'Aurora Borealis Startles Europe—People Flee in Fear'.

Following the vision of 13 July 1917, the children aroused the hostility of the anti-clerical government which since the 1910 revolution had been bent on destroying all forms of religion in Portugal. On 13 August, all three were arrested and were told they would be thrown into a cauldron of boiling oil unless they publicly recanted and said they had been lying; but they refused to be intimidated, nor would Lucia reveal the secret prophecy the Lady had entrusted to her. Meanwhile, some 15,000 people had assembled at the Cova da Iria waiting in vain for the children. They saw the usual small white cloud of light appear from the east and hover for a time over the oak, then it went away and the crowd dispersed.

The whole country had become fascinated by the subject, and an ecclesiastic experienced in such matters was sent by the Catholic Church to investigate. In France, in 1846, two shepherdesses aged 11 and 15, Maximine Giraud and Mélanie Calvar, had claimed to have had similar visions, and he questioned Lucia's mother as to whether she had told the girl about the appearences at La Salette. She had, so he wondered whether that might have caused the trio to invent their own phenomena. Lucia insisted that everything they had said was true.

As 13 October drew near, worldwide attention was focused on the Cova da Iria. The Communist-controlled press in Portugal ridiculed the children, predicting that no miracle would occur, thus finally discrediting religion. The authorities did send soldiers to try and prevent the sightseers from reaching the Cova, but they were too few to hold back the estimated 70,000 people who converged on the spot.

Next day, accounts of what happened appeared in the *Diario de Noticias*, the newspaper with the largest circulation in Portugal, and in another government paper, *O Seculo*. The country's most respected and impartial journalists concluded that what they and other reporters had witnessed could only be described as a miracle. Avelino de Almeida followed his report in *O Seculo* with a further account at the request of a friend in *Illustração Portuguesa* of 29 October 1917. The skies had been overcast since dawn and at 10 o'clock it started to pour with rain in earnest. Then, at the hour foretold, the rain stopped.

The dense mass of clouds parted, and the sun—like a shining disc of dull silver—appeared at its full zenith, and began to whirl around in a wild and violent dance, that a large number of people likened to a carnival display, with such lovely glowing colours passing successively over the sun's surface. A miracle, as the crowd cried out; or a natural phenomenon, as the learned say?

It could not have been a case of collective hallucination, because the phenomenon was witnessed over an area of 600 miles by all sorts of people, including intellectuals and atheists who had kept away from the Cova. The scientist Professor Frederico Oom, director of the Lisbon Observatory, wrote in *O Seculo*:

If it were a cosmic phenomenon, astronomical and meteorological observatories would not have failed to record it. And this is precisely what is missing: that inevitable recording of all the disturbances in the world system, no matter how small they may be.

Quoted in Francis Johnson's book *Fatima: The Great Sign* is the evidence of another eye witness of unimpeachable credentials. Dr Joseph Garrett, professor of natural sciences at Coimbra University, wrote how, when he arrived in Fatima at midday, it was still raining heavily with no signs of stopping and the earth was like a quagmire.

It must have been about half past one when there rose up, on the precise spot where the children were, a pillar of smoke, a delicate, slender, bluish column that went straight up to about two metres, perhaps, above their heads and then evaporated. The phenomenon lasted for some seconds and was perfectly visible to the naked eye. It was repeated yet a second and a third time. On these three occasions, and especially on the last one, the slender posts stood out distinctly in the dull grey atmosphere.

While I continued looking at the place of the apparitions ... with diminishing curiosity, because a long time had passed without anything to excite my attention, I heard a shout from the thousands of voices ... The sun, a few moments before, had broken through the thick layer of clouds that hid it and shone clearly and intensely. I veered towards the magnet which seemed to be drawing all eyes and saw it as a disc with clear-cut rim, luminous and shining, but which did not hurt the eyes ...

It looked like a glazed circular piece cut from a mother-of-pearl shell ... It could not be confused either with the sun seen through fog (for there was no fog at the time), because it was not opaque, diffused or veiled ... The sky was mottled with light cirrhus clouds, the blue coming through here and there, but sometimes the sun stood out in patches of clear sky ... It was a remarkable fact that one could fix one's eyes on this brazier of heat and light without any pain in the eyes or blinding of the retina ... The sun's disc did not remain immobile. This was not the sparkling of a heavenly body, for it spun round on itself in a mad whirl, when suddenly a clamour was heard from all the people. The sun, whirling, seemed to loosen itself from the firmament and advance threateningly upon the earth as if to crush us with its huge fiery weight.

During this solar phenomenon, there were changes of colour in the atmosphere ... Looking at the sun, I noticed that everything around was becoming darkened ... I saw everything an amethyst colour. Objects around me, the sky and the atmosphere were of the same colour. Fearing that I was suffering from an affection of the retina, I turned away and shut my eyes, keeping my hands over them to intercept the light. With my back still turned, I opened my eyes and saw that the landscape was the same purple colour as before ... Soon after, I heard a peasant near me shout: 'Look, that lady is all yellow!' In fact, everything both near and far, had changed, taking on the colour of old yellow damask ... All these phenomena which I have described were observed by me in a calm state of mind. It is for others to interpret and explain them.

Scientists ever since have been puzzled by the 'miracle' at Fatima and unable to find a convincing explanation.

A few years later, Lucia became a Carmelite nun at Coimbra. The 'great secret' was written down at her dictation and kept under lock and key by the Bishop at Leiria. According to Sister Lucia, the Lady had said that the secret could be revealed in 1960. The document was then taken to the Pope in Rome, but he decided not to reveal its contents. The *Neues Europa* of Stuttgart, however, published what they alleged was the text, obtained in a roundabout way. This read:

A great punishment shall fall on the entire human race in the second half of the twentieth century. The human race has sinned ... In no part of the world is life in order. Satan rules in the highest position, laying down how things should be done. He will eventually succeed in seducing the spirits of the great scientists who invent the arms, which in ten minutes could easily wipe out all humanity. He will have under his power the rulers who govern the people and will help them to make an enormous quantity of these arms.

For the Church, too, the time of its greatest trial will come. Cardinals will oppose cardinals and bishops bishops. Satan will march in their midst and there will be great changes at Rome. What is rotten will fall, never to rise again. The Church will be darkened and the world will shake with terror...

Since Fatima there have been many alleged appearances of the Virgin Mary to children in Catholic countries, but none have been accompanied by any spectacular miracles like that of the sun at Fatima. In the Spanish village of San Sebastian de Garabandal in June 1961, Conchita, Maria Dolores, Jacinta, and Maria Cruz claimed to have had a vision of the Virgin Mary and also of the Archangel Michael. Further apparitions followed of both, according to Conchita, the last being on 13 December 1965. The messages were along the same lines as those at Fatima. There would be a miracle, the form of which had to be kept secret and which the girl could only reveal eight days beforehand. It would occur at half-past eight in the evening on a Thursday to coincide with the feast of a holy martyr, and be the greatest ever to be seen in the world, and could be filmed and shown on television. Repeated warnings were also given. People everywhere had been perverted. Many priests, bishops, and cardinals were on the road to perdition taking others with them. They were attaching less and less importance to the Eucharist. If they repented, God would forgive them. Otherwise, there would be a terrible punishment. Conchita said she had been given a vision of this, adding: 'I can assure you that it is worse than if one were surrounded by fire, worse than if one had fire above and below one. I do not know how long it will be before God sends it after having performed the miracle.' The people of San Sebastian de Garabandal are still awaiting the latter event.

In Italy alone, between 1944 and 1972, apparitions of the Virgin Mary were reported from all over the country—in Rome at the Grotto of the Three Fountains, at Montichiari's Little Fountain, at Syracuse where the Madonna of Tears was seen, and at no fewer than 22 other locations.

Some four and a half million people have visited the remote village of Medjugorje in the republic of Bosnia Herzegovina, Yugoslavia, since the summer of 1981. Here the Croatian farming community is staunchly Catholic. It all began when

Ivanka Ivankovic and Mirjana Dragicevic, aged 15 and 16 respectively, went for a walk in the late afternoon on the Feast of St John the Baptist and were astonished to experience a vision of the Madonna dressed in grey and with a white veil, floating on a cloud above a hilltop. Not knowing what to think, they returned home, and later were joined by Ivan Dragicevic and Vicka Ivankovic, both aged 16, who also saw the apparition. Next day they came back again, accompanied by curious relatives and friends, and with them were Marija Pavlovic, aged 16, and Jakov Colo, aged 10, who claimed that they too could see the Madonna.

On the days that followed, the six teenagers ventured up the hill and the Madonna began to speak to them in Croatian. She announced that she was the Blessed Virgin Mary and was appearing to them because they were true believers. The parish priest, Father Jozo Zovko, was away and his assistant, Father Ivan Dugandzic, feared that they were suffering from hallucinations caused by drugs. They were taken away to be examined by doctors and questioned by the police. Soon thousands of devout Catholics flocked daily to watch the young people in ecstasy. Government observers suspected that it was a Fascist plot in religious disguise. On 1 July, the police arrived, broke up the crowds, and tried to take the teenagers into custody, but they fled.

Father Zovko had returned from retreat and was in the church, praying for guidance. He says he heard a voice saying: 'Go and protect the children.' He went to the door and found them pleading for him to hide them, which he did in a room in the presbytery. That evening they had their visitation from the Virgin there as usual. From then onwards, the local people would pack the church, and during the Mass she appeared and through the teenagers called for world peace and urged the faithful to confess their sins and fast each week on bread and water.

On 17 August, the police arrested Father Zovko on the grounds that he had been undermining the state's authority, and he was sentenced to three years' imprisonment. Pavio Zanic, the Bishop of Mostar, was in a difficult position. He visited Medjugorje several times and was impressed with the six young visionaries, but advised extreme caution. He appointed a commission to investigate their claims. Despite his misgivings, the apparitions went on. By now, the

Madonna was confiding 10 secrets to each teenager, which included warnings of future world chastisements. The West, she said, had advanced civilization but had lost God. She prophesied that Russia would come 'to glorify the name of the Lord', and promised that when the apparitions ended a visible sign would be left on the hill where she had first appeared.

On Christmas Day 1982, Mirjana received her tenth and last secret. Her apparitions were now over, though the Madonna consoled her by promising to appear on her birthday and at times of special need. Mirjana was leaving to become a student of agriculture at the University of Sarajevo.

Though the theological commission had not made up its mind about the visions, thousands of believers were still pouring into the parish looking to the visionaries for inspiration and instruction. The new priest, Father Tomislav Pervan, mounted a spirited defence of the apparitions. Distinguished visitors, many of them from Rome, came to look into the events for themselves, and the teenagers were submitted to new medical and psychological tests. They were found to be healthy and sane. The results also suggested that they could not be deliberately lying. Some took this as confirmation that the visions were authentic. Others pointed out that the fact that the teenagers' experience was genuine could not confirm or deny that the Virgin Mary was causing it. The visionaries' testimonies were collected and written up by visiting scholars, journalists, and theologians.

Most reports carried stories of other unusual phenomena which had been observed in the parish. A stone cross stands on a hill opposite that where the apparitions occurred. It was erected in 1933 and is the focus of an annual pilgrimage in September. People claim to have seen it change into a column of light or into a form like that of the Madonna herself. Others say they have taken photographs which seem to reveal a glimpse of a supernatural presence. Many people claim to have been able to look into the sun and to have seen it dancing—as on the last day of the apparitions at Fatima. As at Lourdes, there was evidence of inexplicable healings.

Eventually, after long delays, the Bishop's commission ended their deliberations, but no report was ever published. Rumour had it however, that they regarded the apparitions as false. The Bishop forbade the teenagers to continue using the church. However, thanks to Father Pervan, they were allowed to hold their daily tryst with the Madonna in a study bedroom in the presbytery. Two younger girls in the village were now claiming to have visions. The original group was breaking up. They said the Madonna would like Ivan to become a priest and the others nuns, but nevertheless left it to them to choose their way of life. Ivan's visions were suspended while he did his military service. Ivanka married in December 1986 and no longer sees apparitions. The other three, Vicka, Marija, and Jakov, still live in Medjugorje and experience them. Marija intends to become a nun. BBC television first showed an excellent documentary on *The Madonna of Medjugorje* in their *Everyman* series on 8 February 1987.

Silent apparitions of the Virgin Mary were reported in Cairo in the 1970s, and present-day ones in Kinebo, Uganda. Like everything else in life, imitation in this field can be carried to absurd lengths. In June 1979, *Fate* magazine quoted a report from the Colombian Agriculture Institute stating that they had been given a hen's egg by a peasant woman living in Tebalda, near Bogatá, who found it in her chicken coop in March 1979. The shell of the egg had raised letters that translate as: 'FINAL JUDGEMENT. REPENT. GOD.' *Fate* commented: 'The chicken coop is likely to become a shrine.'

CHAPTER 18

The Rhines and Precognition

In 1932, at his Parapsychology Laboratory at Duke University, North Carolina, Professor J.B. Rhine started experiments in what he termed extra-sensory perception using Zener cards, each pack of 25 containing equal numbers of cards printed with a circle, a cross, a star, a square, or wavy lines.

Various techniques were employed at first. In the 'Basic' technique, a pack would be shuffled, cut, and placed face downward by the tester. The subject tried to guess the first card, which was afterwards put in a separate pile. He then proceeded to do the same in turn with all the other cards. Occasionally, subjects themselves would take the cards from the shuffled and cut pack, hold each face downward, try to guess it, and then lay it in a second pile.

In the 'Down Through' technique, the subject attempted to guess the cards from top to bottom without touching the pack after it had been prepared in the usual way by the tester.

By chance alone, using these techniques, the subject should score an average of five correct guesses in a run of 25 cards. Any scoring over five would make a strong case for telepathy.

The third technique, 'Pure Telepathy', did without the cards. A second person thought of the five Zener symbols in a certain order, and the subject called out his or her guesses.

In his famous book *Extra-Sensory Perception*, first published in 1934, Professor Rhine claimed that he had demonstrated the existence of telepathy by his experiments with these Zener symbols.

That same year, Samuel G. Soal, lecturer in mathematics at Queen Mary College, London, began a similar project, but after spending four years testing 160 persons and assembling a total of nearly 130,000 guesses, the scoring was no better than might be expected through chance.

About the same time as Soal had reached this disappointing conclusion, another researcher, Whately Carington, had been experimenting with drawings. He selected at random from a dictionary a word which could be illustrated by a drawing, which he then pinned up in a curtained room at Cambridge from 7 p.m. to 9 a.m. next day and concentrated his attention on it exclusively for an arranged period of time. A number of percipients living in various parts of the country were asked to send sketches of their impressions of the different drawings exposed on each of 10 successive evenings. The original drawings with those made by the percipients were submitted to an independent judge for comparison.

A series of such experiments, each group consisting of 10 exposures and separated by several weeks, were carried out. It was found that the drawing made on any particular night might not show any significant resemblance to the original displayed on that night, but that the drawings on the 10 nights taken as a whole resembled the 10 originals of that group more than they did the originals of the other groups.

This suggested that the percipients sketching their impressions were often influenced by the original exposed on the previous night or by that which was to be exposed on the next night or, in some cases, the night after that. Carington therefore working independently, and using drawings instead of cards had obtained strong evidence for precognition.

Carington, who was a friend of Soal's, wondered if the apparent failure of the latter's card-guessing experiments was due to the fact that in every case, through concentrating on telepathy, he had looked for *direct* hits and had not investigated the possibility that percipients were in some cases affected by 'time displacement'.

Dr Soal wrote later:

With remarkable pertinacity Mr. Carington insisted that I should re-examine my experimental data. He suggested that I should compare each guess, not with the card for which it was originally intended but with the immediately preceding and the immediately following card and count up the hits. For, according to Mr.

Carington, the faculty of extra-sensory cognition might not always succeed in hitting the object at which it was aimed. Just as a rifleman may show a personal bias which causes him persistently to strike the target at a point to the left or right of the bull's eye, so might it happen that the guesser at E.S.P. cards all unwittingly was guessing correctly—not the card the experimenter was looking at—but a card which was one or two places earlier or later in the sequence. It was, however, in no very hopeful spirit that I began the task of searching my records for this 'displacement' effect. And yet within a few weeks, I had made two quite remarkable finds, which fully confirmed Carington's conjectures. From my records of the guesses of 160 persons, I had discovered two whose results exhibited the kind of effect anticipated by Carington.

One of the two percipients to whom Soal referred was a photographer, Basil Shackleton, who had demonstrated an impressive talent for precognitively describing the card that was about to be chosen. This led to Soal's embarking on a lengthy programme of tests with Shackleton that confirmed his ability to make correct precognitive guesses at a rate far above what might be expected through chance. The tests were done between 1936 and 1943 in London, with Soal replacing Zener cards by his own, depicting five vividly coloured animals. In one series, Shackleton scored 1,101 out of 3,789, about which success Lyall Watson in *Supernature* later commented that one could not get a result like this by chance 'even if the entire population of the world had tried the experiment every day since the beginning of the Tertiary period, sixty million years ago'.

Unfortunately, following Dr Soal's death, examination of the original records has shown that in the latter tests he 'touched them up' to make Shackleton's results better than they were.

Meanwhile, in his Parapsychology Laboratory in North Carolina, encouraged by Whately Carington's discovery of 'time displacement', Professor Rhine embarked on successful precognitive experiments. In his book *The Reach of the Mind*, published in 1947, he wrote:

The conception that the mind might transcend time limitations followed as a natural consequence of the distance tests with E.S.P. For if E.S.P. was space-free, it must also be time-free within our space-time universe of physics. Time is a function of spatial change—that is, physical movement in space requires time, hence to be out of space is to be out of time as well. Perception of past or future events was therefore in line with the perception of distant happenings.

The most important achievements of Professor Rhine's work were, first, to establish that percipients could score not only when the Zener cards and other target materials were known to agents, but also when neither agent nor any other person knew the target order, thus providing evidence for clairvoyance (direct knowledge of some external physical source).

Later, programmes were conducted to ascertain whether such perception could take place only when the targets in question were in existence at the time of the test, or whether they could be accurately identified *before* they were actually selected, which would be so if the mind had precognitive powers. In these experiments, percipients predicted the order in which a deck of cards would be dealt later after being mechanically shuffled. These more difficult tests also produced evidence favourable to the case for precognition.

The Second World War slowed the work of the Parapsychology Laboratory when most of the male staff left for military service. Professor Rhine carried on with the assistance of women experimenters. When peace was restored, Rhine decided that in order to revive interest in the subject the more active co-operation of the general public should be encouraged. People had already without any prompting sent in accounts of their own personal experiences. Rhine decided that instead of merely filing these voluntary contributions they should be studied, and that something ought to be done to show that there was a place for anecdotal evidence of precognition as well as the experimental kind in contemporary research.

In an editorial headed 'The Value of Reports of Spontaneous PSI Experiences' in the *Journal of Parapsychology*, Rhine stated that it was impossible to authenticate each spontaneous happening so as to be sure that all the particulars given were correct and that the desired interpretation of the experience was the only possible one. The material could suggest an extra-sensory method of obtaining information but it could not prove it. Nevertheless, it was because of the questions raised by spontaneous experiences that experimental investigations had begun, and they were still of value.

Ideally, Rhine believed, the kind of spontaneous experiences that had led to experimentation ought to have been kept in mind as research proceeded. Regrettably, they had been disregarded, and he believed that experimenters must go back to them for a fresh outlook. 'And while we are no longer concerned with the original problem of E.S.P. occurrence, the very same types of experience that led to the original experiments in telepathy and clairvoyance may now be of service again in giving us clues as to the nature of these capacities.'

This led to the publication in 1981 of *The Invisible Picture: A Study of Psychic Experience* by Professor Rhine's wife, Louisa. In a foreword, she wrote that her book was a factual account of 10 years spent probing into a great many cases where people appeared to have had psychic experiences. Her purpose was to attempt to explain them. She was and remained a strong believer in the experimental method of modern science as the most dependable way of ascertaining the truth. She had been suspicious of the anecdotal methods of research employed in the past. Nevertheless, she had felt it important to undertake a thorough appraisal of anecdotal phenomena.

In the book, Dr Louisa Rhine maintains that until tests for precognition began to be made in 1933 at the Parapsychology Laboratory, it was not thought to occur amongst most people. Experiments had soon indicated that those who showed signs of being clairvoyant also possessed precognitive ability. Once this was discovered, wrote Dr Rhine, it became evident that everybody was endowed with latent precognitive powers. Those taking part in these tests were mainly university students who until then had no idea that they could apparently see into the future on occasion.

There had been an excellent response from the public to Dr Rhine's appeal for accounts of precognitive dreams. They varied widely in subject matter and importance. It is when a warning affects oneself or one's family that attention is most likely to be paid to it.

In 1932, at the start of the Depression which saw the collapse of so many financial institutions, a woman in Washington DC, dreamed that she saw a man shoot himself in

the temple. He was behind bars, which made her think he
was in a gaol. When she told her husband about it next morning, he merely laughed. Then, suddenly, she saw the scene
again more clearly. It was not a gaol, but the cage occupied
by the president of the bank where they kept all their sav-
ings. As they had no other assets and had three small children to bring up, she became alarmed and told her husband
that he must go to the bank at once and withdraw every cent.
At first the man scoffed at the suggestion, but his wife got
into such a state that in the end he did as she asked. Just
as he was about to leave the bank, the police arrived, and
the president shot himself. He had embezzled the deposi-
tors' money.

Most of the striking dreams came true almost at once. A
woman dreamed one night of two boys fishing. She saw one
shoot the other dead with a rifle and his body then being
carried to a local store she recognized, where it was placed
in a large wooden box. Next day, her brother-in-law visited
the store in question, and on his return he told her that a
small boy had been killed in a shooting affray. She interrupted him by saying that the body had been taken into the
store and put in a large wooden box. Astonished, he asked
how she knew and she explained.

These dreams, Dr Rhine stressed, were not limited to accidents and other violent events, but included trivial happenings as well. In some cases, where fulfilment did not occur
until some time later, the supporting evidence consisted of
a written account of the dream's contents made the morning after.

A warning dream reported by a woman in North Carolina related how she had been very close to her mother, who
had died when the daughter was 12. Years later, grown up
and out shopping, she noticed someone ahead of her dressed
exactly like her mother, but she then lost sight of the woman
in the crowd. A short while later, midway across Main Street,
she heard her mother's voice cry: 'Harriet, Harriet, look out!'
She glanced about her. There was no woman anywhere in
the vicinity, but making straight for her was a street-car.
Springing back, she avoided death by a few inches.

Another, similar warning occurred in the case of a young
woman who was going along a street with her husband
when they both heard a female voice shout 'Mina!' Startled

by the urgency with which her name had been uttered, the young woman seized her husband's arm and held him back. Hardly had she done so than there was a shattering explosion from the spot where they would have been had they not stopped. An enormous block of cement had dropped from high up on a building.

Dr Rhine quotes this as an example of a case where the warning voice was not recognized by the percipient. She goes on to state that out of 188 accounts sent to her where precognitive messages were received from living persons, there was only one where the communication was a warning. This concerned a man at the wheel of a truck travelling to Long Island. Towards 3 a.m. he became very drowsy and was abruptly roused by his mother's voice ordering him to take care just as she used to do when he was a boy. As he looked ahead, he braked in near-panic, for the bonnet of the lorry was only a couple of feet away from the wall of an overpass. He would undoubtedly have been killed had he not awoken in time to avoid crashing into it. His mother, who sent in details of the incident, claimed to have been completely ignorant of her son's near-escape from death until he told her how he owed his life to her warning voice.

Louisa Rhine found that from the start of her project of case collecting, the folder for precognitive dreams filled up faster than any others. This confirmed the conclusion reached by the English psychical researcher Dr D.J. West, who had written in 1944: 'The precognitive dream is by far the commonest reported psychical incident at the present time.' He thought that this was because people had become more interested in dreams since Freud.

According to Dr Rhine, experimenters were reaching the conclusion that the contemporaneous kind of dream (both clairvoyant and telepathic) and precognitive dreams were just different forms of a single talent of the mind to obtain information independently of the known senses. If precognitive dreams were so prevalent, the phenomenon needed explanation. 'And so, with this to explain and also because no study of precognitive experiences had been made since the experimental establishment of precognition, I decided to make one, using the cases in the collection.' Her general objective would be to see if any difference could be shown between the precognitive and the contemporaneous types of cases except that of timing. It was necessary to bear in mind that a dream was often not found to be precognitive until much later. For instance, a New York woman reported how she had dreamed that soldiers bearing rifles were patrolling the refinery where she was employed. There was a tense, excited feeling about the place. She saw herself being driven to the office in a taxi with a soldier on either side standing on the running board. Almost a year later, the dream came true when there was a strike and soldiers moved in to break it.

In another case, a woman from Oklahoma wrote that during the war she dreamed one night that she saw a bomber from a nearby airfield flying alone and suddenly crashing nose first into the ground, killing the entire crew. Next morning, she realized that her dream must have been a telepathic one when she saw in a newspaper a photograph of the wrecked plane complete with a description of the disaster. The plane must have crashed as she was dreaming about it, and the details of the crash corresponded with those contained in the dream.

Dr Rhine states that since 1947 they had received 3,290 cases for study, 1,324 of which were precognitive, and 75 per cent of these were dreams and the rest waking experiences; 60 per cent of the precognitive experiences were realistic. There were 433 cases in which the foreseen events were such that the percipients presumably would have wanted to prevent their happening. In fact, however, almost two-thirds of these percipients made no attempt to do so. An example of this occurred in 1950 in the naval aviation school in Pensacola, Florida.

A young cadet, 'A', dreamed of another cadet, 'B', a complete stranger, who was flying in a training plane when he crashed in a field of mud unlike any at the school and was decapitated. 'A' was very upset for some time after awakening. Five months later, he was transferred to another school for special training, and the first day there he came across the cadet 'B' of his dream and took an instant dislike to him.

Almost a year later, 'B' was killed and mutilated when his plane crashed on a flat muddy plain like the one in the dream. 'A' wrote to the Parapsychology Laboratory what an emotional shock this gave him. 'I sometimes shudder today when I wonder if it might have ended differently had

I swallowed my pride and given a warning before it was too late.'

After eliminating from the survey such cases where no attempt to intervene was made, only 162 remained in which the percipient attempted to stop the event from taking place, so Dr Rhine added 29 cases from the older archives. In 60 cases out of the total of 191, the attempt to prevent the disaster from happening did not succeed. This was in most instances because the warning details received were inadequate and the attempt to prevent the disaster consequently futile.

Sometimes, even when the warning details could be regarded as adequate, a catastrophe could not be avoided. A woman in Oregon woke up one morning with a terrible feeling that her three-year-old son would be seriously injured in a motor accident. She never let him out of her sight for a time, then, as the fear would not leave her, she drove with the child to her mother's house several miles away, taking the greatest care. Having arrived safely, she was immensely relieved. Then, shortly afterwards, there was an urgent ring at the front door, and when she opened it there stood a policeman carrying the unconscious boy, who had been sitting beneath a tree in the yard when a runaway car had jumped the curb and struck him. The mother ended her account: 'How he got out of the house unnoticed is a mystery. But evidently it was to be.'

On the other hand, a man in Illinois claimed that he had had many precognitive dreams that had been fulfilled. He reported how, having dreamed of two men breaking through the doors of his trailer home, which faced the highway, he thought he would 'change the dream' by turning the trailer to face the other way. This involved heavy work moving its contents out and in again as well as altering the plumbing and electrical fixtures. Several years had passed without his trailer being attacked, but as there was no evidence to suggest that an attack had been planned, the dream could not be regarded as precognitive.

Here is one of Dr Rhine's examples where a warning dream made a Californian wife more alert and able to avoid a catastrophe. In it, she saw her husband writhing on the ground after being electrocuted when the television antenna, which he and a friend in green overalls were dismantling, fell on to some electric wires. She described the dream to her husband and tried to persuade him not to proceed with removing the antenna as he intended to do, but he merely laughed and went ahead. With the assistance of a friend wearing green overalls he set to work, but when a strong wind blew down the antenna, they remembered the dream in time and pushed the antenna in the opposite direction.

Commenting on this and similar cases, Dr Rhine stressed that they did not imply that precognized disasters could be prevented from taking place. To prove that, it would be essential to establish in some detail that the warning was precognitive and not telepathic or clairvoyant, and that the preventive steps taken were as a direct consequence of the experience and not ones that would have been employed without it.

For instance, in the following example the girl might have telepathically contacted the unconscious mind of the criminal. She was living with her family in the country and planned to visit the city where they owned a house, sleep there, and return to the country the following day. The night before doing this, she dreamed she was in bed in the city and was roused by a man who was attempting to strangle her. She woke up panic-stricken, but pulling herself together set out in the morning. Then, midway to the city, she let fear get the better of her and travelled back home. Next morning, the police phoned her parents to tell them that the unoccupied house had been burgled the previous night.

The explanation in another case might be psychokinesis, movement caused by the mother subconsciously. She dreamed one night that a large chandelier suspended over her baby's cot in the nursery suddenly broke away from its ceiling fixture and collapsed, killing the child. She saw her husband and herself surrounded by the debris while outside wind and rain lashed against the window panes. She noticed that the hands on a clock showed the time as 4.35 a.m.

The woman woke and roused her husband, but he was not alarmed by her account of the nightmare and, advising her to put it out of her mind and go back to sleep, did the same himself. But she was too upset to do more than doze. Eventually, unable to rest, she hurried into the nursery, took up the baby, and brought her into the bedroom. On looking out of the window, she noticed that it was a clear, quiet night outside with a full moon, just the opposite to what it had been in the dream. This calmed her, but all the same she did not return the infant to the nursery.

Some two hours had gone by when both parents were startled out of their slumbers by a tremendous crash coming from the nursery. Rushing in, they discovered that the chandelier had fallen on to the cot. Had the baby been there still, it would have been crushed to death. The mother stared at the clock. It was 4.35 a.m. And outside the wind howled and the rain pelted against the panes.

After carefully scrutinizing the 131 cases of apparent precognition where percipients tried to prevent the disaster from taking place, Dr Rhine rated nine of them as the most convincing.

There was the mother in New York who dreamed she heard a scream and saw her two-year-old son fall from an open window. This was followed by an ambulance siren approaching the house. Scared, she hardly let the boy out of her sight for the next two days. Then she placed his mattress on the window ledge to air it and pulled down the frame to hold it secure. She was tidying the next room when suddenly she remembered the nightmare and ran back to find that the child had succeeded in raising the frame and had crawled out. She seized him just as he was about to tumble down after the mattress. Although Dr Rhine does not suggest it, psychokinesis might also be the explanation in this case.

Dr Rhine regarded the following as the most impressive of the nine cases. A street-car conductor in Los Angeles dreamed that, travelling south, he drew into an intersection on his usual route, just by a one-way exit for other traffic. At this intersection, motorists occasionally broke the law by crossing both the north- and south-bound street-car tracks and making a left-hand turn.

In the dream, as the conductor crossed the intersection, a no. 5 north-bound street-car passed him. He waved at its driver, and then, without any warning, a large truck painted bright red made an illegal left-hand turn and cut in front of him. The other street-car had screened the exit from his sight, and the irresponsible truck-driver failed to see his street-car for the same reason. There was a shattering collision. Passengers were hurled from their seats; the truck toppled over, and out of it fell two dead men and a woman hysterical from her injuries. Still dreaming, the conductor saw himself approach her, and she stared at him with the biggest blue eyes he had ever seen and shrieked: 'You could have avoided this.'

The street-car conductor woke up at this juncture, most distressed by the nightmare. It was almost time for him to report for work so he rose and set out. However, by his second trip nothing untoward had happened and he regained his composure. And then as the signal changed at the intersection involved in his dream, he saw the north-bound car, no. 5, and as its driver waved to him, he remembered the dream scenario and immediately braked and cut off the power. A truck smaller than the one he had seen in his sleep, and only painted red over an advertising panel, drove at speed right in front of him. Had he not stopped, his street-car would certainly have collided with it.

Inside the vehicle were two men, and also a woman who, as it sped in front of him, peered out of the window at him. She had large blue eyes just like those of the woman in his dream. He was so shaken by the episode that he had to go home, and another man took his place.

Louisa Rhine regards this as a perfect example of a precognitive experience prevented from fulfilment and of 'the occasional intrusion of incorrect details into true and realistic dreams—the description of the truck and the action of the blue-eyed woman'.

Commenting on ancient stories of precognition, Dr Rhine considered that they supported the belief that one could not escape one's fate, and she thought that those stories not in line with this view had deliberately been omitted. Therefore such lore could not be regarded as reliable, especially as most of it had probably been embellished in the retelling. There was a need for tireless research to try and solve the mystery of precognition. She admitted in her book that there were drawbacks to the experimental method employed at Duke University, pointing out: 'Guessing the symbol on cards (which has been a predominant laboratory technique) is a one-dimensional situation, but experiences from life are multi-dimensional.'

In a table showing for 2,878 dreams the frequencies of subject matter for various groups, Dr Rhine demonstrated that in Group I—'Self'—out of 961 cases 27 were about death and 197 about illness, all of them precognitive. There were 484 dreams about 'Important Topics' and 253 about 'Trivial Topics', of which 69 per cent and 92 per cent respectively were precognitive.

In Group II—'Family'—the precognitive percentages were as follows for a total of 1,123 cases: of 365 dreams about death, 71 per cent; of 416 about 'Illness etc.', 41 per cent; of 277 about 'Important Topics', 65 per cent; of 65 about 'Trivial Topics', 75 per cent.

In Group III—'Remote Relationships'—the precognitive percentages were for a total of 409 cases: of 175 dreams about death, 56 per cent; of 108 about 'Illness etc.', 54 per cent; of 107 about 'Important Topics', 56 per cent; of 19 about 'Trivial Topics', 90 per cent.

In Group IV—'Strangers'—the same percentages for a total of 385 cases were: of 85 dreams about death, 48 per cent; of 91 about 'Illness etc.', 56 per cent; of 125 about 'Important Topics', 69 per cent; of 84 about 'Trivial Topics', 94 per cent.

Commenting on these results, Dr Rhine pointed out that Group I, affecting the dreamer personally, included the highest proportion of precognitive cases, but these mostly concerned matters of general but not critical importance, and even of a quite trivial nature. She thought that a repressing influence might be in operation. 'People apparently tend not to look ahead and contemplate these crises of their own.'

Death, which so often had seemed to be one of the main subjects in psychic experience, proved to number only 23 per cent of all the 2,878 cases. The largest single category was 'Important Topics', 34 per cent which included 'other than critical but still important events' and also both 'happy' and 'unhappy' occurrences. The former, however, were not as frequent as the latter.

As regards the 484 dreams about 'Important Topics', of which 69 per cent were precognitive, Louisa Rhine divided them into the following categories: the locating of missing articles, 95; fires of major concern to the dreamers, 20; outcome of bets, races, contests, 52; jobs or professional incidents, 79; the elements, floods, earthquakes, etc., 19; ceremonies, speeches by dreamers, 11; scenes from later life, 76; miscellaneous, 132.

CHAPTER 19

The Stanford Tests—and the Dream Laboratory

The Stanford Research Institute in Menlo Park, California, became independent of the University when some of the academics objected to certain projects being carried on there which they suspected were being conducted for and financed by the Pentagon. Some indication that this might well be the case was provided in June 1981, by a Congressional committee report headed: 'Survey of Science and Technology Issues. Present and Future. Committee on Science and Technology, U.S. House of Representatives.' This read:

Recent experiments in remote viewing and other studies in parapsychology suggest that there is an interconnectedness of the human mind with other minds and with matter...Experiments in mind-matter interconnectedness have yielded some encouraging results...The implication of these experiments is that the human mind may be able to obtain information independent of geography and time...Given the potentially powerful and far-reaching implications of knowledge in this field, and given that the Soviet Union is widely acknowledged to be supporting such research at a far higher and more official level, Congress may wish to undertake a serious reassessment in this country.

Psi research sponsored by the American government had in fact been conducted since the late 1960s. The purpose was to discover techniques capable of producing remote viewing of far distant places, objects, and events. Individuals possessing such telepathic gifts were tested and high rates of accuracy achieved in many instances. Not only that, but some had given accounts of future happenings with remarkable accuracy. It was found that individuals possessing the psi faculty, however slightly, could expand it through mental relaxation.

A report from Washington that appeared in the *Chicago Tribune* of Saturday 13 August 1977 read:

The C.I.A. financed a project in 1975 to develop a new kind of agent who could truly be called a 'spook', C.I.A. Director Stanfield Turner has disclosed.

The C.I.A. chief said that the agency found a man who could 'see' what was going on anywhere in the world through his psychic powers.

Turner said C.I.A. scientists and officials would show the man a picture of a place and he would then describe any activity going on there at that time.

The tight-lipped chief wouldn't reveal how accurate the 'spook' was, but said the agency chopped the project in 1975.

'He died,' Turner said, 'and we haven't heard from him since.'

On 18 October 1976, the Russian pilot cosmonaut Vitali Sevastyanov visited Stanford Research Institute to get the views of those in charge regarding seemingly paranormal occurrences that had happened when he was aboard his spacecraft and when he was being trained for the job. He was accompanied by Professor Lev Lupichev, a director of the Moscow Insitute of Central Problems, and described how he had seemed to be able to communicate telepathically with his fellow consmonaut as they flew in a Salyut spacecraft. He found that hardly had he thought of requiring a certain tool than his companion would pass it to him. Even the contents of intricate plans that only he knew about were uncannily passed on telepathically to the other man.

When training pilots to become cosmonauts, Sevastyanov rode with them in high-velocity centrifuges similar to the ones used by American personnel preparing for space travel, and they would then be exposed to all sorts of unexpected equipment breakdowns during a mock spacecraft shut-off. Sevastyanov disclosed that, while thus engaged, he would find himself putting into operation the necessary emergency secondary systems *in advance* of a specific equipment failure thus arranged during training.

The late K.E. Tsiolkovsky, one of the greatest of the Russian space pioneers and inventor of their first space rocket, believed that the further out into the universe men sped, the more important telepathy would become as a means of communication over vast distances. He wrote in his published diaries that they would have 'to develop latent psychic abilities to function efficiently in the strange environment of space'.

The Popov parapsychologist, the late Dr I. Gellerstein, agreed. In 1966, he told a congress of astronautic scientists in Paris that since cosmonauts would be speeding at such a rate into space it would become essential for them to foresee what was going to happen. In order to be able to take avoiding action before trouble occurred, they must develop their precognitive faculties.

The psi research programme at SRI was begun by two physicists, Russell Targ and Dr Harold Puthoff, who believed that the psychic faculty worked best when those participating were enthusiastic and relaxed. The remote viewing experiments conducted by Puthoff and Targ were devised to achieve this and did so with significant success, so that they served as a model for others undertaken at Princeton University, Mundelein College in Chicago, and the Institute for Parapsychology in Durham, North Carolina, all of which produced notable results, too.

In the first tests at SRI, the outward experimenter, using a random number generator, would select a target site from a pool of 60 different ones, drive to it, take a photograph, and stay there for a quarter of an hour. Meanwhile, the interviewer would tell the person acting as the viewer to concentrate on trying to visualize the unknown target and what the outward experimenter was doing there and then describe or sketch the scene on paper.

In 1974, when Harold Puthoff and Russell Targ were in the middle of their first programme of remote viewing trials aimed at investigating the case for present time telepathy, evidence supporting that for precognition occurred instead. They were joined at SRI by Pat Price, previously a police commissioner at Burbank, California, whose psychic ability had helped him to track down criminals. He began his contribution to the programme by acting as viewer in nine remote viewing trials and gave correct descriptions in seven of them. The likelihood of this happening by chance was less than one in a hundred thousand. Moreover, in one test, he even told his questioner the site's name.

For the fourth test, Price and Targ, together with Dr Hugh

Crane, a staff scientist, were in a second-floor room in the Engineering Sciences building, while the target selectors were Harold Puthoff and Dr Bonnar Cox, the laboratory director, who decided to choose the target by driving at random, taking turnings left or right as determined by the way the traffic moved. They set out at 3 p.m. Five minutes later, Targ switched on the tape recorder and was dictating that the other couple would reach their target at 3.30 p.m. when Price broke in with: 'We don't have to wait till then. I can tell you right now where it will be. What I'm looking at is a little boat or a little boats dock along the bay. In a direction about like that from here.' He pointed in what was to prove the right direction and said that he could now see clearly the boats as well as motor launches, little sailing ships with furled sails, a little jetty or little dock, and crumbling granite slabs leading down to the water. 'Funny thing—this just flashed in—kinda looks like a Chinese or Japanese pagoda effect. It's a definite feeling of Oriental architecture that seems to be fairly adjacent to where they are.'

It was then 3.10 p.m. Twenty minutes later, the outward experimenters, Puthoff and Cox, having driven on their random route as if in a maze, looked at their watches and stopped. They were four miles north-east of SRI at the Redwood City Marina, and all around were sailing boats. There was a small dock, and near to where they stood was a glass and redwood restaurant built in Oriental style. As arranged, the two men remained here for a quarter of an hour, only to learn that Pat Price had described in such impressive detail the random target 20 minutes *before* they arrived at the site.

This was only one of the many occasions on which Price displayed his precognitive gift before his death in 1975. Harold Puthoff and Russell Targ state that almost every day he would make some prediction that proved accurate. These were mostly about world events, such as telling them a long while in advance the exact date and hour of the cease-fire in the Yom Kippur War.

In 1975, Puthoff and Targ conducted four purposely precognitive tests with Hella Hammid. She had to describe half an hour ahead a target to be chosen by chance and then reached by the outward experimenter, who was known as the 'beacon'. At 10 a.m. the interviewer would record on tape Hella's description of the site where the beacon would be at 10.30 a.m. Targ states that the most striking feature of these experiments was that when following a route picked for them by a random number generator, Targ and Puthoff stopped at precisely half-past ten and played the recording of Hella's earlier description not only of the place where they found themselves but also of what she had predicted they would be doing there.

On one occasion, the two men ended their journey in a courtyard at Stanford University Hospital. They listened to Hella's voice saying that she foresaw them walking along a path with colonnades on both sides, then emerging out of the shade into strong sunlight and into a formal garden with well-cared-for trees and shrubs—which to their astonishment was an exact description of where they were and what they were doing. Targ insists that there was no possible way in which Hella could have learned in advance where the random number generator would pilot them, particularly since the selecting had taken place in a car far away from her after they had driven off with the tape-recording.

Hella Hammid underwent three other tests, in all of which she displayed similar ability to predict what the targets would turn out to be. She foresaw the outward experimenters stopping by 'a large, black iron triangle' and could hear squeaking about once a second. This was an excellent description of the target they reached later—a swing supported by a 'black triangular frame which squeaked as a child used it'.

In other experiments, 35mm slides were used as targets instead of actual places. At SRI the viewer would be left alone in an upstairs room with paper on which to draw and a recording machine to take down his or her impressions. Meanwhile Professor Charles Tart of the University of California and Russell Targ were in a trailer at the back of the building choosing slides at hazard and projecting the scenes they depicted on a screen after the viewer had earlier predicted on tape what would be displayed. On one occasion, the viewer correctly described in advance a picture of a building with a pointed roof that had stars painted on its windows.

Tart and Targ thought that this might provide them with the opportunity to ascertain whether the viewer saw the scene depicted on the slide or the place itself. As the stars were for advertising purposes and the photograph was fairly old, it might be that they had been removed, so they visited the place and found this was the case. This gave convincing support to their belief that what the viewer foresaw being shown on the screen was the picture on the slide.

As a result of Harold Puthoff and Russell Targ's reporting on their successful experiments in precognition at a conference at the Parapsychological Association in Santa Barbara, one of those present, John Bisaha, a professor of psychology at Mundelein College in Chicago, became keenly interested, and with his colleague, Brenda Dunne, embarked on precognitive projects using locations in that city. Two women students new to such work acted in turn as viewers, and each was allowed 15 minutes to record her description of where she predicted Brenda would be half an hour later. This site would be chosen by Brenda taking at random one of 10 numbered slips of paper from a sealed envelope, and then being given travelling instructions bearing the same number. Eight tests were held and produced such successful results that the fourth was filmed and shown on CBS television in 1977.

The last test provided the most remarkable result. The Angel Guardian Orphanage Florist Shop was the target chosen at random. This was in a square-shaped building with a pointed roof and a front entirely made of glass except for four columns covered with tiles of blue mosaic, and behind which were displayed brightly coloured flowers and plants. The student viewer recorded that she foresaw Brenda reaching a place where there were 'A lot of colors, small groups of colors. Lots of reds and yellows, greens, pinks. Probably flowers. They look like they are all bunched together. On display. There's some kind of building. Windows, poles, glass. Concrete around, that she is walking on. . .A sensation of blue.'

Such a successful beginning led to Brenda Dunne and John Bisaha engaging in many more precognitive experiments, and with the intention of attempting some over a considerable distance he went beyond the Iron Curtain in 1976. Three of these had targets in Moscow and two in Bratislava. The viewer in Chicago would start recording at 8.30 a.m. local time the description of the predicted target that John Bisaha would photograph twenty-four and a half hours later at 3 p.m. Three independent judges regarded the results as strong evidence for precognition.

For the opening experiment, the viewer was in Wisconsin, and Bisaha in Bratislava. He stood next day before a restaurant resembling a flying saucer built high in the air on heavy pillars above a bridge near the River Danube. This was close to the experimenter's recorded prediction, which was that Bisaha would be standing near a very large expanse of water on which there were boats. The description continued 'Vertical lines like poles. A circular shape like a merry-go-round or gazebo. It seems to have height, maybe with poles...A dark fence along a walk...at the top of the steps, like a walkway...A boardwalk and there is a fence along it.'

Brenda Dunne and John Bisaha conducted similar experiments which they claimed proved that precognition was in no way adversely affected by distance or a long lapse of time.

Later Brenda Dunne, together with Professor Robert Jahn, Dean of the School of Engineering, and R.D. Nelson of Princeton University, published a long evaluation of 227 precognitive trials. They concluded that 'precognitive remote perception techniques can acquire statistically significant amounts of compounded information about spatially and temporally remote target locations by means currently inexplicable by known physical mechanisms'.

Commenting on these and other experiments conducted on similar lines, Russell Targ and Keith Harary, in their excellent book *The Mind Race*, maintained that the results justify the belief that if you predict that a person will do something there is a strong possibility, given the right conditions, that this will occur. On the other hand, if you were to take your prediction and reveal it to whoever might be affected, fulfilment might be prevented by their taking the appropriate action. There cannot therefore be an infallible prophet unless he possesses superhuman powers.

These authors advance three possible explanations for how precognitive information can be obtained. The first is that the future is already in being and one can tap it. The second is that through telepathy or clairvoyance one can gather knowledge not available to others and deduce what is likely to happen. Their third theory, and they admit that it is the least likely, is that the successful precognitive remote viewer scores by psychokinetically influencing the random number generator.

Some of the most impressive laboratory experiments in ESP

have been conducted since 1962 at the Dream Laboratory of the Maimonides Medical Center in Brooklyn by Dr Montague Ullman, who was joined in 1964 by Stanley Krippner. A person believed to possess psychic powers would be invited to sleep all night in a sound-proof room with electrodes fastened to his or her head which would transmit brain waves to an electroencephalograph (EEG) in another room, where an investigator watched for rapid eye movements (REM) signifying that the sleeper was dreaming, and would then rouse him or her over an intercom and ask for the dream to be described as fully as possible on to a tape recorder.

Immediately the dreamer had started to doze off at the commencement of the experiment, a sealed envelope containing a print reproduction of a painting chosen by a random number generator (RNG) would be handed to a third person acting as an agent, who was not to open it until locked into a room for the night. He or she then concentrated on the print, writing down a description of what it represented and trying to convey this information by the power of thought to the mind of the sleeper. This room was at first some 30 feet away, then three times that distance, and later several miles away in another building. It was found that distance in no way lessened the success rate of these experiments.

In the morning, the recordings would be compared with the target print to see of there were any evidence to support telepathy. Exceptionally high scores came from some subjects. Tests were then extended to cover precognition. In 1969, Malcolm Bessent, the English psychic, took part in novel experiments. There would be no agent concentrating on a print during the night while Bessent slept, because it was not chosen until next morning. The agent's function was limited to waking Bessent every time the apparatus indicated he was dreaming, and recording the descriptions he then gave of his dreams.

Next morning, another researcher, who had not in any way communicated with the night team, would arrive and use the RNG to select numbers leading to a phrase in a book of dream descriptions. He would then choose a print of a painting from the Laboratory's collection that was best described by this phrase. If precognition had occurred, then this should correspond with what Bessent had dreamed about during the previous night.

Sixteen such tests were undertaken with Bessent, who one night dreamed that he was in a mental hospital and had seen a woman patient escape from where she was being detained and run down a corridor. In the morning, Dr Krippner chose the word 'corridor' and then a print of Van Gogh's *Corridor of the St Paul Hospital*. When the target was Cokovsky's *Fruits and Flowers*, Bessent's dream was of a bowl of fruit. On some nights he had previsions not of the next morning's target but of that for a morning two or three days ahead.

At the Foundation for Mind Research in New York, a psychic volunteering to experiment would stand, blindfolded, on a platform suspended from the ceiling by cables and, securely strapped on to this, be swung gradually higher and higher. The invention of the Foundation's director, R.E.L. Masters, the 'Altered States of Consciousness Device' became known as the Witch's Cradle because in the Middle Ages witches would swing in a bag hanging from the branches of a tree so as to get themselves into a state of trance and in touch with Satan. The Witch's Cradle was used by Masters to probe deep into the unconscious and cause the subject to lose all sense of time and space.

Alan Vaughan of New York is a psychic whose predictions, sent regularly to the Central Premonitions Bureau, have proved mostly accurate. Some of these sent there on 5 December 1969 were in reply to questions from Masters as Vaughan swung and gyrated in the Witch's Cradle. He was right in foretelling when the Vietnam War would end, that there would be an attempt on the Pope's life in 1970, and that Jacqueline Kennedy would become estranged from Aristotle Onassis.

CHAPTER 20

Fateful Numbers

The idea that numbers can play a vital role in one's future would seem absurd to the sceptic. It was Pythagoras who in the fifth century BC wrote: 'The world is built upon the power of numbers.' Since then numerologists have maintained that numbers are occult symbols of a person's destiny. They point out that there are seven colours in the rainbow, seven days in the week, and that seven is the number of seals in Christendom and of Devas in Hinduism, and so on.

King Edward VII was extremely superstitious and often consulted Cheiro, who told him that the numbers 6 and 9 were the most important in his life. He had been born on the ninth day of the month. His names, Albert and Edward, each had six letters. His marriage took place in 1863, which reduces to 9 by adding the numbers together until a single digit is reached, and his bride's name, Alexandra, had nine letters, and so did that of her father, Christian IX. When Edward succeeded to the throne his coronation had to be postponed because he fell ill with appendicitis. The new king feared that he was going to die, but Cheiro predicted that that could not happen until the numbers 6 and 9 came together. Reassured, Edward asked the seer to select a date for the coronation and 9 August was chosen. Edward VII died in his sixty-ninth year—and nine kings walked behind his coffin.

In more recent times, John Lennon firmly believed that the number 9 affected everything in his life. He and his son Sean both had the same birthday, 9 October. Brian Epstein first attended a Beatles concert at the Cavern in Liverpool on 9 November 1961, and clinched their record contract with EMI on 9 May 1962. The group's first record, *'Love Me Do'*, was on Parlophone 4949.

John Lennon regarded it as significant that he first met Yoko Ono on 9 November 1966, that their New York apartment was on West 72nd Street, and that their Dakota one also was numbered 72 (7 + 2 = 9). As a student, he had taken the 72 bus to and from his home to Liverpool Art College. Three of his songs were entitled, *'Number 9 Dream'*, *'Revolution 9'*, and *'One After 909'*, written at his mother's house—9 Newcastle Road, Wavertree, Liverpool.

When John was killed late on the evening of 8 December 1980, in New York, the five-hour difference meant that it was 9 December in Liverpool. His body was removed to the Roosevelt Hospital on Ninth Avenue.

Nine was also the fadic number of Abraham Lincoln and John Kennedy and is regarded as that of high achievement, of romantic visionaries over-fond of the limelight.

In the case of the British Prime Minister Margaret Thatcher, we get 4 as her fadic number. She was born on 13 October (1 + 3), married on 13 December, her two children were baptized on 13 December, and her son, Mark, announced his engagement on 13 November.

The most unlucky of numbers is believed to be 666, and the experience of Michael Gardner, who lived with his family in Altringham Road, Brooklands, certainly lent credence to this superstition. It was reported in the *Sunday Express* by Gordon Ducker, who was told by Gardner that for 27 years he enjoyed trouble-free motoring until he bought a £15,000 silver-grey Vauxhall Senator with the registration number B666 VVR. Soon after this, watching from the window of his fourth-floor room in a Cologne hotel, he saw a youth stabbed to death on the boot of the car.

Back in Brooklands, as Gardner waited to turn right in a wide main road, another car hit his head-on, breaking two of his ribs and injuring his back and legs. The culprit raced off and has not been traced. Next, as Gardner drove down a quiet side road, two large black dogs suddenly sprang from behind a parked van. He braked but hit one. His number plate was cracked—but the figures 666 were undamaged. In the nine months after acquiring the vehicle, Michael Gardner also had other troubles with it. Then, one weekend, he visited his father's grave in the cemetery of the parish church at Timperley, Cheshire, and found that the two-foot-high headstone had unaccountably fallen, crushing the flowers his mother had placed there.

As Mr Gardner was wedging the stone upright, Canon Desmond Probets came out of the church and they started to talk. The Book of Revelation was mentioned, and chapter 13, verse 18, which states that 666 is the number of 'the beast', meaning Satan. It was arranged for the Canon to bless the car, and since then apparently no other major mishaps have occurred.

This story attracted a letter in a later issue of the newpaper from a Mr E.S. Taylor of Lyme Regis, who wrote that having read about the supposedly doom-laden number 666 he felt compelled to record at least one exception. In 1970 he had bought a 1966 'S' type Jaguar, registration number HDD 666D, which when he sold it after 13 years at a £400 profit had done 102,000 miles with no trouble, not a scratch and only normal servicing and replacements. Mr Taylor ended his letter: 'Perhaps I am the Devil himself!' When I drew this to the attention of a believer in numerology, she suggested that he had been protected through the influence of the planets ascendant at the time of his birth.

CHAPTER 21

The Great Pyramid Prophecies

Of the Seven Wonders of the Ancient World only one remains, the Great Pyramid. It is remarkable in many ways as regards position, construction, and measurements—and there are those who maintain that the latter provide a key to the course of events since it was built and into the future. For this purpose, all its dimensions are taken into account, such as height, width, and length of passages, galleries, and chambers. The study of these prophecies has come to be known as Pyramidology. Although believers have been able. to link past occurrences with positions in the pyramid's chronological line, when it comes to foretelling even the near future their success rate has been poor. For example, at the commencement of this century, the date of the Second Coming was given as 1911, then 1936, and now 2040.

We were told that by 1982 a world cataclysm would shift the earth's axis. During the next five years, sea levels would rise through melting ice-caps and excessive rainfall, followed until the end of the century by violent natural disasters and wars leading to the extermination of three-quarters of the earth's population, including all the people of Israel. Despite this—or perhaps because of it—the world's leaders will become spiritually enlightened. Civilization will finally collapse about 2030, after which a new society will come into being, culminating in the reappearance of the promised Messiah in human form.

A Melbourne business man, John Strong, published a book, *The Doomsday Globe*, based on Pyramidology, in which he predicted that the Russians would bombard its enemies with nuclear weapons in October 1978. As a result, nearly

100 of his middle-class adherents sought refuge on a remote ranch with deep reinforced shelters and provisions for a year. When no such attack occurred, it was suggested that Strong might have made a mistake in interpreting the pyramid's measurements.

Moira Timms in *The Six O'Clock Bus* points out how according to St Matthew (24:29), Jesus reiterated the old prophecies of Isaiah, Joel, and Habakkuk about the earth trembling, the sun and moon darkening, and the mountains being crushed to dust, then he added that 'the stars shall fall from the heavens'. In this passage, she states, the original Greek word for 'heavens' is *ouranos*, the root word for uranium. The phrase should therefore read instead: 'The powers of uranium shall be shaken.' She regards it as a curious coincidence that the first nuclear tests were known as 'Project Trinity', while the result of that dynamic fusion was code-christened 'Baby Jesus'.

Moira Timms claims that this interpretation corresponds completely with what is predicted in the King's Chamber of the Great Pyramid, for right in the middle, as the last but one date before the record ends, 3–4 March 1945 is indicated. That was when the first atomic bomb experiments took place.

CHAPTER 22

Writers as Prophets

Are novelists and other writers really tapping Jung's 'collective unconscious'? Certainly their predictions often turn out to be more accurate than those of many who make foretelling their business. Long before Jules Verne, Cyrano de Bergerac in his *Voyage to the Moon*, published in 1656, had predicted that men propelled by a rocket would reach it. So much of what Verne himself wrote in his two futuristic novels *From the Earth to the Moon* (1865) and *Round the Moon* (1870) proved to be descriptions in astonishing detail of space travel in this century that some have doubted whether it could be put down to coincidence, a lively imagination, and a natural bent for science, and believe that, without being aware of it, he possessed the gift of precognition.

The similarities between Verne's moon adventure and that of the Americans make intriguing reading. His spacecraft, the *Columbiad*, was launched from Tampa in Florida, which is only some 120 miles from Cape Kennedy. Its name is almost identical with that of *Apollo XI's* command module, the *Columbia*. Both were cone-shaped and were crewed by three men. The *Columbiad*, travelling at 25,000 miles an hour, reached the moon in 97 hours 13 minutes 20 seconds, while *Apollo XI* took 97 hours 39 minutes 17 seconds. The flight calculations for the former were supposed to have been prepared by the observatory in Cambridge, England, while for *Apollo XI* they were computed at the Astrophysical Laboratory in Cambridge, Massachusetts. Rockets were fitted to both fictional and real crafts to jerk them out of lunar orbit and lessen the speed of return into the earth's atmosphere.

The astronauts in *Columbiad* fed on meat and vegetables

hydraulically compressed as small as possible, while those in the Apollos to save space took with them capsules and concentrated liquids.

Verne's spacecraft was made of aluminium, which until then had been regarded as a semi-precious metal. It was only at the beginning of our century that it was first used in airships, and in 1917 in the fuselages of planes.

Verne had *Columbiad's* progress tracked by a telescope placed on Long's Peak in Missouri, while NASA's telescopes are sited in the mountains of California. It splashed down in the Pacific and the three astronauts were taken aboard an American ship, just as was to happen with *Apollo XIII*. *Columbiad's* nearly fatal disaster was caused in a surprisingly similar way to that which endangered the lives of the astronauts aboard the same American spacecraft. When their supply of oxygen starts to escape, *Columbiad's* crew are almost asphyxiated and, owing to loss of heat, they narrowly escape being frozen to death. In the case of *Apollo XIII*, an explosion in the oxygen tank threatened a catastrophe for its crew. That of the *Columbiad* hoped to land on the moon but could not, and therefore went into orbit round it, fearful that they would remain doing so until they crashed. Fortunately, like the astronauts in *Apollo XIII*, its personnel managed to get out of orbit by igniting rockets and diving back to earth.

It is remarkable that Jules Verne should have set his moon shot in the United States, then regarded by Europeans as lagging far behind in scientific knowledge. In one respect, the *Columbiad* differed from *Apollo XIII*—there were two dogs on board. It was to be the Russians that did this for the first time in real life before sending up cosmonauts.

In *Twenty Thousand Leagues under the Sea* (1866), Verne describes an advanced type of submarine the crew of which are able to travel beneath the ocean for months without surfacing. It was only with the invention of the nuclear-powered submarine that this became possible. Other improvements in everyday living that he foretold were the discovery by scientists of ways in which to regulate the climate, and how to capture the sun's heat so as to supply all our energy requirements. Grim and already in existence are the instruments of destruction that he described as capable of obliterating entire communities in a flash.

Lecturing in Amiens nine years later, his theme 'In the 29th

Century—the Day of an American Journalist', Jules Verne proved wrong— but only on when his visions would become fact. He should have said 'in the twentieth century' when he predicted that in the United States there would be streets 300 feet wide and tall buildings over 1,000 feet tall wherein the temperature could be kept always equable. He might have been describing the Empire State Building. Many in his audience were sceptical when he predicted the skies 'furrowed by aero-cars and buses', and professors crouched over their computers, 'engrossed in equations of the 59th degree'. Perhaps we will have to wait until the twenty-ninth century for 'pneumatic trains operating under the oceans' and taking us from London to New York or Tokyo at speeds of 1,000 miles an hour.

Arthur C. Clarke, the celebrated space consultant and author, has an impressive track record as a predictor of scientific inventions. When serving as a radar operator with the RAF, he suggested in 1945 that 'synchronous orbit communication satellites' should be launched into the sky, and in 1963 such a satellite, *Syncom II*, came into existence and a stream of these followed, culminating in *Comsat*, which enabled spacecraft and ground technicians to communicate with ease.

In 1947, Clarke even gave the year when he foresaw a rocket reaching the moon, 1959, and indeed the Russian *Lunar II* landed there that September. He was out only by a year in foretelling that astronauts would walk on the lunar landscape in 1970.

According to Clarke's vision of the future, satellites will have a far greater effect on communication than the telephone ever had, and they will be connected with huge information banks through which much of the world's business will be conducted. These, he predicts, will be situated beneath the Arizona desert and the Mongolian steppes 'or wherever land is cheap and useless for any other purpose'. In the Third World, he pictures life transformed even in the most isolated communities by one lone antenna capable of picking up 'microwave broadcasts'. Satellite power will enable the most complicated surgery to be performed in remote places. A specialist, miles away, will in this way be able to operate by employing robot arms remotely controlled.

It may take a little longer than 1990 for Clarke's forecast

to come true that cargo ships will be replaced by freighter submarines and trains by hovercraft, while men will be busy colonizing the planets—or than 1995 for cars to be driven by electric motors in each wheel, manual steering having been forbidden by law and replaced by computers.

That brilliant professor A.M. Low, writing in the magazine *Tomorrow* in 1938, predicted that Britain would eventually be run by a Minister of the Future, whose duty it would be to collect data from all over the world to be tabulated, correlated, and compared. 'He will be like a spider sitting in a web, drawing towards him all knowledge, and working out, on scientific lines, the effect that the latest developments and discoveries will probably have upon the human race.'

Government 'think tanks' have already attempted to do this, and industry, too. Their success record has been mixed. In 1951, Bertrand de Jouvenel, whose brain-child was the International Futuribles Association, urged the French government in vain to take the necessary action to avoid the rebellion which he correctly foretold would break out in Algeria. An American analyst, George Whitman, of the Hudson Institute, confidentially reported in 1978 not only that the Shah was bound to be overthrown but gave a date for it and asserted that a religious fanatic would then take over in Iran.

Ray Bradbury in his *Fahrenheit 451* depicts a world in which everything is fireproofed except books, which are banned by totalitarian rulers who control the populace through television and tiny transistors stuck permanently in their ears. Some of his predictions already seem to be coming true: 'School is shortened, discipline is relaxed, philosophy, historic languages dropped. English and spelling gradually neglected, finally almost completely ignored. Life is immediate ... Why learn anything save pressing buttons, pulling switches, fitting nuts and bolts?' Nightmarish is Bradbury's forecast that the average person's living-room will have every wall covered from ceiling to floor with television screens. This is not an incongruous and impossible conception of his fancy, but based on study of social and scientific trends.

The winner of the 1913 Nobel Prize for Physiology and Medicine, Professor Charles Richet, wrote in his book *In One Hundred Years*, published in 1892: 'If we knew the totality of things in the present, we should know the totality of things to come. Our ignorance of the future is the result of our ignorance of the present.' And demonstrating his own far-sightedness he added: 'The United States and Russia will be the most powerful nations in 1992 with a combined population around six hundred million which will be much larger than that of all Europe.'

It should be mentioned that Richet's other work, *Thirty Years of Psychical Research*, is full of remarkable examples of precognition. One of the oddest concerns a Mr Banister, who, as a schoolboy in 1813, saw in a dream a tombstone engraved with his name and the date, lacking the *e*, 'Jun 9, 1883'. On 9 June 1835, his eldest son, also a schoolboy, died. The father's own death occurred nearly 48 years later and was shown on his tombstone as 'Jan 9, 1883'. It was as if in a macabre way the dream had mixed up the months of the two deaths.

Even more macabre is Arthur Koestler's anecdote in his book *The Challenge of Chance* which was related to him by an English schoolboy. Edgar Allan Poe, who died in 1849, wrote a book, *The Narrative of Arthur Gordon Pym*. In it, the ship on which Pym was travelling sank, and he and three survivors drifted in an open boat for days. Then starvation forced them to kill and eat the cabin boy, whose name was Richard Parker. Koestler's informant wrote: 'Some years later in the summer of 1884, my grandfather's cousin was cabin boy in the yawl, *Mignonette*, when she foundered and the four survivors were in an open boat for many days. Eventually senior members of the crew killed and ate the cabin boy. His name was Richard Parker.'

The writer Peter Lemesurier reached a similar conclusion to that of Professor Richet when he said that the prophet's role seemed to be 'to feel the pulse of the present'.

Max Beerbohm, critic and caricaturist, shocked London in June 1923 when he exhibited at the Leicester Square Galleries a cartoon which he claimed was his prevision of the then Prince of Wales in 1972, when having abdicated after a short reign he had eventually become a pathetic old man married to the socialite daughter of an American landlady. Although widely condemned for such *lèse-majesté*, Beerbohm was unrepentant and the cartoon was later bought by Sir Gerald Du Maurier, the actor-manager.

Mark Twain once consulted Cheiro, the celebrated palmist, and wrote in his Visitors' Book: 'Cheiro has exposed my character with humiliating accuracy.' When Twain was born in November 1835, Halley's comet blazed in the night sky. The novelist often mentioned this, and came to regard himself and the comet as 'unaccountable freaks' which having arrived together must depart together. He was correct, for when he died in April 1910 Halley's comet had briefly returned.

CHAPTER 23

A Chapter for Cynics

It has been estimated that there are at least 10,000 full-time and 50,000 part-time astrologers in America. The cynic finds it astonishing that anybody can take seriously the contents of the astrological features published in the popular press. If everybody born, say, under Leo were to receive a letter on the same day, the postal service would break down. It is the writer who can give a new look to the subject who leaps to the fore, such as Sydney Omarr, thanks possibly to the Armour Meat Company giving away a free copy of his *Cooking with Astrology* to every purchaser of a packet of their bacon. Linda Goodman's *Sun Signs* became a best-seller because she avoided all the clichés of the old fashioned astrologer and wrote in a breezy style. She made the woman born under Leo feel she would go places by telling her: 'You are no wall-flower—you are a sun-flower!'

With so many astrologers active, one might have expected their successes to have been more numerous. Take earthquake predictions. Roger Hunter, a geophysicist with the US National Ocean Survey, after a thorough investigation of astrologers' claims concluded that throwing darts blindfold at a calendar would give similar results. He found that although 17 major earthquakes took place between January and August 1970, the forecasters in the *American Astrology Magazine* missed every one. Of the 16 earthquakes predicted by them, they were right for only three minor upsets and failed to give any advance warning of the worst disasters of the century to strike Peru on 21 May when some 30,000 people perished.

In 1968, more and more Americans began taking seriously

the predictions of some psychics that California would be destroyed by an earthquake and tidal waves in April of the following year. Members of spiritualist churches in Los Angeles and elsewhere were urged by their ministers to take refuge in the hills of Georgia and Tennessee, and many obeyed. Andrew Widrovsky of Santa Barbara described to reporters his awesome prevision of 'two titanic earth convulsions, followed by five tidal waves and a deluge of radioactive ash that will cover the entire south western part of the state', and he announced that he had invented an 'anti-radiation belt' which if worn would save people's lives. These could be purchased direct from him.

There was some confusion as to the date of the expected disaster. When the news broke that California's then Governor, Ronald Reagan, would be going away to Arizona on 4 April, the rumour spread that he had received a confidential warning from a friendly top psychic. But nothing untoward occurred that day, and the favourite date then became 18 April—the date of the terrible earthquake of 1906 that had destroyed San Francisco. Enterprising shopkeepers urged customers to buy protective helmets and fireproof clothing, while one store put on a 'How to be Best Dressed for the Earthquake' fashion show.

The event was expected by most astrologers to begin at 3.15 p.m., and at 5 a.m. Joseph Alioto, San Francisco's Mayor, gave a great 'Earthquake Party' in its Civic Center Plaza. Undeterred by having to rise so early, over 7,000 gathered to await the predicted havoc with song, dance, and drink, and were entertained with earthquake scenes shown on a giant screen from the MGM movie *San Francisco*. But the elements did not rage that afternoon, neither did they next day at 8.19 a.m., the time chosen by a group of mystics supported by the hippies of Haight-Ashbury.

Not all scientists have derided the claims of astrologers. In 1959, Dr Rudolf Tomascher, president of the International Geophysical Union, startled more orthodox colleagues by claiming that planetary positions did appear to be linked to earthquake incidence. His claim, based on a study of 134 earthquakes, was published in the scientific journal *Nature*. Tomascher selected Uranus as the planet to keep under close observation. Its position in relation to earthquake epicentres was the same far more frequently than it should have been by chance, the odds being 10,000–1.

Within a short while, following the publication of Dr Tomascher's paper, an earthquake destroyed Agadir in Morocco. He then commented that if its population had read *Nature*, they would have taken the necessary precautions while Uranus neared meridian after the minor precursor shocks. Thus they might have saved their lives when the main quake occurred at 11 p.m. leading to over 20,000 deaths.

Dr Tomascher stressed that there was something unique about Uranus. 'It is the only planet the direction of whose axis coincides with the plane of its orbital revolution, so that any magnetic field issuing from it must have an influence quite unlike that of any other planet.'

It has already been mentioned in connection with Edgar Cayce's career how some 35 years earlier he drew attention to the fact that all the planets would be bunched together on the same side of the sun in 1982 and that this would disturb its equilibrium, leading to earthquakes. Astrologers agreed with him, and even the Astronomer Royal in Britain gave it as his opinion that it might cause quakes and volcanic eruptions wherever the earth's crust was thinnest, but fortunately natural disasters in 1982 were not on the scale predicted.

Every New Year, many popular newspapers and magazines indulge in a welter of forecasting for the year ahead, enlisting the services of experts in various fields. The psychics most adept at publicizing themselves point out their past successes, carefully ignoring their failures. Take the year 1980. Seven out of 10 interviewed by the *National Enquirer* confidently predicted that Senator Ted Kennedy would sweep into the White House in a landslide victory. Clarissa Bernhardt of California added, 'after selecting a woman as his running mate', and that Prince Charles would cause a political crisis in Great Britain by announcing his intention to marry a divorced woman, which Parliament would reluctantly allow.

Astrologer Frederick Davies predicted that John Wayne's ghost would materialize at the Alamo before the disbelieving eyes of visitors. Shawn Robbins of New York foresaw John Travolta taking over the controls of an airliner, moments after the pilot had a heart attack, and landing it safely—also that Arab-financed mercenaries would raid Fort Knox, making off with an astonishing amount of gold. Dorothy Allison of New Jersey asserted that Bob Hope would become US Ambassador to China, while astrologer Jack Gillam of Orlando believed that an inventor would produce an electronic device that massaged the sleep centre of the brain doing away with the need for sleep, and that Lassie would be kidnapped and only released after a ransom of $1 million was paid.

All these predictions misfired. Another paper, the *Globe*, asked some leading psychics to concentrate on making cheerful ones. Lou Wright, who earlier that year had correctly foretold five of the Oscar winners, was cautiously vague in predicting the discovery of a herbal cure for diabetes. Barbara Donchess of Canton, Massachusetts, had more or less the same impression as Frederick Davies in the *National Enquirer* but was less specific, saying that there would be new evidence of life after death 'when the ghost of an actor who has passed away will be seen by many'.

Ken Burke, former editor of the *Psychic News*, was fairly safe in assuring the *Globe*'s readers that someone would report the landing of visitors from outer space in a UFO. 'They will land near a school and smile and talk to kids in a strange, high pitched language before taking off again.' Dallas-based astrologer Patti Tobin predicted that a terrorist group would kidnap and hold to ransom the Ayatollah Khomeini, and that a mass exodus of people from Cuba would force Fidel Castro to seek asylum in South America. Maria Graciette pleased dog-lovers by promising that Congress would order the striking of a special medal for the Canine Hero of the Year that would carry four small children to safety from a blazing building. None of these auguries have so far been fulfilled—and neither, much to the disappointment of TV addicts, has Mario Papapetros's forecast that the price of sets would plummet 'after an amazing technology break-through in America that will bring last-forever circuits and picture tubes'.

Many psychics predicted a violent end for the Ayatollah in 1980, and the same sources then said it would happen in 1981, when a flying saucer would buzz the UN headquarters in New York, Frank Sinatra would be appointed American Ambassador to the Vatican, King Solomon's legendary mine would be discovered, a 'Dallas' fan would attempt to kill Larry Hagman, who would then give up the role of J.R. to become an evangelist.

In the summer of 1981, Jeane Dixon announced that she had seen in a vision the flag flying at half-mast over the White House in 1983, and another clairvoyant, Tamara Rand, who had correctly predicted President Reagan's shooting, now also said that he would die in 1983. When this did not happen, it was suggested that, aware of the Presidential 'jinx' and being, as Linda Goodman phrases it, 'a secret astrology freak, he got sworn in at some strange time like six minutes after midnight' thus protecting himself against maleficent aspects. When questioned about his attitude to astrology by the press, Ronald Reagan has avoided committing himself, saying: 'I am no more interested in the subject than the average man.'

Thanks to the use of audio or video tape, psychics making predictions on radio and television were now able to provide recorded evidence when challenged for proof. So when the attempt on the life of Pope John Paul II was made in 1981, five American psychics were able to substantiate their claims. Shawn Robbins, interviewed on 26 February by Norman Mark on Chicago's WIND radio station, predicted that the Pope would be 'shot within a few weeks' but that he would live and that others in the crowd would be injured. Lou Wright of Denver made similar predictions during the same month on the radio stations in Memphis, Mobile, and Denver; Evelyn Paglini of Chicago on WKRS radio in Waukegan, Illinois, on 24 March; Gloria James to Wayne Braverman during his show broadcast on WJUL radio in Lowell, Massachusetts, on 5 March; and in the previous year, on 8 August, Bill O'Hara on Station KFMK. But was this true precognition—or could the assassin have been telepathically influenced to attempt the crime?

The knowledge that Halley's comet was due to make one of its rare returns near to the vicinity of the earth led to a plethora of predictions that it would cause great destruction. Jeane Dixon declared:

Towards the middle of the 1980s the earth will be struck by a comet. Earthquakes and tidal waves will be the result of this tremendous collision which will take place in one of the great oceans. It will be one of the worst disasters of the twentieth century. Although the approximate point of impact has already been revealed to me, I believe that I should not reveal it yet, but at a future date I will give more detailed information.

Mrs Dixon wisely did not do this, and was later hard put to find excuses for the catastrophe's non-occurrence.

Another American psychic, Elizabeth Van Buren, claimed to receive warnings from her spirit friends through suspending a pendulum over the letters of the alphabet arranged in a circle. Consequently, she advised people to leave California before November 1982, when it would be devastated by a massive sliding of the San Andreas fault that would cause the same to occur in other fault zones throughout the globe and the North Pole to be moved to a new position in the vicinity of the old United States frontier with Mexico. The spirits urged Elizabeth to start a survival community somewhere in South America, the location of which she must keep secret.

The fact that earlier prophets of doom had drawn blanks did not deter some from believing in this prediction, just as Australian psychic John Nash of Adelaide found followers when the New Year dawned in 1976 and he announced that that city had become such a haunt of the wicked that an earthquake reinforced by a tidal wave would wipe it out at midday on 19 January. Nash packed his family off to the safety of Melbourne, while the credulous took refuge in high country, but Don Dunstan, Prime Minister of South Australia, supported by other cynics dawdled on the foreshore daring the tide to attack them. In the city itself, others crowded the churches or bolstered their courage with booze while brazen belles with bare breasts paraded the waterfront inviting the men 'to sin before it's too late', according to one newspaper report, which also informed its readers that some regarded as a signal from Heaven the fact that even snails had been spotted hurrying up to the roofs of houses.

American mortician Cresswell claimed to have foretold the outbreak of the Six Days War between the Arabs and the Israelis in 1967, but he was wrong in predicting that most of the women living in St Louis would go bald between 11 February and 11 May 1983; that a woman styling herself the Lady of Light would band together the people of the Orient under her leadership in 1985; that a meteor would almost destroy London on 8 October 1988, and that between May 1988 and March 1989 people in the United States would go sex-crazy through an aphrodisiac having been pumped into the country's water and heating systems.

The *Daily Telegraph*'s 'Peterborough' on 24 January 1987 quoted this extract from the *Bournemouth Evening Echo*: 'A blaze ripped through a Bournemouth store early today causing damage estimated at £10,000. The cause of the fire at Harper's is still being investigated. A clairvoyant at the store, George Lewis, said he did not predict the blaze because "Sundays are my days off".'

CHAPTER 24

I Ching

I Ching or *Book of Changes* has been described as a crystal ball between hard covers, but it is much more than that. Compiled over 4,000 years ago, its theme is that the entire universe and events in it depend upon interaction between two forces, *Yin*, which is negative, and *Yang* which is positive. It is a distillation of the ancient Chinese teachers' wisdom and has been used down the ages by all types in the human hierarchy seeking guidance as to how best to pilot their lives through the uncharted future.

The body of the book consists of 64 numbered hexagrams or oracles made up of six lines, either broken in the middle (*Yin*) or unbroken (*Yang*). Every pattern of lines has significance, and this formation is decided either by letting 49 yarrow stalks fall or by tossing three coins. If there are more 'heads' than 'tails', a *Yang* line is formed, and if 'tails' exceed 'heads' a *Yin* line is put down; and so on until there are six lines in all in the shape of a hexagram. While doing this, one must repeat to oneself the question to which one is seeking an answer, which will be found in the key to the hexagram. There are 64 possible combinations of *Yin* and *Yang* lines, and each of the hexagrams has a name and a fixed interpretation.

Admirably translated into English by Richard Wilhelm in 1951, *I Ching* was described by him in an introduction as one of the most important books in the world's literature in which both of the branches of Chinese philosophy, Confucianism and Taoism, have their common roots. It has been consulted down the years by all sorts of people, from politicians to peasants, seeking answers to their problems.

I Ching gained a certain intellectual prestige in the West through Carl Jung's interest in it. He was astonished by the relevance of the book's answers to his enquiries. Its advice was often so appropriate that he agreed to write a foreword to Richard Wilhelm's translation. He revealed that for more than 30 years he had found 'uncommon significance' in 'this oracle technique or method of exploring the unconscious'. In order to understand the book, it was imperative to cast off certain prejudices of the Western mind. It was a curious fact that such a gifted and intelligent people as the Chinese had never developed what we call science. Ours, however, was based upon the principle of causality, but a great change in our standpoint was setting in. The axioms of causality were being shaken to their foundations by modern physics. We now knew that what we term natural laws are merely statistical truths and thus must necessarily allow for exceptions. Every process in nature is partially or totally interfered with by chance, so much so that under natural circumstances a course of events absolutely conforming to specific laws is almost an exception.

The Chinese mind, as Jung saw it at work in *I Ching*, seemed to be exclusively preoccupied with the chance aspect of events. What we called coincidence was apparently the chief concern of this peculiar mind, and what we worshipped as casuality passed almost unnoticed. Jung considered that there was something to be said for the immense importance of chance. An incalculable amount of human effort was directed at combating and restricting the nuisance or danger represented by chance. Theoretical considerations of cause and effect often compared to disadvantage with the practical results of chance. The moment under actual observation appeared to *I Ching* more of a chance hit than a clearly defined result of concurring casual chain processes. While the Western mind carefully sifts, weighs, selects, classifies, isolates, the Chinese picture of the moment encompasses everything down to the minutest nonsensical detail, because all of the ingredients make up the observed moment.

Therefore, continued Jung, when one threw the three coins, or counted through the 49 yarrow stalks, these chance details formed a part of the moment of observation. With Westerners it would be almost meaningless to say that whatever happens in a given moment inevitably possesses the quality peculiar to that moment. This was not an abstract argument but a very practical one. There were certain connoisseurs who could tell merely from the taste, and so on, of a wine the site of its vineyard and the year of its origin. In the face of such facts, it had to be admitted that moments could leave long-lasting traces—like the astrologer who without any previous knowledge about you could say what zodiacal sign rose above the horizon in the moment of your birth.

In other words, wrote Jung, whoever invented *I Ching* was convinced that 'the hexagram worked out in a certain moment coincided with the latter in quality no less than in time'. To him it was 'the exponent of the moment in which it was cast—even more so than the hours of the clock or the divisions of the calendar could be—inasmuch as the hexagram was understood to be an indicator of the essential situation prevailing in the moment of its origin'. Thus, the meaning in the enquirer's question would be overpoweringly attracted to the meaning contained in the most apposite of *I Ching's* hexagrams.

Jung stressed that the *I Ching* method of self-knowledge was not for the frivolous or immature, nor was it for the intellectual or rationalist. It was appropriate only for 'thoughtful and reflective people'. Colin Wilson in *The Occult* thought its real purpose was to restore circulation to the unconscious mind, whilst Lyall Watson in *Supernature* considered consulting it at a time of personal crisis amounted almost to 'a session with your favourite analyst'.

Danah Zohar in *Through the Time Barrier* gives two examples of *I Ching's* possibly precognitive ability. In 1978, a London couple worried about all the complications that were holding up the purchase of a house asked the book whether this would finally go through. The tossing of the three coins selected hexagram 28, 'Preponderance of the Great', which reads: 'The ridgepole sags to the breaking point.' The commentary explains: 'The weight of the great is excessive. The load is too heavy for the strength of the supports. The ridgepole, on which the whole roof rests, sags to the breaking point because its supporting ends are too weak for the load they bear.'

A few days later, the couple received a letter from a building society rejecting their application for a mortgage because the society's surveyor had found major cracks in the house's support walls due to subsidence.

Danah Zohar's second case concerned a member of the Society for Physical Research who was upset by a feeling of foreboding the night before her brother and sister-in-law were due to fly to Turkey. Unable to sleep, the woman asked *I Ching* if it were safe for them to do so. The reply came in two stages. The final answer was given in hexagram 18, 'Work on What Has Been Spoiled', which reads: 'Has supreme success. It furthers one to cross the great water. Before the starting point, three days. After the starting point, three days.' The commentary adds: 'What has been spoiled through man's fault can be made good again through man's work. It is not immutable fate.'

Later, the woman heard from her sister-in-law in Istanbul that their departure from Heathrow had been delayed for several hours because while their plane was taxiing for take-off an indicator on the pilot's instrument panel signalled a fault and the plane had to return to the terminal for this to be put right.

CHAPTER 25

Theories of Time

Some people have tried to explain cases of apparent precognition as nothing more than coincidences. Schopenhauer describes the latter in his book *On the Apparent Fate of the Individual* as 'the simultaneous occurrence of causally unconnected events'. He regarded events as forming a pattern similar to lines of latitude and longitude; the latter stood for the causal connections of events, and the former the cross-connections of acausal meaningful coincidences.

Both kinds of connections exist simultaneously, and the self-same event, although a link in two totally different chains, nevertheless falls into place in both, so that the fate of one individual invariably fits the fate of the other, and each is the hero of his own drama while simultaneously figuring in a drama foreign to him—this is something that surpasses our powers of comprehension, and can only be conceived as possible by virtue of the most wonderful pre-established harmony. Everyone must participate in it. Thus everything is interrelated and mutually attuned.

Dr Paul Kammerer of the Institute of Experimental Biology in Vienna was fascinated by the subject, and from his early twenties carried a notebook wherever he went in which he recorded coincidences he experienced. Sitting on park benches for long periods of time, observing passers-by, he found that certain types, people carrying the same objects and so on, came in definite groupings. He decided that this was caused by a law which he named 'seriality', and in 1919 he brought out a book on the subject, *Das Gesetz der Serie*. This phenomenon was responsible for attracting together whatever had some affinity, thus forming 'a world mosaic or cosmic kaleidoscope, which in spite of constant shufflings and rearrangements' ended up by achieving this.

In 1952, Kammerer's theory of seriality was developed further, when the quantum physicist and winner of a Nobel Prize in this field Wolfgang Pauli and Carl Jung collaborated and published *The Interpretation of Nature and the Psyche*, which was prefaced by Jung's essay 'Synchronicity: An Acausal Connecting Principle', and followed by Pauli's 'The Influence of Archetypal Ideas on the Scientific Theories of Kepler'. The combined theme is that there is an absolute cosmos where space and time do not exist and where the psyche and the material universe are both evident. It was through attempting to find an explanation for the way in which, in his own experience, people and events apparently unconnected were brought together by extraordinary coincidences that Jung put forward his theory of synchronicity, attributing their occurrence to an 'acausal principle' at work.

A young woman patient had been telling Jung how she had dreamed that a man had handed her a golden scarab, when something tapped lightly on the window-pane. Jung opened the window and a golden-coloured scarab beetle flew in, which he caught and handed to her, saying: 'Here is your scarab.' Apart from arriving at the right moment, it had acted contrary to its natural instinct in seeking admission to a darkened room.

Another patient of Jung's, who had shown no signs of ill-health, had a heart attack while walking home. When carried into his house and about to die, the man found his wife in the same critical condition due to her having been scared by the flocking of hundreds of birds on the roof of the house, which had occurred before the death of both his mother and his grandmother.

A remarkable coincidence was reported in the *Daily Telegraph* of 3 June 1982, of a duck farmer in Lincolnshire who employed two people named Crow, four called Robbins, a Gosling, a Sparrow, and a Dickie Bird. Another occurred in Derby, where a Canadian goose crashed through the window of a house while the owner was listening to a record by singer Frankie Laine, 'Cry of the Wild Goose'.

The Comorro Islands, lying between the coast of Africa and Madagascar, became independent in 1975. It was not long before their elected President was overthrown in a coup staged by a cruel character, Soilih, assisted by a French mercenary, Colonel Denara. A witch doctor told the repressive new ruler that only a man with a dog could put an end to his life, with the result that he ordered all dogs on the islands to be destroyed. Three years later, however, his ruthless regime collapsed when there was a rebellion and he was shot dead by its leader, Denara, who had returned bringing his pet Alsatian with him. This is the sort of anecdote where thorough investigation is needed to ascertain whether it was a mere coincidence, precognitive, or even if the witch doctor was in collusion with Denara.

In his book *Riddle of the Future*, Andrew Mackenzie includes the case of an eminent surgeon, whose identity he cloaked under the name of 'Donald Wilson'. One Saturday night in 1964, the surgeon dreamed that he was in his consulting-room on the following Monday morning and that his first patient was a stranger on whose buttock he found a large discoloured patch. On the actual day, his receptionist ushered in not the patient he expected, but a hospital nurse he had never seen before who had been added at the last minute ahead of everyone else. When Wilson examined her, he discovered a tumour on her right buttock as in his dream, except that it was two inches lower down. He removed the tumour, which proved to be malignant. Had he not done so, she would have died. Was this merely a coincidence, or could it have been a precognitive dream? A third possibility is that the nurse, concerned about her health, had telepathically communicated to him her intention to consult him urgently.

In 1932, Sigmund Freud conceded that telepathy might be 'the original archaic method' through which primitive men understood each other. He hoped that the cause might prove to be rays emitted from the human brain and so far unknown. Seven years earlier, he had written in an essay, 'The Occult Significance of Dreams', that he had concluded from personal experience that telepathic communication took place between himself and his patients when he was analysing them. Even some professional fortune-tellers were good telepathists. They predicted the future that those visiting them craved consciously or unconsciously, but did not talk about.

After joining both the Society for Psychical Research in London and its sister society in New York, Freud wrote to his disciple, Ernest Newman: 'When any one adduces my fall into sin, just answer him calmly that my conversion to telepathy is my private affair like my Jewishness, my passion for smoking.' Also, in his essay 'Psychoanalysis and Telepathy', published after his death, he added 'If I had my life to live ever again, I should devote myself to psychical research rather than to psycho-analysis.'

However, Freud maintained that precognition was impossible, and this once led to an extraordinary scene when he was in Jung's study. He was enumerating his reasons for thinking this when Jung felt, to quote his words, as if his diaphragm 'were made of iron and were becoming red-hot, like a glowing vault', and a moment later there was a loud bang inside his bookcase. Quickly availing himself of this phenomenon to support his own views, Jung declared: 'There, that is an example of a so-called catalytic exteriorization.'

'How can you talk such nonsense!' Freud retorted.

'It isn't nonsense,' Jung insisted. 'You're wrong—and to prove my point, I now predict that there will be another explosive sound.'

There was. This alarmed Freud, who left soon afterwards, never to visit Jung's house again.

In Benjamin Wolman's *Handbook of Dreams, Research, Theories, and Application*, the distinguished parapsychologist Dr John Beioff has written that even some of his fellows 'in the teeth of the empirical evidence have preferred to resort to certain expedients, at no matter what cost in deviousness and general implausibility, rather than acknowledge as meaningful a literal awareness of future events'. He maintained that none of their objections were valid. If precognition did occur, then the common-sense view of time must be at fault.

In *Paranormal Foreknowledge*, Dr Jule Eisenbud deals with its problems and perplexities and said that over the years researchers had put forward 'a considerable assortment of conceptional gimmicks designed to enable the precognition theorist to wriggle out of the seemingly iron-clad constraints of the physical world as we know it'. But none had attracted a following, with the possible exception of the hypothesis that everything exists in the mind of God and that 'He is able to vouchsafe to us glimpses into what He is thinking'.

According to the late Madeleine Montalban, writing in *Prediction* in April 1982, so long as the mantle of prophecy was upon an Old Testament prophet's shoulder, he knew the past and the future, but once it was lifted he was like a child who has seen a scientific wonder and tries to describe it in baby talk, lacking the necessary words for it. Thus we get the rich but tangled imagery of Ezekiel, Elijah, and of Revelation, with the prophecy depicted in symbols rather than words, and forces as beasts.

The God hypothesis is a 'passive' one as it requires only precognitive ability on a person's part. There are 'active' hypotheses such as that of Dr Tanagras, who in his book *Psychophysical Elements in Parapsychological Traditions* suggested that a paranormal force existed that could carry out the conscious and unconscious aims of certain people. He believed that any deep impression which is driven back into the subconscious mind and which strives for expression can release an emanation which is demonstrated by telekinetic phenomena and which, after a fortuitous premonition, tries to express this fulfilment in three ways: (a) by direct unconscious telekinetic action on inorganic matter (on motor cars, trains, or ships, for example, with resulting breakdowns, derailments, shipwrecks, etc.); (b) by action on living organisms in the form of telepathic suggestion (for example, unconscious influence on the brain of the driver of a car or on an individual's will-power); (c) by a temporary or permanent influence on an individual's life.

According to Dr Tanagras, this 'psychobolic' force is normally repressed, but it can escape and work on others. The future therefore is not foreseen but is created by it. His theory received scant support, and the part played in it by psychokinesis received most criticism. Variations on it advanced later by W.G. Roll and also E.D. Drew were similarly regarded as implausible.

The chief objection to the theory that the future already exists is how can it if we dream of a disaster and act successfully to avoid it? P.D. Ouspensky had an ingenious explanation. He regarded time as having a third dimension—its 'unactualised possibilities'. If we rise up into the sky in a balloon or climb a mountain, he said, we can see several things happening simultaneously that one cannot witness from below—such as two trains speeding towards each other and almost certain to collide as a sharp bend in the track makes each driver unaware of the other's approach. One can observe what is going on in two cities, which their inhabitants are unable to do even by telescope because of the formation of the land. In a dream, we become that observer on the heights and can warn those in peril of the dangers ahead. As Ouspensky wrote in *Tertium Organum*: 'So consciousness rising above the plane in which it usually operates must see simultaneously the events divided for ordinary consciousness by *periods of time*. These will be the events which ordinary consciousness *never* sees together as cause and effect...Vision will enlarge during such an ascent, the *moment* will enlarge.'

In *Foreknowledge* H.F. Saltmarsh maintained that the present occupies a space of time, however tiny. This may be greater in the subconscious part of our minds than in the conscious part. He illustrated the point he was making thus. If one were to peer through a large hole at a moving picture of a fox running across a screen, one would see that hounds were chasing it before a man could who was looking through a smaller hole, and therefore one would be able to predict what would happen next. According to Saltmarsh, when we are awake the exigencies of life force us to concentrate our attention on the immediate 'now', but when we are relaxed or asleep our vision expands and enables us to see more.

There is some psychological backing for Saltmarsh's theory. The older people get, the quicker time seems to pass. When we are bored, it drags, and when emotions are stirred, it flies—and it is often when the latter happens that people get glimpses into the future.

Professor C.D. Broad regarded time as running in two-dimensional planes from the past to the future. Imagine you are driving a car along a straight road with hedges so high that you cannot see what is happening beyond them, and that at intervals there are crossroads, representing future events. You would see what was happening on these roads only when they were reached, but if suddenly the hedges were lowered, then looking diagonally ahead one could observe what was taking place on the crossroads before reaching them. This, Professor Broad suggested, was what might occur when one was asleep or in a state of trance, enabling one to see into the future.

Zelma Bramley-Moore in her fascinating *Strange Diary* suggested that, in cases of precognition, it is not the future that is being looked into but the past. It took time for the unconscious mind to become aware of events and transmit them to the conscious mind 'A split tenth of a second? No, it takes longer than that,' she wrote. 'It may vary with the individual; but it may take hours, days, weeks, months, or even years! And, if this should be the case, we are, all of us, in a sense, living behind Time.' She compared the mind, conscious and unconscious, to telegraph wires running parallel to each other.

'The unconscious mind-wire vibrates strongly under the stimulus of great excitement or agitation...In the normal human being these wires are laid too far apart from each other for them ever to come into contact, no matter how violently the unconscious mind-wire should vibrate.'

But there are other people with mind-wires nearer together than is usual, so should anything cause the mind-wire to vibrate violently, it might come into contact with the conscious mind-wire for a moment or longer, and this would allow the conscious mind to become aware of an event out of its ordered sequence, giving it the impression that it is peeping into the future.

Dr G.D. Wasserman of Durham University was associated with Dr S.G. Soal and F. Bateman in conducting precognitive tests, and in their *Modern Experiments in Telepathy* Soal and Bateman describe his hypothesis. He thought that world events have 'mental patterns' already in existence, and that it is these patterns, and not the events, that are contacted in moments of precognition. It might be that the latent patterns of all possible events pre-exist, both those which will be brought into being and those which won't. Dr Wassermann considered that we might unconsciously be in touch with the mental patterns. The priests of ancient Hawaii had somewhat similar ideas. They maintained that the future was fixed to a certain point, beyond which it resembled an architect's plan for a building and could be changed.

In *The Challenge of Chance*, Arthur Koestler stressed how the physicist's notion of time has entirely changed from what it was a century ago. He quoted the astronomer Fred Hoyle, who had said that the concept of time as a steady progression from past to future is false and had added: 'I know very well we feel this way about it subjectively, but we are the victims of a confidence trick.'

Einstein started the revolution in human thought in 1905 with the publication of his *Special Theory of Relativity*, followed 11 years later by his *General Theory of Relativity*, from which the logical conclusion must be that if space is curved, so, too, is time, which upsets our common sense and gives the scientists more puzzles to try and solve. As Danah Zohar states in *Through the Time Barrier*, there is much controversy among theoretical physicists regarding the apparently static nature of the universe in Relativity Theory—that the future is already as fixed as the past. Many argue that it need not be so, and that there is scope for flux and change. Physicist David Bohm argues that even the past, as we know it, is not fixed.

Einstein emphasized that it was wrong to describe events occurring at a distance from each other as taking place at the same time unless one specified who was watching them. This was obvious when one studied the stars. The closest star was four light years away, and it took four light years for its light to reach the earth. So what we see is the star as it was then. Our present happens at the same time as its past, whilst for a star dweller our present remains in the future.

All this implies that if we could fly away from the earth as fast as light, then at whatever time we started out it would always remain the same time. If we flew faster than light, we would catch up with light signals emitted before our departure. Looking back at the earth, we should witness historical events of the past. We could film them as if they had just happened, return to earth, and show them in the cinema or on television. And back here, barely older, one would be astonished to find that centuries had elapsed during one's absence.

As Arthur Koestler has written, if 'on the macro-cosmic scale of very large distances and high speeds, the paradoxes of Relativity play havoc with our earthly notions of time, on the micro-cosmic scale they do the same'. Parapsychologists are looking increasingly at the researches and discoveries of quantum physics. They have been encouraged by the fact that the principal objections to precognition have been negated, for it has been established that, in the atom, neither causality nor time have any significance as formerly accepted. Psychokinesis is no longer considered far-fetched.

The quantum theory led Dr Ninian Marshall to put forward in 1960 the first detailed physical theory of precognition, which he described in detail in the *British Journal for the Philosophy of Science* in that year. Then, in 1974, Evan Harris Walker, the American physicist, published a paper entitled 'Consciousness and Quantum Theory' in a book edited by J. White, *Psychic Exploration*. This was the first of what has been termed 'the observation theories', and since then it has aroused considerable interest. Other physicists have been inspired to bring out their own variations on his original, which he himself has revised. These were discussed by Brian Millar under the heading 'The Observational Theories: A Primer' in the *European Journal of Parapsychology* in 1978. But despite the enthusiasm in many circles, some critics have accused these theories of lacking explanatory power, and of seeming largely nonsensical.

There are, of course, dozens of theories attempting to solve the mystery of precognition. Most are complex and difficult for the lay reader to follow, and all can be flawed. Perhaps one day a sufficiently developed computer will come up with a convincing answer. The purpose of this book has been to assemble some of the global evidence, both anecdotal and experimental. Whether precognition has been proven is for the jury, the readers, to debate. Perhaps it will be an 'Open Verdict'?

Bibliography

Abbreviations
JASPR *Journal of the American Society for Physical Research*
JSPR *Journal of the Society for Psychical Research*
PSPR *Proceedings of the Society for Psychical Research*

Barker, J.C., *Scared to Death* (Muller, London, 1968).
Beloff, J., *The Existence of Mind* (MacGibbon & Kee, London, 1962).
___, *New Directions in Parapsychology* (Elek, London, 1974).
Bentine, Michael, *Doors of the Mind* (Grafton, London, 1985).
Besterman, Theodore, *Crystal Gazing* (Rider, London, 1927).
Bisaha, J.P., and Dunne, B.J., 'Precognitive Remote Viewing in the Chicago Area: A Replication of the Stanford Experiment', in J.D. Morris, W.G. Roll, & R.L. Morris (eds.), *Research in Parapsychology* (Metuchen, New Jersey, 1975).
___'Multiple Subject and Long Distance Precognitive Remote Viewing of Geographical Locations, in C.T., Tart, H.E. Puthoff, and R. Targ (eds.), *Mind at Large* (Praeger, New York, 1979).
Bohm, David, *Quantum Theory* (Constable, London, 1951).
Bramley-Moore, Zelma, *Strange Diary* (Rider, London, 1937).
Braude, Stephen, 'The Observational Theories in Parapsychology: A Critique, *JASPR*, vol. 73 (1979).

Bridge, Ann, *Moments of Knowing* (Hodder, London, 1970).

Broad, C.D., *Lectures on Psychical Research* (Routledge & Kegan Paul, London, 1962).

Buck, Alice C., and Palmer, F. Claude, *The Clothes of God* (Peter Owen, London, 1956).

Carington, Whately, *Telepathy* (Methuen, London, 1945).

Carter, M.E., *Edgar Cayce on Prophecy* (Paperback Library, New York, 1968).

Clarke, A.C., *Profiles of the Future* (Gollancz, London, 1962).

Cooke, Aileen H., *Out of the Mouths of Babes: Extrasensory Perception in Children* (James Clarke, Cambridge, 1968).

Cox, W.F., 'Precognition: An Analysis II', *JASPR*, vol. 50 (1956), pp.99-109.

Dixon, Jeane., *My Life and Prophecies* (Muller, London, 1971).

Dobbs, H.A.C., 'Time and ESP' *PSPR*, vol. 54 (1965).

Dunne, J.W., *An Experiment with Time* (Faber, London, 1929).

Einstein, Albert, *Ideas and Opinions* (Harper, New York, 1949).

Eisenbud, Jule, *Paranormal Foreknowledge* (Human Sciences Press, New York, 1982).

Elwell, Dennis, *Cosmic Loom* (Unwin Hyman, London, 1987).

Feinberg, G., 'Precognition—A Memory of Things Future? *Proceedings on Quantum Physics and Parapsychology at Geneva, Switzerland* (Parapsychology Foundation, New York, 1975).

Fraser, J.T. (ed.), *The Voices of Time* (Allen Lane, London, 1968).

Freedland, N., *The Occult Explosion* (Michael Joseph, London, 1972).

Gardner, Jeanne, *A Grain of Mustard Seed* (Simon & Schuster, New York, 1969).

Garrett, Eileen J., *Many Voices, the Autobiography of a Medium* (George Allen & Unwin, London, 1969).

Glass, Justine, *The Story of Fulfilled Prophecy* (Cassell, London, 1969).

Godley, John, 'Dreams of Winners', *JSPR* (June 1947).

Goodman, J., *The Earthquake Generation* (Turnstone, London, 1979).

Greenhouse, H.B., *Premonitions: A Leap into the Future* (Turnstone, London 1972).

Gribbin, J., *Timewarps* (Dent, London, 1979).

_____, and Plagemann, S.H., *The Jupiter Effect* (Macmillan, London, 1974).

Gris, Henry, and Dick, W., *The New Soviet Psychic Discoveries* (Souvenir Press, London, 1979).

Hannah, Jack W., *The Futility God: Spiritist Power, Occultism and Futility* (Didactic, Mansfield, Ohio, 1975).

Heywood, Rosalind, *The Sixth Sense* (Chatto & Windus, London, 1959).

_____, *The Infinite Hive* (Chatto & Windus, London, 1964).

_____, 'Apparent Precognitions by Juliet, Lady Rhys-Williams, DBE', *JSPR*, vol. 42 (1964).

Holzer, Hans, *The Prophets Speak* (Manor Books, New York, 1975).

Howe, Ellic, *Urania's Children* (Kimber, London, 1967).

Hurkos, Peter, *Psychic* (Arthur Barker, London, 1961).

Inglis, Brian, *Natural and Supernatural* (Abacus, London, 1979).

Johnson, Francis, *Fatima: The Great Sign* (Augustine Publishing Company, Chulmleigh, Devon, 1980).

Jung, C.G., *Synchronicity* (Routledge & Kegan Paul, London, 1972).

_____, *Psychology and the Occult* (Princeton University Press, 1977).

_____, with Pauli, Wolfgang, *The Interpretation of Nature and the Psyche* (Routledge & Kegan Paul, London, 1955).

Kinsman, F., *Future Tense: A Prophetic Consensus for the Eighties* (Pendulum, London, 1980).

Koestler, Arthur, *The Roots of Coincidence* (Hutchinson, London, 1972).

_____, *The Challenge of Chance* (Hutchinson, London, 1973).

Krippner, S., Ullman, M., and Honorton, C., 'A Precognitive Dream Study with a Single Subject', *JASPR*, vol. 65 (1971), pp.192-203.

_____, 'A Second Precognitive Dream Study with Malcolm Bessent', *JASPR*, vol. 66, (1972), pp.269-79.

Le Vert, Liberté E., *The Prophecies and Enigmas of Nostradamus* (Firebell Books, Glen Rock, New Jersey, 1980).

Lemesurier, P., *The Great Pyramid Decoded* (Element Books, Shaftesbury, 1977).

Lyttelton, Dame Edith, *Our Superconscious Mind* (P. Allan, London, 1931).

_____, *Some Cases of Prediction* (G. Bell, London, 1937).

Mackenzie, Andrew, *The Unexplained: Some Strange Cases of Psychical Research* (Barker, London, 1966).

_____, *Frontiers of the Unknown* (Barker, London, 1968).

_____, *Riddle of the Future* (Barker, London, 1974).

Megroz, Rodolphe, *The Dream World* (John Lane, London, 1939).

Millar, Brian, 'The Observational Theories: A Primer', *European Journal of Parapsychology*, vol. 2 (1978).

Millard, J., *Edgar Cayce* (Fawcett, New York, 1967).

Montgomery, Ruth, *A Gift of Prophecy* (Morrow, New York, 1965).

Nichols, Beverley, *Powers That Be* (Jonathan Cape, London, 1966).

Ostrander, Sheila, and Schroeder, Lynn, *PSI—Psychic Discoveries Behind The Iron Curtain* (Prentice-Hall, New York, 1970).

Osty, Eugene, *Supernormal Faculties in Man* (Methuen, London, 1923).

Ouspensky, P.D., *Tertium Organum* (Kegan Paul, London, 1934).

_____, *In Search of the Miraculous* (Routledge & Kegan Paul, London, 1950).

Pauwels, Louis, and Bergier, Jacques, *The Morning of the Magicians* (Stein & Day, New York, 1964).

Pollack, J.H., *Croiset the Clairvoyant* (W.H. Allen, London, 1965).

Pratt, J.G., *Parapsychology Today: An Insider's View* (Doubleday, New York, 1964).

Priestley, J.B., *Man and Time* (Aldus, London, 1964).

Puharich, Andrija, *Beyond Telepathy* (Doubleday, New York, 1962).

Randles, Jenny, *Beyond Explanation* (Robert Hale, London, 1985).

Rhine, J.B., *The Reach of the Mind* (Wm. Sloane, New York, 1947).

___, *New World of the Mind* (Wm. Sloane, New York, 1953).

___, and Pratt, J.G., *Parapsychology: Frontier Science of the Mind* (Blackwell, Oxford, 1958).

___, and others, *Extra-Sensory Perception After Sixty Years* (Humphries, Boston, 1966).

Rhine, Louisa E., *Hidden Channels of the Mind* (Gollancz, London, 1962).

___, *ESP in Life and Lab* (Macmillan, New York, 1967).

___, *Mind Over Matter* (Macmillan, New York, 1970).

___, *The Invisible Picture: A Study of Psychic Experience* (Metuchen, New Jersey, 1981).

Ryzl, Milan, 'Parapsychology in Communist Countries of Europe', *International Journal of Parapsychology*, New York, vol. 10, no. 3 (1968).

Salisbury, Harrison E. (ed.), *The Soviet Union: The Fifty Years* (Harcourt, Brace, New York, 1967).

Saltmarsh, H.F., *Foreknowledge* (G. Bell, London, 1938).

Schopenhauer, Arthur, *On the Apparent Fate of the Individual* (Watts, London, 1913).

Simovet, Dragomir, Series on Bulgarian Parapsychology, *Svet*, Belgrade, nos. 533–7, (January–February, 1967).

Soal, S.G., and Bateman, F., *Modern Experiments in Telepathy* (Faber, London, 1954).

Stearn, J., *The Door to the Future* (Muller, London, 1964).

Stevenson, Ian. 'A Review and Analysis of Paranormal Experiences Connected with the Sinking of the Titanic, *JASPR*, vol. 54 (1960).

___, 'Seven More Paranormal Experiences Associated with the Sinking of the Titanic', *JASPR*, vol. 59 (1965).

Strong, John, *The Doomsday Globe* (Clarendon Press, Sydney, 1973).

Tanagras, Angelos, *Psychophysical Elements in Parapsychological Traditions* (Parapsychology Foundation, New York, 1967).

Targ, Russell, and Harary, Keith, *The Mind Race* (Random House, New York, 1984).

Targ, R., and Puthoff, H., *Mind-Reach* (Paladin-Granada, London, 1978).

Taylor, John, *Science and the Supernatural* (Temple Smith, London, 1980).

Timms, Moira, *The Six O'Clock Bus* (Turnstone Books, London, 1979).

Ullman, M., and Krippner, S., *Dream Studies and Telepathy: An Experimental Approach* (Parapsychology Foundation, New York, 1970).

Warcollier, René, *Mind to Mind* (Collier, New York, 1963).

Watson, Lyall, *Supernature* (Hodder, London, 1973).

Wilhelm, Richard, *I Ching*, with a Foreword by C.G. Jung (Routledge & Kegan Paul, London, 1951).

Wilson, Colin, *The Occult* (Hodder, London, 1971).

Wolman, Benjamin, *Handbook of Dreams, Research, Theories, and Application* (Van Nostrand Reinhold, New York, 1979).

Woodruff, Maurice, *Woody* (Cassell, London, 1967).

Wulff, Wilhelm, *Zodiac and Swastika* (Barker, London, 1973).

Zohar, Danah, *Through the Time Barrier* (Heinemann, London, 1982).

Index

Of further interest...

Visions of the Future

The Definitive Study of Premonitions

DR KEITH HEARNE

Many people experience premonitions, yet little research has been carried out to determine exactly what they are, how they occur and how reliable they can be. The author investigates this fascinating subject and comes up with some startling discoveries.

Starting with an account of premonitions throughout recorded history, he proceeds to an in-depth study of contemporary cases. By authenticating and examining up-to-date accounts, he concludes that scientists are being unscientific by refusing to acknowledge this valid area of parapsychology.

A revolutionary new theory is suggested to explain the clear-cut evidence for premonitions but which challenges the modern scientific view of the universe as a material reality.

Dr Keith Hearne is an internationally known psychologist and world leader in research into lucid dreaming. He specializes in parapsychology and has established the Hearne Research Organization to further investigations into a number of areas of scientific study.

Frontiers of Reality

Where Science Meets the Paranormal

Edited by HILARY EVANS

We are living at an exciting moment in time when all kinds of findings are pouring in, which show that fact and fantasy are not so distinct as has traditionally been supposed. Ever since the study of dreams showed that these experiences, generally regarded as a synonym for everything that is unreal, have their foundations in reality, it has become increasingly clear that the boundary between what is real and what is unreal must be redrawn.

This book sets out to chart that boundary area, the FRONTIERS OF REALITY. Already researchers have made sufficient discoveries to show that, contrary to traditional belief, the mysteries do not fade away into nothing when the light of science is turned on them. And the more thorough the investigation, the more stringent the research, the more certain it becomes that the phenomena we label 'paranormal' really do occur.

Written by top people in their fields, from Europe, America and Australia, the book provides an excellent summary of man's understanding as we enter the last decade of the twentieth century.